Astrology
Birthday Book

Astrology
Birthday Book

a guide to your personality and destiny

Michele Knight

spruce

contents

What's in a birthday? Each day of the year has a unique magic, and your birthday can reveal your strengths and weaknesses, helping you discover how to reach your full potential and make the most of your journey here on Earth.

The power of your birthday is determined not only by your ruling planet, but also by the numerology of the date of your birth. By combining your birth date ruler with your ruling planet, you will be able to understand why you are not just a typical Taurus or Aries. For instance, an Aries whose birth date is ruled by Neptune, planet of dreams and visions, is likely to be far more sensitive and intuitive than the average Aries. A Sagittarius whose ruling planet and birth date ruler are both Jupiter, planet of good fortune, is destined to be a natural performer and will gain recognition easier than their peers. Perhaps you are touched with the ability to make people laugh, or have the makings of a scientist or artist, but are unaware of this side of your character. Sometimes ability is hidden within, but once you are given an insight into what is inside you, you are free to evolve and develop into your full potential.

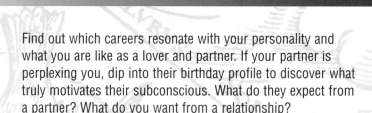

Find out which careers resonate with your personality and what you are like as a lover and partner. If your partner is perplexing you, dip into their birthday profile to discover what truly motivates their subconscious. What do they expect from a partner? What do you want from a relationship?

Discover important events that happened on the day of your birth throughout history. Perhaps they'll give you a greater appreciation of the day you were born on. Find out which famous people share your birthday and see if you can pinpoint any similarities between your character and theirs. If they made it so can you!

"Know thyself" was the inscription carved over the door at the great temple of Delphi, and your birthday numerology will help you develop a deeper understanding of your own personality and to work towards creating all the wondrous birthday gifts the Universe has bestowed on you.

Embrace your full potential and fly!

aries

march 21–april 20

color mauve ★ **number** 1, 3, 33 ★ **stone** ruby—spark your passion with this stone that the ancient hindus believed was for lovers ★ **flora** dahlia ★ **animal** horse ★ **occupation** long-distance runner, firefighter, hunter ★ **key features** unconventional, powerful, feisty ★ **naturally good at** seeing things through to completion

march 21

character ★ You have an iron will to succeed that is based not on dreams of material success but on wanting a sense of personal achievement. You have your own set of values and will not let anyone tell you what to do. The good news is that your single-mindedness nearly always works. You do not care about convention but always follow your own unique path.

life path ★ You are here to impress upon others that free-thinking action can reap rewards. All your friends have become more maverick and spontaneous thanks to you. You love people and can be an active group member as well as an individual if you feel passionately about the activity.

love ★ Unusually for an Aries you do have loner tendencies, but ultimately you want a mate who is an equal. You do not like clingy partners and prefer the hunt and chase to settled marital bliss. Your birth date ruler,

Jupiter, planet of good fortune, is also the ruling planet of Sagittarius, and a Sagittarian would make an ideal lover.

best present ★ Surprise party, engraved silver compass.

birthday share ★ 1685 Johann Sebastian Bach, composer; 1946 Timothy Dalton, actor; 1958 Gary Oldman, actor; 1962 Matthew Broderick, actor.

on this day ★ In 1963, Alcatraz prison in San Francisco Bay, a harsh maximum security jail which once housed gangster Al Capone, closed when the last 27 prisoners were transferred.

color silver, gold ★ **number** 4, 13, 22 ★ **stone** diamond—this hardy stone inspires strength in you and matches your multifaceted personality ★ **flora** angelica ★ **animal** bloodhound ★ **occupation** adventurer, traveler, mime artist ★ **key features** unusual, free, rebellious ★ **naturally good at** creating success from adversity

march 22

character ★ You have had an unusual life that has involved strange adventures and a sense of destiny. Where you live and what you are doing seem to be inescapable givens. Your pals may find it downright spooky that life just seems to happen for you. However, you never like to get too settled and have a wandering spirit.

life path ★ You keep changing your mind about what you want from life. Sometimes it is to have kids and settle down, but then you break out in a cold sweat and want to run off with the circus or discover a new continent. Take each day as it comes.

love ★ You are unpredictable in relationships—adoring one minute and detached the next, so your partner may find it difficult to keep up. Your birth date ruler is Uranus, so perhaps a freedom-loving Aquarius, whose ruling planet is also Uranus, will suit you.

best present ★ Racing-car lessons, driving gloves.

birthday share ★ 1931 William Shatner, actor; 1943 George Benson, singer; 1959 Matthew Modine, actor; 1976 Reese Witherspoon, actress.

on this day ★ In 1903, Niagara Falls slowed to a trickle during a severe drought.

march 23

character ★ You have a big personality and it is often difficult for other people to get a word in edgewise. You have a side-splitting laugh. If you are a woman, you are one of the boys, and if you are a man, you are right there with the gals. You love to be admired and have a wicked sense of humor.

life path ★ You love life and love talking about life, but be careful not to gossip too much. You delight in telling tall tales and you don't mean any harm, but your conquests would be mortified if they knew the degree of detail you reveal. Be careful what you say and you will avoid a lot of trouble.

love ★ No doubt about it: you have had many lovers singing your praises. You are generous and affectionate but prone to being unfaithful. Try a Gemini whose ruling planet is Mercury, the planet of communication, the same as your birth date ruler.

best present ★ Engraved ring, magazine subscription.

birthday share ★ 1904 Joan Crawford, actress; 1921 Donald Campbell, land-speed record breaker; 1953 Chaka Khan, singer; 1968 Damon Albarn, singer.

on this day ★ In 1983, President Ronald Reagan announced plans for a new space-based defense system, later known as "Star Wars."

color pink, light green ★ **number** 1, 6, 66 ★ **stone** rose quartz—the stone of unconditional love ★ **flora** sea lavender ★ **animal** ginger tomcat ★ **occupation** beauty contestant, dancer, student ★ **key features** innocent, charming, naive ★ **naturally good at** lighting up the room with your dazzling smile

character ★ You have countless admirers who adore you, but you are a strange enigma. On the one hand you are like a five-year-old child, eager, innocent, and in awe of the world, but if someone crosses you or takes advantage of your pure spirit, you will not stop until you have crushed their ego.

life path ★ You were sent to light up other people's lives. You have a sweet charisma that makes even the most cynical grump grin and feel 16 again. You are so genuine that no one could get the wrong impression of you unless they were very bitter indeed.

love ★ Many gravitate toward you but you are looking for an extremely talented and intelligent partner. You need someone as gentle, kind, and sweet as you. Suffice to say you have been disappointed in the past with princes who turned into frogs after the first kiss! Try your opposite sign, Libra, whose ruling planet is Venus, your birth date ruler.

best present ★ PlayStation, digital camera.

birthday share ★ 1874 Harry Houdini, escape artist; 1887 Fatty Arbuckle, actor; 1911 Joseph Barbera, animator; 1930 Steve McQueen, actor.

on this day ★ In 1958, Elvis Presley enlisted in the U.S. Army.

color sea green ★ **number** 1, 7, 16 ★ **stone** aquamarine—will soothe your spirit and draw the truth to you ★ **flora** hydrangea ★ **animal** tadpoles ★ **occupation** speedboat racer, motorcross rider, marine biologist ★ **key features** fantasizing, exploring, wistful ★ **naturally good at** mountain climbing

march 25

character ★ You tend to live in the past and in a dream world, which is quite unusual for an Aries. You see the past through rose-tinted glasses and always feel a need to move on. This is partly because you have no time for relationships and go through them quickly or long for the unobtainable.

life path ★ Quirky and original, you need to mix with other eccentric or unique people. Otherwise you will always be a big fish in a small pond, and that is no good to anyone. You have a keen desire to see the world and need travel to expand your horizons.

love ★ You avoid relationships on the whole but love to fantasize about them, particularly the one that got away or the one you cannot have. If you want love, there is plenty around for you. Try a sentimental Pisces to bring you romance; Pisceans' ruling planet is the same as your birth date ruler, dreamy Neptune.

best present ★ Divining rod, trip to an exotic location.

birthday share ★ 1925 Flannery O'Connor, author; 1942 Aretha Franklin, singer; 1947 Elton John, singer; 1965 Sarah Jessica Parker, actress.

on this day ★ In 1949, Laurence Olivier's *Hamlet* became the first British film to win an Oscar at the Academy Awards, winning five in total.

color hunter green ★ **number** 8, 17, 35 ★ **stone** red jasper—grounds you and gives you a sense of security ★ **flora** love lies bleeding ★ **animal** wild boar ★ **occupation** army major, mayor/mayoress, industry boss ★ **key features** bossy, bold, loud ★ **naturally good at** shouting commands and orders

march 26

character ★ People don't mess with you; you're strict, powerful, and quite frightening! You lay down the law and will not back down if you feel you are right. You also find it difficult to apologize. You tend to take control of situations and don't stand for any nonsense. Calm down and open your heart.

life path ★ You're a born leader, but there is a time and place to lead. You do let your hair down with your friends and can enjoy a good drink and a chat. Even though you charm strangers, you never really trust someone until you have known them for at least ten years.

love ★ You need to be gentle with your partner—you sometimes bark orders and expect them to jump as if they are in boot camp. You are a big softie underneath but start showing it! Your birth date is ruled by strict Saturn, so seek out a wise Capricorn whose ruling planet is also Saturn.

best present ★ CD of classical music, history book.

birthday share ★ 1931 Leonard Nimoy, actor; 1944 Diana Ross, singer; 1948 Steve Tyler, singer; 1960 Jennifer Grey, actress.

on this day ★ In 1969, John Lennon and Yoko Ono spent their week-long honeymoon in bed in Room 902 of the Amsterdam Hilton, the first of their "bed-in" protests against the Vietnam War, during which they recorded antiwar songs with friends.

color scarlet ★ **number** 9, 18, 36 ★ **stone** fire opal—a rare opal that will act as a talisman and inspire you ★ **flora** lisianthus ★ **animal** pitbull terrier ★ **occupation** race-car driver, dentist, bouncer ★ **key features** powerful, dynamic, unstoppable ★ **naturally good at** being heroic

march 27

character ★ Sassy, sizzling, and brash, you are a true one-of-a-kind. Nothing can hold you back, but you can be so eager to achieve your goal that you trample over other people. You have true grit, but make sure that you use it for good.

life path ★ You have the power of a Viking warrior, and whether male or female you have astounding physical presence and strength. Your natural heroism makes you a great person to deal with a dangerous situation. You instinctively take control and save everyone else before yourself.

love ★ You are naturally tactile but can overdo those bear hugs sometimes! You need to learn the softer side of pleasure. Your double ruler, Mars, gives you all that energy. Try another Aries for true love.

best present ★ Paintball session, kickboxing lessons.

birthday share ★ 1863 Sir Henry Royce, car designer; 1942 Michael York, actor; 1963 Quentin Tarantino, director; 1970 Mariah Carey, singer.

on this day ★ In 1794, the U.S. government established a permanent navy and authorized the building of six vessels.

color orange, gold ★ number 1, 11, 22 ★ stone carnelian—the romans' favorite talisman, used to energize, stimulate, and protect ★ flora gladioli ★ animal tiger ★ occupation visionary, artist, builder ★ key features focused, intense, fanatical ★ naturally good at creating magnificence

march 28

character ★ You have a burning desire to create something special or to do your very best to be at the top of your field. You have a deep sense of the spiritual in life but may not talk about this, as you prefer to keep some sides of yourself private. Your career is very important to you, and a job well done is a matter of personal pride for you.

life path ★ Rarely superficial, you are intense or dismissive with very little middle ground. You believe with total conviction and have no time for ignorant or small-minded people. Those close to you are extremely protective of you, seeing you as very pure and good.

love ★ You can be rather elusive in love—you can give your all and love sincerely but the next day, hour, or minute you may be distracted by some important plan or event, leaving your lover perplexed as to your feelings. Your birth date ruler is the Sun, so choose a Leo whose ruling planet is also the Sun, and who will understand you.

best present ★ Oil paints, trip to an art gallery.

birthday share ★ 1899 August Busch, beer magnate; 1921 Dirk Bogarde, actor; 1964 Salt, rap artist; 1981 Julia Stiles, actress.

on this day ★ In 1986, 6,000 radio stations worldwide simultaneously broadcast the song "We Are the World" to raise awareness for hunger relief in Africa.

march 29

character ★ You are very authentic and do your best in life to help others. You can feel your partner's thoughts and have an uncanny telepathic connection with those you love. In personal relationships you can get a little oversensitive and perhaps even paranoid.

life path ★ You have a genuine desire to give of yourself careerwise; not the mundane for you but a job that uplifts people, or raises awareness of injustice. You are perhaps a little too wise, which can lead you to becoming disillusioned if you are not careful. You will study later on in life, as you have a hunger for knowledge.

love ★ Love is essential for you but you can be a little too intense too soon. You know the minute you set eyes on someone if they are for you. You tend to sweep your lovers off their feet and rarely meet resistance. Your birth date ruler is the Moon, so perhaps choose a Cancer whose ruling planet is also the Moon.

best present ★ Deck of tarot cards, book on runes.

birthday share ★ 1918 Pearl Bailey, jazz singer; 1943 John Major, former British prime minister; 1964 Elle Macpherson, model; 1976 Jennifer Capriati, tennis player.

on this day ★ In 1974, the first close-up pictures of the planet Mercury were taken by the U.S. spacecraft *Mariner 10*.

color purple, lavender ★ **number** 3, 21, 33 ★ **stone** jade—a stone sacred to the chinese that will draw wealth to you ★ **flora** catkin ★ **animal** mouse ★ **occupation** painter, carpenter, surgeon ★ **key features** luck, dynamism, vitality ★ **naturally good at** overcoming obstacles

character ★ Unusually lucky, you often find yourself in the right place at the right time. You're attractive and energetic but have a mild manner, so people only sense your burning sensuality rippling under the surface. Sometimes you forgo relationships to focus on a personal ambition.

life path ★ Your life is quite cyclical, with two-year periods every 12 years or so when you are touched by magic. During these fairy-tale years you will be able to obtain all of your desires, but if you don't cherish them they could vanish as quickly as they arrived.

love ★ You are irresistible and will often have partners more successful, rich, and attractive than you who will adore you and help you. Don't be insecure or these relationships will pass you by. Your birth date ruler is Jupiter, so choose a Sagittarius who has Jupiter as their ruling planet.

best present ★ Sunglasses, wristwatch.

birthday share ★ 1853 Vincent van Gogh, artist; 1937 Warren Beatty, actor; 1945 Eric Clapton, singer and rock guitarist; 1968 Celine Dion, singer.

on this day ★ In 1981, Ronald Reagan was shot and gravely wounded by John W. Hinckley Jr. on leaving the Washington Hilton Hotel. Hinckley was later found not guilty for the shooting by reason of insanity.

color silver, red ★ **number** 4, 13, 22 ★ **stone** hematite—gives you genuine confidence ★ **flora** basil ★ **animal** dragonfly ★ **occupation** property developer, stockbroker, director ★ **key features** commanding, influential, rugged ★ **naturally good at** taking charge of groups

march 31

character ★ If you're a guy you will have a very masculine aura, and if you're a girl you will be powerful and equal to, if not stronger than, most men. You have an air of authority that is quite awesome and you command respect. When you smile, people will do anything for you.

life path ★ You're a little fierce sometimes but you are also fair. You like to have power and will always be a leader rather than a follower. You draw people to you and are generous to a fault with those you love.

love ★ Generous but controlling in relationships, you rarely let any lover get the better of you and are usually the one with the upper hand. You have a kind and sweet nature under your gruff exterior. Your birth date is ruled by Uranus, so aim for an Aquarius who shares this ruler and won't be fazed by you.

best present ★ Dinner at the best restaurant in town, leather diary.

birthday share ★ 1732 Joseph Haydn, composer; 1943 Christopher Walken, actor; 1948 Al Gore, former U.S. vice president; 1971 Ewan McGregor, actor.

on this day ★ In 1918, daylight saving time went into effect for the first time in the United States.

color orange, yellow ★ **number** 1, 11, 22 ★ **stone** topaz—this fiery stone oozes allure ★
flora bluebell ★ **animal** wild deer ★ **occupation** mountaineer, writer, magician ★
key features impetuous, spontaneous, brave ★ **naturally good at** meditation, inventions

character ★ You can be a bit of a loner, which is unusual for an Aries. You love to sit and think for hours and come up with wild plans for the future. You are capable of unexpected spontaneity that surprises those around you. Your moods always show on your face so you're incapable of lying.

life path ★ Learn to trust and to speak your mind. You have fantastic ideas but you tend to keep them to yourself until they are fully formed, which means they sometimes remain in your mind and never materialize. If you open up, others can help you.

love ★ You have an extremely warm heart and you love to be kissed and cuddled by the right partner. You tend to cause your friends to fall in love with you and you have a tendency to put lovers on pedestals. Your birth date is ruled by the Sun, so why not choose a beaming Leo whose ruling planet is also the Sun?

best present ★ Walking boots, fountain pen.

birthday share ★ 1932 Debbie Reynolds, actress; 1938 Ali McGraw, actress; 1939 Rudolph Isley, singer; 1948 Jimmy Cliff, reggae musician.

on this day ★ In 1924, a court sentenced Adolf Hitler to five years in jail for high treason after his abortive 1923 Munich beer-hall putsch.

color red ★ number 2, 22, 26 ★ stone opal—some people consider this stone unlucky, but it intensifies your mood, so carry it with you when you are feeling happy ★ flora orchid, moonflower ★ animal siamese cat ★ occupation politician, public speaker, director ★ key features dreamy, humanitarian, loving ★ naturally good at inviting people to parties

april 2

character ★ You're a big kid with a heart of gold. You love other people and can chat with just about anyone, but you can also be a tad opinionated and headstrong, and you always stand up for your point of view. In relationships you are a fantastic lover but can be a bit domineering.

life path ★ Your life path is all about balance and learning to share. You will throw yourself into love with wild abandon but need to let your partner be independent, with his or her own views and interests. Remember that they are quite capable of looking after themselves and stop being overprotective.

love ★ You are an emotional and playful partner and have a big heart. You will travel long distances to help a partner in trouble, and although you can be hard work you are worth it. Why not try a Cancer whose ruling planet is the same as your birth date ruler, the sensitive Moon?

best present ★ Trip to a romantic city, tickets to a concert.

birthday share ★ 1805 Hans Christian Andersen, author; 1928 Serge Gainsbourg, singer; 1939 Marvin Gaye, singer; 1947 Emmylou Harris, singer.

on this day ★ In 1982, Argentina invaded the Falkland Islands and overthrew the British administration. Britain responded by sending a task force to retake the islands.

color green ★ **number** 6, 9, 33 ★ **stone** adventurine—brings adventure into your life ★
flora dahlia ★ **animal** bulldog ★ **occupation** teacher, charity worker, personal assistant ★
key features sociable, generous, naive ★ **naturally good at** mediation

april 3

character ★ You love to join in, and get a buzz from working with others. You are always on the go, helping other people and up for any party or social gathering; perhaps you need to spend a little more time on your own or you could end up burning out. You are fit and strong and loved by most people who meet you.

life path ★ You were born lucky but tend to be overly generous so could give away too much, particularly to those who spin you a sob story. Use those fabulous humanitarian instincts to work with others, but spoil yourself as well and wait a little longer before you give others your trust.

love ★ Generous to a fault and very committed when you fall in love, your ideal match is probably a wild and spontaneous Sagittarius whose ruling planet is the same as your birth date ruler—Jupiter, the planet of good fortune.

best present ★ Bicycle, surprise birthday party.

birthday share ★ 1783 Washington Irving, author; 1924 Marlon Brando, actor, and Doris Day, actress; 1961 Eddie Murphy, actor.

on this day ★ In 1882, in St. Joseph, Missouri, the infamous outlaw Jesse James was shot in the back by his cousin Robert Ford and killed.

april 4

character ★ You have a genuine wacky streak that makes you unique and unusual. People are drawn to your extraordinary view of the world and love to hear you telling stories about the adventures you have had. You also tend to have a mesmerizing voice. You often achieve success quite easily, as other people are fascinated by you.

life path ★ You could never fit into a normal job or routine, as you crave excitement from life and want to experience more than others. You have the ability to come up with new ideas and crave to express them. You are here to bring a splash of color to the world so should always be your unique self and not allow anyone to put you in a box.

love ★ You love the unusual in a partner and find it hard to settle down and commit. It takes a unique and complex lover to pin you down. You are drawn to the equally eccentric Aquarius whose ruling planet, Uranus, is also your birth date ruler.

best present ★ Trip to an observatory, dinner at an unusual restaurant.

birthday share ★ 1915 Muddy Waters, singer; 1928 Maya Angelou, author and poet; 1932 Anthony Perkins, actor; 1965 Robert Downey Jr., actor.

on this day ★ In 1968, Martin Luther King Jr. was assassinated by James Earl Ray in Memphis, Tennessee.

color silver ★ **number** 3, 23, 41 ★ **stone** aquamarine—helps you express yourself ★ **flora** violet ★ **animal** parrot ★ **occupation** journalist, writer, telephone operator ★ **key features** hardworking, communicative, lively ★ **naturally good at** problem solving

character ★ Thoughtful and fairly introverted for an Aries, you tend to focus on work and career. You are an asset to any company, so perhaps it would be a good idea to work for yourself! You have exceptional writing abilities and can talk almost nonstop.

life path ★ Share your views with the world and learn to have faith in your own ideas and your ability to communicate. Make sure that you balance work and play, as you can easily get stuck in a rut. Remember that you're an Aries and have the drive and spontaneity to leap forward. There is a whole world of adventure out there if you have the courage to accept change.

love ★ You spend hours communicating and chatting to your partner, you are never off the telephone to them when they are away, and you email them regularly, too. You need to find a Gemini, who will love this attentiveness as their ruling planet, Mercury, is the same as your birth date ruler.

best present ★ Cell phone, day at a writing workshop.

birthday share ★ 1900 Spencer Tracy, actor; 1908 Bette Davis, actress; 1916 Gregory Peck, actor; 1937 Colin Powell, secretary of state.

on this day ★ In 1960, the movie epic *Ben-Hur*, starring Charlton Heston, won 10 Oscars at the Academy Awards.

color green, pink ★ **number** 15, 24, 33 ★ **stone** rose quartz—the love stone that heals your heart ★ **flora** rose ★ **animal** lovebird ★ **occupation** florist, poet, actor ★ **key features** humorous, romantic, idealistic ★ **naturally good at** calming others and healing

april 6

character ★ You are quite gentle and loving for an Aries and always look out for your friends. You have a strong affinity with the underdog and always lend a helping hand to those in need. You seek to explore the meaning of life and are a deep and philosophical thinker. You also have a great sense of humor and enjoy making people laugh.

life path ★ Your mission on Earth is to share your love and knowledge with those around you—and possibly with the whole world. Acting or writing is a likely form of communication. You are a spiritual explorer as well and may get involved in healing. You have a huge heart overflowing with great compassion and you also have empathy with animals.

love ★ You are supremely romantic and although always on the go you make time for serious loving. You are drawn to sentimental Libra, whose ruling planet is Venus, planet of love, which is also your birth date ruler.

best present ★ Book of love poems, gold heart locket.

birthday share ★ 1929 André Previn, musician and conductor; 1947 John Ratzenberger, actor; 1969 Paul Rudd, actor; 1976 Candace Cameron, actress.

on this day ★ In 1917, the United States entered World War I by declaring war against Germany.

color aquamarine, sea green ★ **number** 7, 14, 16 ★ **stone** coral—takes you into your emotions ★ **flora** waterlily ★ **animal** koi (carp) ★ **occupation** diver, psychic, fisherman/woman ★ **key features** deep, intense, spiritual ★ **naturally good at** sailing and all water-related pursuits

character ★ Bold and forthright, you have very deep beliefs and will fight to the death to defend them. You have experienced strange coincidences and always seem to bump into deep or unusual people. You are a strong believer that there is more to life than the superficial and seek to acquire knowledge on all things spiritual.

life path ★ You have always felt that there is a meaning or purpose to your life and that you must set out to find it. You are a bit of a dreamer and have often rushed into what you thought was your destiny, only to be knocked back or lose interest, so some people don't take you seriously. Don't listen to them—your true destiny will soon be revealed, so keep looking.

love ★ You are dreamy and romantic but you don't necessarily show your partner this side of you because you regard it as a weakness and hate to lose control. Try a Pisces lover whose ruling planet is also your birth date ruler, Neptune.

best present ★ Horseback-riding lessons, deck of tarot cards.

birthday share ★ 1770 William Wordsworth, poet; 1915 Billie Holiday, jazz singer; 1939 Francis Ford Coppola, director; 1964 Russell Crowe, actor.

on this day ★ In 1906, the Italian volcano Vesuvius erupted, destroying the town of Ottaiano.

color dark blue, blood red ★ **number** 17, 26, 62 ★ **stone** smoky quartz—helps you face your fears ★ **flora** starflower ★ **animal** scorpion ★ **occupation** psychologist, missionary, private detective ★ **key features** responsible, deep, hard ★ **naturally good at** unmasking people, research

april 8

character ★ You are very deep but tend to swing from being broody and mysterious to outgoing and spontaneous. You often have difficulty keeping up with your own intensity, as you feel things so deeply. You are determined to succeed, no matter how long it takes, and are tenacious if you desire something or someone.

life path ★ Don't get lost in your own fears—you are naturally outgoing when you allow yourself to trust, but you can suffer from self-doubt. If you can overcome your fear, you will be capable of anything and could be a great righter of wrongs. You have the potential to make great strides in bringing harmony to the world.

love ★ You can be quite obsessive and almost tyrannical in relationships, as you have the unfortunate attitude that those you love are your property. Try to remember that they are not, and that if you allow them to

be free, love will deepen. Lighten up and choose a Capricorn whose ruling planet is the same as your birth date ruler, Saturn.

best present ★ Book on unexplained mysteries, trip to a museum.

birthday share ★ 1918 Betty Ford, U.S. first lady; 1938 Kofi Annan, secretary general of the United Nations; 1963 Julian Lennon, singer; 1968 Patricia Arquette, actress.

on this day ★ In 1974, at the Atlanta-Fulton County Stadium, Henry "Hank" Aaron hit the 715th home run of his career, breaking baseball great Babe Ruth's record.

color orange, red ★ **number** 18, 36, 72 ★ **stone** ruby—this stone will raise your libido ★
flora red-hot poker ★ **animal** alsatian dog ★ **occupation** race-car driver, hunter, firefighter
★ **key features** energetic, strong, impulsive ★ **naturally good at** all areas of fitness

april 9

character ★ Over the top and overwhelming, you have a huge personality and are a party animal. You love to have a good time and have a remarkable capacity for working and playing hard. You need to relax, as this overindulgence may cause health problems. You aim to keep fit but need to match your diet with your exercise.

life path ★ You have to win in all battles and can be aggressive. Be very careful of outbursts of rage—your anger passes quickly but others may hold a grudge. You are easily led into passionate liaisons and need to stop and think before you leap.

love ★ You love like a whirlwind and are hungry for all sorts of romantic delights. You are insatiable in this area and have fantastic stamina. Both your birth date ruler and your ruling planet are Mars so you have a double dose of fire. Try another Aries, who will probably be able to keep up!

best present ★ Sneakers, exercise machine.

birthday share ★ 1926 Hugh Hefner, founder of *Playboy* magazine; 1954 Dennis Quaid, actor; 1957 Severiano Ballesteros, golfer; 1966 Cynthia Nixon, actress.

on this day ★ In 1865, the American Civil War ended.

color yellow, orange ★ **number** 1, 11, 22 ★ **stone** citrine—this yellow stone increases your self-esteem ★ **flora** sunflower ★ **animal** horse ★ **occupation** wildlife photographer, actor, comedian ★ **key features** foolhardy, extrovert, outrageous ★ **naturally good at** winning competitions

april 10

character ★ You have a dazzling personality and love to be the center of attention. You ooze charisma and charm and relish life's challenges. You are always showing off or doing something adventurous, like skateboarding down hillsides or white-water rafting. Male or female, you have an impulsive streak that could land you in hot water.

life path ★ You are a born leader and like nothing more than taking control and winning. You need to learn about cooperation, though, and must try to balance that independent wild streak with sensitivity and patience. There is no doubt that you will go far, but your life tends to be a self-created roller coaster and however much you complain about it, you seem to prefer it this way.

love ★ You can be a little arrogant and you demand to be adored and worshiped—in fact, you usually inspire this—but don't let it go to your head. Why not try a Leo who will be an equal, as Leos are ruled by the dazzling Sun, your birth date ruler?

best present ★ Parachute lessons, Swiss army knife.

birthday share ★ 1847 Joseph Pulitzer, journalist and publisher; 1932 Omar Sharif, actor; 1951 Steven Seagal, actor; 1988 Haley Joel Osment, actor.

on this day ★ In 1972, more than 50 countries signed a treaty outlawing the stockpiling of biological weapons.

color silvery blue ★ **number** 2, 11, 22 ★ **stone** fluorite—brings you intuitive wisdom and flashes of the future ★ **flora** poppy ★ **animal** chinchilla ★ **occupation** lawyer, ornithologist, social worker ★ **key features** intuitive, emotional, kind ★ **naturally good at** dealing with other people's problems

april 11

character ★ You are assertive but warm-hearted and may have a career caring for others less fortunate. You have the ability to communicate to the masses and focus much of your energy on your career. You will probably settle down early, as you have a craving for family life.

life path ★ You see situations in a practical and emotional way and are an excellent problem solver; you love to see results and will work longer hours than you are paid for. You are fond of food, are always happy to cook for your loved ones, and see nutrition as important.

love ★ You are loyal and trustworthy but do tend to flirt! Attractive and appealing, you exude charisma. You have many admirers but tend to stay faithful. Your birth date ruler is the Moon, which is also the ruling planet of Cancer, making Cancerians excellent partners for you.

best present ★ Cookbook, candleholder.

birthday share ★ 1939 Louise Lasser, actress; 1941 Ellen Goodman, journalist; 1947 Peter Riegert, actor; 1957 Jim Lauderdale, singer.

on this day ★ In 1968, President Lyndon B. Johnson signed the Civil Rights Act, prohibiting discrimination in the sale, rental, and financing of housing.

april 12

character ★ Your affable manner allows others to open up to you and, like David Letterman, who shares your birthday, you can gently rib people without them taking offense. You are well liked but often do not reach your goals until after the age of 30.

life path ★ Your intellect and humor will help you go far. Always remain optimistic, as you do have luck on your side. If sudden calamity or change occurs, this is probably just to make way for even greater good fortune, so learn to accept whatever comes and to go with the flow.

love ★ Have faith—you will end up with the perfect partner if you haven't already met them. You are very fortunate in the love stakes, and it is probably preordained that you will end up with someone who exceeds your expectations. Look out for a Sagittarius whose ruling planet is the same as your birth date ruler, Jupiter.

best present ★ Night in Las Vegas, bottle of champagne.

birthday share ★ 1947 Tom Clancy, author, and David Letterman, talk show host; 1950 David Cassidy, singer and actor; 1971 Shannon Doherty, actress.

on this day ★ In 1961, the Soviet Astronaut Yuri Gagarin became the first person to orbit the Earth.

color violet, amethyst ★ **number** 4, 22, 31 ★ **stone** geode—to increase your creativity ★
flora iris ★ **animal** leopard ★ **occupation** architect, chess player, surgeon ★ **key**
features clever, stimulating, diverse ★ **naturally good at** performing detailed tasks

april 13

character ★ You have a brilliant mind and usually very beautiful and dextrous hands. Even though you are generally quite impatient, you can handle exacting or difficult jobs. You would make a good engineer or mechanic, as you excel at resolving technical problems. You spend lots of time experimenting with new technology and you love gadgets.

life path ★ You constantly seek mental stimulation and get bored quickly; you may have a habit of tapping your foot and are generally a restless creature. Friends find your impatience amusing and put up with your foibles because you can be very entertaining when you relax.

love ★ You are a good lover, if a little unpredictable. You can be very affectionate one day but play the cool cat the next, which may confuse potential partners. You need to find the middle ground in this because it

doesn't do you or them any good. Try a broadminded Aquarius whose ruling planet, Uranus, is your birth date ruler.

best present ★ Palmtop computer, latest cell phone.

birthday share ★ 1743 Thomas Jefferson, 3rd U.S. president; 1942 Bill Conti, composer; 1946 Al Green, singer; 1963 Garry Kasparov, chess player.

on this day ★ In 1796, the first elephant brought to the United States arrived from Bengal, India.

color sky blue ★ number 5, 14, 32 ★ stone angelite—imbues you with a feeling of oneness with your surroundings ★ flora daisy ★ animal eagle ★ occupation singer, songwriter, party host ★ key features chirpy, eloquent, vital ★ naturally good at making speeches

april 14

character ★ Lighthearted and fun-loving, you have a wonderful way with people. You are self-effacing but very popular, and your humble nature and vitality serve you well. You can probably sing and have a heavenly voice. You are not very good with money but are quite lucky. If you want to be a writer, you should give it a try, as you definitely have it in you.

life path ★ When inspired you are an excellent speaker and a great mouthpiece for any organization or group. Even though you are nervous as a prairie dog, you live to communicate. Put those skills to good use, because all forms of communication energize and enhance your life.

love ★ You need someone who can protect your vulnerability because everyone else sees you as strong. In reality you are a sensitive soul, but once you trust a lover, you open totally to reveal the child within. Find

yourself a Gemini who is ruled by Mercury— the same ruler as your birth date ruler.

best present ★ Laptop computer, plant.

birthday share ★ 1904 Sir John Gielgud, actor; 1941 Julie Christie, actress, and Pete Rose, baseball player; 1961 Robert Carlyle, actor.

on this day ★ In 1912, the *Titanic* struck an iceberg on its maiden voyage and began to sink.

color lime, pink ★ **number** 6, 33, 42 ★ **stone** rose quartz—the stone that should fill you with unconditional love ★ **flora** geranium ★ **animal** donkey ★ **occupation** chef, songwriter, bar owner ★ **key features** sensitive, insecure, brave ★ **naturally good at** being a loving partner

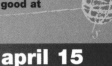

april 15

character ★ You can be addicted to relationships and can also party a little too much. Love easily becomes an obsession for you, which may stem from childhood experiences when you did not feel loved for yourself. You are outgoing, warm, and very sensitive to other people's feelings.

life path ★ You need to overcome the insecurity you feel; other people see you as brave, bold, and charismatic but you feel clumsy and unlovable. It is as if you are still seven years old. Nurture the child within but also value the adult you are now. You are truly gorgeous and adorable—so wake up and smell the coffee!

love ★ Lovers are drawn to you because you are strong and funny, yet when you fall in love you tend to give all your power away and become possessive and needy. Aspire to a relationship with a Libra whose ruling planet is Venus, your birth date ruler.

best present ★ Charm bracelet, yo-yo.

birthday share ★ 1452 Leonardo da Vinci, artist; 1843 Henry James, novelist; 1938 Claudia Cardinale, actress; 1959 Emma Thompson, actress.

on this day ★ In 1865, President Abraham Lincoln died at 7:21 a.m. after being shot at Ford's Theater in Washington D.C. by John Wilkes Booth the previous night.

april 16

character ★ You have a deeper understanding of life's mysteries than most, and are constantly talking about the meaning of life. At the same time you are wolfish, seductive, and very demanding. Generous to the point of stupidity, you love to share all of yourself with your friends and loved ones. You tend to overindulge in anything you truly enjoy.

life path ★ You need to find a balance between your extremes—the spiritual and the earthy—but you will still have a good time. You have a certain childlike quality, which is endearing and lets you get away with being difficult. You see yourself as a knight in shining armor and would walk to Timbuktu for those you love.

love ★ A highly emotional and idealistic lover, you dream of a once-in-a-lifetime relationship and seek a spiritual union. Because your birth date ruler is Neptune you can sink into the depths of your partner and see their soul, which they may find exhilarating but scary. Try a Pisces who will capture your attention and your heart.

best present ★ Antiquarian poetry book, white-gold ring.

birthday share ★ 1867 Wilbur Wright, aviator; 1889 Charlie Chaplin, actor and director; 1954 Ellen Barkin, actress; 1965 Martin Lawrence, actor.

on this day ★ In 1982, Queen Elizabeth II of England proclaimed Canada's new constitution, severing the last colonial links with Britain.

color hunter green ★ **number** 8, 17, 44 ★ **stone** amazonite—brings power and invites adventure into your life ★ **flora** stargazer lily ★ **animal** dalmatian dog ★ **occupation** headhunter, concert promoter, manager ★ **key features** willful, authoritative, dependable ★ **naturally good at** success in business

april 17

character ★ Domineering in the extreme, you need to realize that even if you are right, you have to respect other people. You demand good manners from those around you but can be brash and rude yourself. You tend to speak your mind without thinking but would be mortified to know you had hurt someone's feelings.

life path ★ You thrive on a challenge and make either loyal friends or viperous enemies. You are either adored or despised for your larger-than-life personality. However, you love a good battle, so it doesn't bother you if people are against you—you just fight harder.

love ★ You're a passionate lover, but if you get married you miss the thrill of the hunt and may be tempted to flirt with strangers. Although you don't consider this disloyal because you love your partner, you would go crazy if your partner did the same. Your

birth date ruler is Saturn, which is also the ruling planet of Capricorns, who would make a compatible match.

best present ★ Signet ring, silver pen.

birthday share ★ 1894 Nikita Krushchev, Soviet leader; 1918 William Holden, actor; 1951 Olivia Hussey, actress; 1974 Victoria Beckham, former Spice Girl.

on this day ★ In 1524, Italian navigator Giovanni Verrazano discovered New York harbor.

color crimson ★ **number** 9, 63, 72 ★ **stone** lapis lazuli—a sacred stone that represents the heavens and brings wisdom ★ **flora** apple blossom ★ **animal** horse ★ **occupation** army officer, athlete, pianist ★ **key features** influential, sturdy, fearless ★ **naturally good at** fighting battles and winning them

april 18

character ★ Powerful and strong, you stand firm in your beliefs. Be careful that you do not go to extremes or become fanatical. You have boundless energy and physical strength. You will have very strong political or moral views of either right or left. You always take the lead in conversations and consider yourself confident.

life path ★ You are intuitive and have finely tuned psychic antennae that you call gut instincts, and you always listen to your inner voice. You could do with being a little more gentle and open. At parties you will be the last man or woman standing.

love ★ Love is not a game but you love the thrill of the chase and are attracted to men or women who spurn you or are elusive. You have no time for people who roll over and offer themselves to you. Your birth date ruler is the same as your ruling planet, fiery Mars, so why not check out another Aries?

best present ★ Hiking boots, skis.

birthday share ★ 1882 Leopold Stakowski, conductor; 1946 Hayley Mills, actress; 1953 Rick Moranis, actor; 1968 Christian Slater, actor.

on this day ★ In 1906, an earthquake destroyed most of San Francisco.

color orange, gold ★ **number** 1, 11, 22 ★ **stone** carnelian—a roman talisman that will fire you up ★ **flora** canna lily ★ **animal** giraffe ★ **occupation** comedian, horse rider, ice-hockey player ★ **key features** cheerful, charismatic, attractive ★ **naturally good at** turning heads

april 19

character ★ You always smell fabulous, have loads of magnetism, and know how to use it. You are drawn toward famous people and may work in the entertainment industry. You love fast cars and beautiful people but must work hard to avoid being superficial.

life path ★ Money comes easily to you and you know how to squander it. It may be boring but you should put some by for a rainy day, as all this living to excess could leave you broke in years to come. You have beautiful, compelling eyes and the gift of gab.

love ★ You could take your pick from a host of glamorous admirers but prefer to be footloose and fancy-free. There is sometimes an on-off element to your relationships and there may well be someone in the background whom you toy with. Your birth date ruler is the Sun, Leo's ruling planet, so a Leo is sure to make your heart beat faster.

best present ★ Mirrored sunglasses, linen shirt.

birthday share ★ 1933 Jayne Mansfield, actress; 1935 Dudley Moore, actor; 1946 Tim Curry, actor; 1949 Paloma Picasso, perfume and fashion designer.

on this day ★ In 1956, Grace Kelly married Prince Rainier of Monaco, and became Princess Grace of Monaco.

color silver ★ **number** 2, 11, 22 ★ **stone** moonstone—a fertility stone that will also balance your mood ★ **flora** daffodil ★ **animal** hawk ★ **occupation** actor, counselor, telephone operator ★ **key features** sensitive, profound, charming ★ **naturally good at** seeing into the souls of others

april 20

character ★ You are strong but sensitive, and although you are often caught up in the superficial you have a longing to experience the profound in life. You may seek answers via spiritual workshops and self-help groups but in fact this knowledge lies within you. You are a wise soul and are very good at understanding people.

life path ★ You will end up doing something worthwhile and important, but this usually comes later in life. You have a strong connection to your mother for good or bad and may have felt that your parents were very different from each other. You want a family life but usually don't settle until your thirties.

love ★ Loving and understanding, you make an excellent partner. You get to the heart of your spouse and can talk about their vulnerabilities, but be careful not to become their therapist or to take on a parental role. Your birth date ruler is the Moon, the ruling planet of Cancer, so try a Cancerian for an unbreakable connection.

best present ★ Silver heart key ring, trip to the countryside.

birthday share ★ 1889 Adolf Hitler, German dictator; 1941 Ryan O'Neal, actor; 1949 Jessica Lange, actress; 1951 Luther Vandross, singer.

on this day ★ In 1841, *The Murders in the Rue Morgue* by Edgar Allan Poe, considered the first detective story, was published in *Graham's Magazine* in Philadelphia.

aries

your ruling planet **Mars** is the planet of war and you are quick to do battle. This hot and fiery planet is also known as the red planet and is the closest to the Sun. Mars imbues you with passion and hot-headedness. It is responsible for your aggressive side but also for your huge romantic streak. Mars gives you your drive and unlimited energy but you must be careful not to burn yourself out. Your warrior spirit comes from your ruler, as does a certain raw, primal energy that carries you through life and allows you to go after your dreams and goals fearlessly. It is impossible for you to conceal your true emotions and feelings—you spout them out quite bluntly and often at inappropriate moments when they can be hurtful. You are only trying to be honest but perhaps you need to learn some diplomacy and develop greater sensitivity. Do not use the truth as a weapon. Mars takes no prisoners and is relentless in its pursuit of pleasure, success, and passion.

your natural habitat If you are male and single you will tend to have a real bachelor pad where you can indulge your love of boys' toys and gadgets. You are as masculine as they come, a real macho guy or tomboy. You are not the tidiest of people and expect others to clear up after you. If you are female you, too, like to have a home of your own that is decorated exactly to your taste. If you live with someone else, whether you are male or female, you tend to take over and even relegate your partner's stuff to the attic. You cannot live with an interior you don't like—it causes you immense irritation and with that big Aries mouth of yours, you don't hold back when sledgehammering your partner's taste in wallpaper and soft furnishings. Ideally you would like a super-cool city apartment that is smart and minimalistic, as well as a country cottage, complete with fireplace.

are you a typical aries?

You're wild, impulsive, and mouthy. You speak your mind and hate being ignored. A natural leader, you cannot stand anyone telling you what to do. Life is an impulsive joy ride and you refuse to be tamed. You enjoy the thrill of the chase and rush around from one exciting adventure to another. You are something of a hero and will always defend the underdog. Playful and extravagant, you have loads of friends who adore you.

Why you're wonderful! You are generous to a fault and will always share what you have. You are kind and a big kid at heart. This childlike charm captivates all who meet you, although you can be very uncooperative, which is less than charming. Your enthusiasm is infectious and you are great at empowering other people; you have a strong belief that we can all make it. You like to lead and others trust you and follow. You are also a fantastic and exuberant lover with a heart of gold.

Why you're impossible! You can be demanding, petulant, and overcompetitive. You like things your own way. Although you have a volcanic temper that can spring from nowhere, you are also quick to forgive. You love to boss people around and always think you are right. Because you act impulsively you can sometimes do the wrong thing and find yourself in a lot of trouble.

Your secret side Underneath that overly confident exterior you have a modicum of shyness and insecurity. You cannot bear to be misunderstood, and even though you are rebellious and independent on the surface, you need a lot of love. You crave someone you can trust because loyalty is important to you, and someone who can support you emotionally. This vulnerability is hidden under a large dollop of bravado, but it is very real.

aries love compatibility chart

	aries	taurus	gemini	cancer	leo	virgo
fun	🍾	🍾	🍾	🍾	🍾	🍾
romance	💘	💘	💘	💘	💘	💘
loyalty		🔗			🔗	
adventure	🎈	🎈	🎈		🎈	🎈
	💋	💋		💋	💋	💋
	🪑	🪑	🪑		🪑	🪑
	💡		💡		💡	💡
		👥		👥	👥	

	libra	scorpio	sagittarius	capricorn	aquarius	pisces
	🍾		🍾		🍾	🍾
	❤	❤	❤	❤		
	⭕					
	🎈	🎈	🎈		🎈	
	👄	👄	👄	👄		
	🪑		🪑			
	💡		💡		💡	💡
	👥					

  passion **chilling out** **spontaneity**  **attentiveness**

taurus

april 21–may 21

color lavender ★ number 3, 12, 30 ★ stone herkimer diamond—said to reduce stress and help you remember your dreams ★ flora bluebell ★ animal jack russell dog ★ occupation garden designer, judge, politician ★ key features potent, regal, dignified ★ naturally good at being a leader

april 21

character ★ Majestic and noble, you inspire others with your hardworking attitude and stamina. You always stick to your word and have some loyal friends who have been close to you for years. You love fine food and wine but are prone to overindulgence and as a result possibly suffer from a fluctuating weight.

life path ★ Others might say you are lucky but actually you have worked hard to get where you are. You inspire trust, so people like to help you professionally because they know you will do a good job. You have it in you to reach the top, so do not let emotional ties stop you.

love ★ Faithful and with high moral values, you sometimes stay in relationships when it would be better to move on, and this sense of misplaced loyalty may hold you back emotionally. Anyone would be lucky to have you as a partner even though you can get stuck in a routine. Your birth date ruler is Jupiter, so perhaps look out for an eccentric Sagittarius whose ruling planet is also Jupiter.

best present ★ Pool table, digital camera.

birthday share ★ 1816 Charlotte Brontë, author; 1915 Anthony Quinn, actor; 1926 Queen Elizabeth II of Great Britain; 1958 Andie MacDowell, actress.

on this day ★ In 1828, Noah Webster published his first *American Dictionary of the English Language*, standardizing U.S. English and distinguishing it from British English.

color silver ★ **number** 4, 22, 31 ★ **stone** kunzite—clears the mind and prevents memory loss ★ **flora** sage ★ **animal** piranha ★ **occupation** leader, actor, entrepreneur ★ **key features** charismatic, mesmerizing, compelling ★ **naturally good at** capturing all the attention in a room

character ★ The number 22 is a master number and sets you aside from the masses. You exude power but usually in a quiet, understated way. You can persuade people to change their minds about the most fundamental things and have a hypnotic charm that is impossible to resist.

life path ★ You are here to create something special—special to you, anyway. However, if you wanted to have an effect on society as a whole it would be relatively easy for you. You are touched with a certain magic and simply need to be more aware of your own power.

love ★ Basically faithful, you have such an aura of sensuality and mystery that temptation is always on the cards. Your partners need to keep a close eye on you because you can get carried away with flirting. Your birth date ruler is Uranus, so check out an Aquarius whose ruling planet is also Uranus.

best present ★ Portable CD player, training weights.

birthday share ★ 1724 Immanuel Kant, philosopher; 1870 Vladimir Lenin, Soviet Communist leader; 1899 Vladimir Nabokov, author; 1937 Jack Nicholson, actor.

on this day ★ In 1889, a single gunshot at midday started the Oklahoma land rush, with 200,000 people racing to stake claim to 160 acres each of prairie.

april 23

character ★ You are an excellent communicator and can talk to anybody about anything. You have friends from all walks of life and enjoy variety in your social life. You love to socialize but mainly with trusted friends over dinner rather than at clubs or bars. Your home is a sanctuary but you may not get to spend enough time there.

life path ★ The Bard, William Shakespeare, shared your birthday and like you he had lots to say! You have brilliant observational skills and are something of a people watcher. You have your friends in stitches with your witty take on life, but you can occasionally sink into despair because you crave to be understood more deeply.

love ★ You are romantic and old-fashioned; you like to woo partners and value the journey of seduction, sometimes more than long-term security. You would do anything for the one you love and are very faithful, but you sometimes chase unobtainable beauties or hunks. Try a Gemini whose ruling planet is also your birth date ruler, Mercury.

best present ★ Engraved key ring, silver heart pendant.

birthday share ★ 1564 William Shakespeare, playwright and poet; 1891 Sergei Prokofiev, composer; 1928 Shirley Temple, child actress and U.S. ambassador; 1936 Roy Orbison, singer.

on this day ★ In 1933, the Gestapo, the secret state police of the Nazi party, was established in Germany.

color pink, coral ★ **number** 6, 15, 33 ★ **stone** rose-quartz—the stone that brings unconditional love ★ **flora** carnation ★ **animal** poodle ★ **occupation** actor, singer, fashion designer ★ **key features** faithful, dedicated, devoted ★ **naturally good at** loving others with your very soul

character ★ You have deeply held spiritual beliefs and feel that magic exists underneath everything. You believe the world should be a place of universal love and equality, are fiercely protective of your family, and have an enormous heart.

life path ★ You have a strong shielding instinct for those you love, even when they are in the wrong, but you can feel let down or disappointed if they fall from the lofty pedestals you place them on. Occasionally it is necessary to be more objective or you could end up going against your own principles. Put yourself first sometimes.

love ★ Venus, the planet of love, is both your birth date ruler and your ruling planet. Venus bestows on you great magnetism and abundance in the love stakes. Choose wisely, because you tend to be lovestruck rapidly and completely, becoming so committed that you are blind to any faults. Why not choose a Libra whose ruling planet is also the gentle Venus?

best present ★ Love letter, home-cooked meal.

birthday share ★ 1934 Shirley MacLaine, actress and author; 1940 Sue Grafton, author; 1942 Barbra Streisand, singer; 1952 Jean-Paul Gaultier, fashion designer.

on this day ★ In 1704, the *Boston News-Letter*, one of the earliest newspapers in the U.S. colonies, was first published.

april 25

character ★ You are sometimes called lazy because you sit around pondering your options and getting nothing practical done. You can become involved in emotional situations that have a mystery or secret connected to them. On the one hand you enjoy these trysts, but you can also become directionless and confused.

life path ★ You tend to let things happen to you rather than control your destiny. You need to gain clarity or there is a danger that you will float from situation to situation through your life without ever taking hold of the reins.

love ★ There is no doubt that you love to love, but you can be quite changeable. Often attracted to someone you know full well you cannot have, you tend to stay in stable relationships while craving a grand passion.

Neptune is your birth date ruler, so ideally you should choose a Pisces who has Neptune as their ruling planet.

best present ★ Snorkel and flippers, surfboard.

birthday share ★ 1917 Ella Fitzgerald, singer; 1940 Al Pacino, actor; 1964 Hank Azaria, actor; 1969 Renée Zellweger, actress.

on this day ★ In 1950, Chuck Cooper became the first black man to play in the National Basketball Association (NBA).

color burgundy ★ **number** 8, 17, 62 ★ **stone** alabaster—purifies your emotions and brings peace when anger throbs ★ **flora** ivy ★ **animal** stallion ★ **occupation** farmer, horticulturist, long-haul truck driver ★ **key features** dogged, dominant, inflexible ★ **naturally good at** pushing yourself to the highest levels of physical endurance

character ★ You're powerful and stubborn and never give in, particularly in business. You work your fingers to the bone and expect rewards. You can be a little naughty in your determination to get to the top and will manipulate if you need to, considering this as sometimes necessary to achieve the best results.

life path ★ Power is not about money, assets, or Armani suits, but how open you can allow your heart to be. You may get caught in a trap of materialism if you are not careful, but no amount of wealth can truly fulfill you. Finding some kind of spirituality is essential for the growth of your soul.

love ★ You have high ideals and want a lover who will be as faithful to you as you are to them, and who will look after you. They must be a very attentive man or woman, and know how to pamper you. Your birth date ruler is stern Saturn, so look around for a Capricorn whose ruling planet is also Saturn.

best present ★ Golf clubs, calculator.

birthday share ★ 1894 Rudolf Hess, Nazi official; 1900 Charles Francis Richter, earthquake seismologist; 1936 Carol Burnett, comedienne; 1967 Kane (Glen Jacobs), WWF wrestler.

on this day ★ In 1986, the fourth reactor at the Chernobyl nuclear complex in the Ukraine exploded and caught fire, spreading a radioactive cloud across Europe in the world's worst nuclear disaster to date. As a result of the explosion, 31 people were killed, and thousands more were exposed to harmful radioactive material.

color red ★ number 9, 18, 45 ★ stone aragonite—amplifies your dreams and thoughts, bringing great personal power ★ flora peony ★ animal red squirrel ★ occupation gardener, landscape architect, literary agent ★ key features energetic, sturdy, earthy ★ naturally good at working on the land

april 27

character ★ You are very strong and have a prodigious capacity for heavy physical labor. You take your strength for granted and fuel it with a hearty appetite, but you need to watch your diet. You often spend periods of time alone but don't seem to mind this. Your support of others is unswerving if you believe in what they are doing. You may get frustrated that others are not as supportive as you, but you must avoid bitterness at all costs.

life path ★ You may be tempted to get involved in some form of fundamentalism or extreme views at some point in your life. This would hold you back and you need to remember that we are all unique and equal. This tendency comes from a place in you where you feel neglected, but love is actually all around you if you want it.

love ★ You may have periods of celibacy, but once you meet your dream lover you will blossom physically and spiritually. Devoted relationships suit you, and you are darned good at them. Love will bring you many answers if you let it in. Look for it from a passionate Aries who has Mars, your birth date ruler, as their ruling planet.

best present ★ Gardening tools, Italian meal.

birthday share ★ 1791 Samuel Morse, inventor of the Morse code; 1822 Ulysses S. Grant, 18th U.S. president; 1932 Anouk Aimée, actress; 1959 Sheena Easton, singer.

on this day ★ In 1956, Rocky Marciano retired as undefeated world heavyweight boxing champion.

color orange, yellow ★ number 1, 11, 22 ★ stone apophyllite—banishes negative energy and helps you connect with your spirit guide ★ flora daisy ★ animal lion ★ occupation filmmaker, advertising executive, campaigner ★ key features gregarious, focused, radiant ★ naturally good at making things happen

april 28

character ★ You go for it in life and your motto is probably carpe diem (seize the day). When you have decided on action, nothing can divert you from your path. You're great at motivating others to action and handling big projects. Life for you is an orchestra and you're the conductor.

life path ★ Opportunities in life come easily to you. You will enter into something only if you feel strongly about it, so your career should be quite smooth. If you are a rare 28th April person in that you are doing something you detest, you should change quickly because it will never work. You're talented and attractive and programmed for a charmed life.

love ★ Love comes naturally to you, and, unless you are overwhelmed by your career, you are usually in a pretty good relationship where you have the power. Security is important to you. Your birth date ruler is the Sun, so why not choose a Leo whose ruling planet is also the Sun?

best present ★ Bottle of vodka, silk shirt.

birthday share ★ 1878 Lionel Barrymore, actor; 1924 Kenneth Kaunda, president of Zambia; 1941 Ann-Margret, actress, singer, and dancer; 1974 Penelope Cruz, actress.

on this day ★ In 1789, after a mutiny provoked by his harsh treatment, the British sailor William Bligh, commander of the *Bounty,* was cast adrift near the Friendly Islands in a small open boat with 18 men.

color silvery blue ★ number 2, 11, 22 ★ stone beryl—the crystal that is said to give you a glimpse of the future ★ flora carnation ★ animal barn owl ★ occupation lecturer, nanny, model ★ key features gentle, kind, caring ★ naturally good at gaining the trust of other people

april 29

character ★ If you are male you should have loads of women friends and confidantes. If you are female you should exude femininity. This is a very womanly birth date, as you are ruled by the Moon and Venus. You also have an affinity with babies and children, and you bring out the caring instincts in others.

life path ★ You're adorable and lovable, and it is a lucky family indeed that has you in it. You are a giver not a taker, love to look after others and pamper them, and always have a kind word for those you love. You can feel vulnerable sometimes for no reason, but you're simply an emotional person, so go with the flow.

love ★ You can get carried away in love and often it strikes you like a thunderbolt. Once you feel it you pursue it, showering your partner with gifts and demanding adoration in return. Cool it just a little.

Try a Cancer who has the Moon, your birth date ruler, as their ruling planet. This will promote mutual emotional understanding.

best present ★ Cocktail shaker, ice bucket.

birthday share ★ 1954 Jerry Seinfeld, comedian; 1957 Daniel Day-Lewis, actor; 1970 Uma Thurman, actress, and André Agassi, tennis player.

on this day ★ In 1992, a jury acquitted four Los Angeles police officers accused of beating motorist Rodney King. The verdict sparked rioting and looting.

april 30

character ★ You are a pillar of the community and take an interest in your neighborhood. You may feel inclined to take up a charitable cause or generally do good deeds. You have friends of all ages and always take care of older family members, respecting them even when they are difficult.

life path ★ You could be accused of taking life a little too seriously. Try sharing some of the responsibilities you take on. If you're a woman you have a strong maternal instinct, and if you're a guy you may be drawn to mother figures or have older female friends.

love ★ Your partner may feel you are not around enough because you have so many commitments. Take time out to be a little more romantic. Your birth date ruler is Jupiter, so choose a free-spirited Sagittarius whose ruling planet is Jupiter, as they will respect your need for freedom.

best present ★ Wallet/purse, baseball cap.

birthday share ★ 1870 Franz Lehar, composer; 1908 Eve Arden, actress; 1933 Willie Nelson, singer; 1982 Kirsten Dunst, actress.

on this day ★ In 1900, U.S. railroad engineer Casey Jones died while saving passengers as the *Cannonball Express* was about to crash into another train at Vaughan, Mississippi.

may 1

character ★ You have a sunny personality but can be a bit finicky when it comes to work. You like to be in charge and do not take orders well unless you consider your boss a friend. You are imaginative and able to come up with creative ideas at the drop of a hat.

life path ★ You need to have more faith in your own abilities; you tend not to push yourself and could achieve more than you do. You like the familiar and are alarmed by change or new situations, although on the surface you don't show it.

love ★ You like relationships that resemble an old pair of slippers, comfortable and worn in. You may complain about the boring nature of your love life, but really you wouldn't have it any other way. Your perfect partner could well be a Leo, as your birth date ruler is the Sun, Leo's ruling planet.

best present ★ Air-hockey table, tickets to a rock concert.

birthday share ★ 1916 Glenn Ford, actor; 1923 Joseph Heller, author; 1925 Scott Carpenter, astronaut; 1944 Rita Coolidge, singer.

on this day ★ In 1931, New York City's Empire State Building was completed and opened by President Herbert Hoover.

color silver ★ **number** 2, 11, 22 ★ **stone** calcite—a good luck gem bringing opportunities your way ★ **flora** tulip ★ **animal** mouse ★ **occupation** lawyer, doctor of naturopathy, psychologist ★ **key features** emotional, balanced, profound ★ **naturally good at** relating to other people's problems

character ★ You have a strongly compassionate spirit and will always lend a hand to those in need. Your home can be a sanctuary for friends with problems, but putting more effort into others than into yourself means you tend not to follow your dreams.

life path ★ Listen to the advice you give others and apply it to yourself. You are so intuitive and caring. If you were to turn that inward, your life would turn around. You have a heart of gold and need to work on your self-esteem because others think you are great. An inspirational job in which you can help and advise people would suit you.

love ★ You often fall for the underdog or for people with problems. Try not to be their therapist and healer. Your birth date ruler is the Moon, so perhaps a Cancer, whose ruling planet is also the Moon, would be the one for you.

best present ★ Set of runes, crystal pendulum.

birthday share ★ 1936 Engelbert Humperdinck, singer; 1945 Bianca Jagger, human rights activist; 1955 Donatella Versace, fashion designer; 1975 David Beckham, soccer player.

on this day ★ In 1969, the British passenger liner *Queen Elizabeth II* left on her maiden voyage to New York.

may 3

character ★ You may have felt restricted when you were younger, but in your thirties life seems to fly and all of a sudden shapes up in the way you would like. Do not rest on your laurels, though; keep pushing to achieve your aspirations and Lady Luck will give you a helping hand.

life path ★ Your birth date is ruled by Jupiter, planet of good fortune, so if you make the effort, good things will just fall into your lap. However, don't take this for granted—although you were born lucky, it is up to you to transform your life. Laziness can be a weakness.

love ★ When you love, you love forever and give your heart and soul, but you can lose passion slightly as the relationship progresses, so make sure that you put effort into maintaining the sparkle. Sagittarius, whose ruling planet is your birth date ruler, Jupiter, would make a perfect partner.

best present ★ Tennis racket, gold bracelet.

birthday share ★ 1906 Mary Astor, actress; 1921 Sugar Ray Robinson, boxer; 1933 James Brown, singer; 1937 Frankie Valli, singer.

on this day ★ In 1937, author Margaret Mitchell won a Pulitzer Prize for her novel *Gone With the Wind*.

color copper ★ **number** 4, 13, 22 ★ **stone** peacock ore—gives you energy and optimism ★
flora delphinium ★ **animal** wild turkey ★ **occupation** charity worker, singer, spiritual guide ★
key features caring, strong, intense ★ **naturally good at** spotting future trends

may 4

character ★ You have a deeper personality than most and could find yourself in situations where you are asked to be a public figure or leader. You may be reluctant to take on this role, but follow this path if you can and you will have a rewarding life. Unusual opportunities are destined to come up, so be prepared.

life path ★ For some reason you are not allowed to settle down and live a mundane existence. No matter how hard you try to live a quiet life you will always be confronted with excitement and opportunity. This is partly because your birth date ruler is wacky Uranus, which cannot stand to be settled. Surrender to it and enjoy the ride.

love ★ You are turned on by what people think, not by what they look like, and may have had partners in the past who were very different or eccentric. Your perfect match may well be an Aquarius, whose ruling planet, Uranus, is also your birth date ruler, and who is just different enough.

best present ★ Giant hop ball, telescope.

birthday share ★ 1928 Hosni Mubarak, president of Egypt; 1929 Audrey Hepburn, actress; 1959 Randy Travis, country singer; 1979 James Lance Bass, singer.

on this day ★ In 1904, work began on the Panama Canal.

color cobalt blue ★ number 14, 23, 32 ★ stone iolite—a blue-purple stone said to increase intuition ★ flora starflower ★ animal rabbit ★ occupation journalist, personal assistant, clerk ★ key features vocal, professional, amiable ★ naturally good at expressing your thoughts

may 5

character ★ You have great communication skills and love a good argument, usually just for the mental banter. This can cause friction in your personal relationships, but you don't mean any harm and are quickly forgiven. Perhaps you should learn to bite your tongue and listen a bit more?

life path ★ You have a vague feeling of dissatisfaction, which goes back as far as you can remember. Use this to change the things that are stuck in your life. Studying Buddhism or another philosophy may help you deal with the melancholy side of your personality.

love ★ Being in a partnership suits you. You are not afraid of commitment but can take your lover for granted or see them as an extension of yourself. Your birth date ruler is Mercury, Gemini's ruling planet, so a Gemini would make an understanding partner.

best present ★ Candle lantern, meditation stool.

birthday share ★ 1818 Karl Marx, philosopher; 1942 Tammy Wynette, singer; 1943 Michael Palin, Monty Python member, author, and travel commentator; 1957 Richard E. Grant, actor.

on this day ★ In 1961 Alan B. Shepard Jr. became the first U.S. astronaut in space during a 15-minute ride aboard the Mercury capsule *Freedom 17*.

color pink ★ **number** 15, 27, 33 ★ **stone** peridot—this green heart stone gives mental clarity and protects against nightmares ★ **flora** rhododendron ★ **animal** cow ★ **occupation** relationship counselor, internet entrepreneur, poet ★ **key features** loving, creative, trustworthy ★ **naturally good at** understanding human emotions

character ★ Venus, planet of love, is your double ruler, making relationships and love extremely important to you. You tend to have a very kind personality and the ability to give generously of yourself. You are a fantastic cook and entertainer, an all-around domestic god or goddess. Food is a passion so you should keep an eye on your weight.

life path ★ Your life will be transformed by love in some way. This could be the love of a partner or the love of a child, but love is your life lesson. Do not become obsessive or possessive of loved ones as you follow the path of unconditional love. Real love is all about freedom and trust, so do not let your baser instincts get the better of you.

love ★ Because this is such a strong motivating force in your life you may be tempted to play games or manipulate partners out of insecurity. The sooner you learn to have faith in others, the happier you will become. Choose another loyal Taurus for a good match, as their ruling planet, Venus, is also your birth date ruler.

best present ★ Heart-shaped pendant, tank-driving course.

birthday share ★ 1856 Sigmund Freud, psychologist; 1915 Orson Welles, actor and director; 1953 Tony Blair, British prime minister; 1961 George Clooney, actor.

on this day ★ In 1957, Massachusetts senator John F. Kennedy received the Pulitzer Prize for his *Profiles in Courage*.

may 7

character ★ You live in a fantasy world and should focus on making some of your fantasies reality. You have a strong spiritual streak and believe in destiny, but you do need to give destiny a helping hand sometimes and put your high ideals to good use. You were given a fantastic imagination and should do something with it.

life path ★ Finding your spirituality or meaning for being here is a lifelong mission. You have natural intuition and should develop this gift. Writing will put you in touch with your inner wisdom and could be very rewarding for you.

love ★ You want to experience spiritual merging and union but perhaps don't really believe this exists anywhere. Yes, you do have a soul mate and yes, you will find them, so remain open to the possibility. Try a Pisces whose ruling planet, Neptune, is also your birth date ruler.

best present ★ Crystal ball, meditation cards.

birthday share ★ 1840 Pyotr Ilyich Tchaikovsky, composer; 1901 Gary Cooper, actor; 1919 Eva Peron, former first lady of Argentina; 1923 Anne Baxter, actress.

on this day ★ In 1994, the Channel Tunnel was officially opened, linking Britain to France.

may 8

character ★ Strong-willed and like an immovable object, you never back down. You are respected and sometimes feared—people often feel they have to handle you with kid gloves. Your bark, however, is worse than your bite. You genuinely love those close to you but see vulnerability as weakness. Open up and let love in.

life path ★ Your lesson is to discover that strength is gentleness, not dominance. Whether male or female you can be too strong-willed and need to learn flexibility. Nevertheless, you are also quite attractive in a serious sort of way and have no shortage of admirers, whom you probably don't even notice. Discover your playful side and allow yourself to be frivolous sometimes.

love ★ Love is a serious business for you and you need a partner who is an equal. If you are a woman, you will be drawn to powerful partners, but often end up with someone weaker than you, and men will tend to control their loved ones a little too much. Choose a Capricorn whose ruling planet is also your birth date ruler, Saturn.

best present ★ Hip flask, red wine.

birthday share ★ 1884 Harry S. Truman, 33rd U.S. president; 1930 Gary Snyder, poet and author; 1941 James Mitchum, actor; 1975 Enrique Iglesias, singer.

on this day ★ In 1945, Victory in Europe Day (VE Day) was declared, marking the end of World War II in Europe.

may 9

character ★ You may experience some hardships in your life but you have the capacity to survive in situations that would defeat others. You are brave and true and have a powerful aura. Although you can often lose your temper you are quick to forgive. You will always succeed with the strength of your personality, but underneath that forceful exterior you're really a pussycat.

life path ★ Sometimes you think that someone above is having a laugh at your expense, as you encounter so many problems and battles. However, you generally sail through and must keep an optimistic and positive front. Wealth comes to you over time and life gets easier after the 40 milestone.

love ★ When you love it is for life, even if the relationship does not last. You will not let anyone put your partner down and are very protective of them. You are a tactile and generous lover. Try an Aries whose ruling planet, Mars, is also your birth date ruler.

best present ★ Locket containing a picture of a loved one, playing cards.

birthday share ★ 1860 J. M. Barrie, playwright; 1936 Albert Finney, actor; 1946 Candice Bergen, actress; 1949 Billy Joel, singer.

on this day ★ In 1926, U.S. aviators Richard E. Byrd and Floyd Bennett became the first to fly over the North Pole.

color orange, yellow ★ **number** 1, 11, 22 ★ **stone** chrysolite—a stone related to the sun that makes you even more charming than you are already ★ **flora** dandelion ★ **animal** tiger ★ **occupation** nightclub singer, dancer, athlete ★ **key features** athletic, agile, glamorous ★ **naturally good at** dance and movement

may 10

character ★ You love your body and become very depressed if you get out of shape. You need to do plenty of exercise to keep you happy and admire others who are fit. If you are one of the rare May 10th people who don't do much physical activity, try it—it will change your life!

life path ★ You have natural rhythm and should always have music playing around you. You have a spiritual connection to movement and it is almost a meditation for you. Your body is your temple and you need to treat it as such—this is more important to you than for people born on any other day. This also makes you a fine lover.

love ★ You adore beautiful people but it is important that you avoid going for a trophy partner. When you are younger you can be quite superficial in this area, but as you mature you will discover that beauty is only skin deep. Your ideal match would be a gorgeous Leo whose ruling planet, the radiant Sun, is also your birth date ruler.

best present ★ Tap-dancing lessons, gym membership.

birthday share ★ 1899 Fred Astaire, dancer, actor, and singer; 1922 Nancy Walker, actress; 1960 Bono, singer and campaigner; 1965 Linda Evangelista, model.

on this day ★ In 1869, the east and west coasts of the United States were linked when the Central Pacific Railroad from the west met the Union Pacific Railroad from the east in Utah.

color silver ★ number 2, 11, 22 ★ stone celestite—an angelic stone that eases away tension and fills you with gentleness ★ flora waterlily ★ animal dove ★ occupation choreographer, photographer, lawyer ★ key features artistic, sensitive, trusting ★ naturally good at having a sense of the aesthetic

may 11

character ★ You pride yourself on your ability to turn the drabbest environment into a paradise of comfort, and naturally you have a stunning home. You love beautiful objects but beware: too many can look like clutter. Even where you work, your little touches will make it feel homey. You have a slightly mysterious air about you, which makes others wonder what you are thinking.

life path ★ Because you are so intuitive you can be too caught up in your own point of view; you feel when things are right. This can frustrate people who expect a more rational response. So what! You are usually quite right in your opinions but you could deliver your verdicts with more love and humility.

love ★ You have periods of long-term relationships alternating with periods of being alone, which, at the time, you feel will last forever. As the Moon is your birth date ruler you will instinctively know when you meet the right partner. Try a Cancer, who also has the Moon as their ruling planet.

best present ★ Book on the *I Ching*, aromatherapy bath oil.

birthday share ★ 1888 Irving Berlin, composer; 1904 Salvador Dali, artist; 1911 Phil Silvers, actor; 1932 Valentino Garavani, fashion designer.

on this day ★ In 1997, IBM's supercomputer Deep Blue made chess history by defeating Gary Kasparov. It was the first time a reigning world champion had been beaten in a match by a machine.

color lilac ★ **number** 3, 21, 33 ★ **stone** rhodonite—for self-healing and to remove feelings of guilt ★ **flora** waterlily ★ **animal** chicken ★ **occupation** business manager, real estate agent, flight attendant ★ **key features** patient, nonconformist, free ★ **naturally good at** getting your own way

character ★ You are a free spirit who may have a normal job but still maintains a strong individual streak. You are quite lucky but your luck comes in chunks that are difficult for you to anticipate. You can be self-destructive or overindulgent because you are easily bored and want adventure.

life path ★ You hate the mundane and your life can be just that. Find ways of expressing your inner being or you may start to feel sorry for yourself when there is no need. There are solutions and you will be able to balance your free spirit with your responsibilities if you truly want to.

love ★ When in a long-term and committed relationship you are never absolutely sure that it is for you and always keep back a part of yourself. You would be like this with any partner, so enjoy what you have. Your birth date ruler is Jupiter, planet of good fortune and the ruling planet of Sagittarius, so choose a Sagittarius for long-lasting romance.

best present ★ Acting lessons, weekend in New York.

birthday share ★ 1820 Florence Nightingale, nursing pioneer; 1907 Katharine Hepburn, actress; 1928 Burt Bacharach, composer; 1962 Emilio Estevez, actor.

on this day ★ In 1935, Alcoholics Anonymous was founded in Akron, Ohio, by William Wilson.

color light blue ★ **number** 4, 13, 22 ★ **stone** lapis lazuli—the highly prized stone of the ancient egyptians that brings wisdom and increases intuition ★ **flora** pansy ★ **animal** boxer dog ★ **occupation** advertising executive, guitarist, stand-up comic ★ **key features** stubborn, funny, charming ★ **naturally good at** making people laugh

may 13

character ★ You could charm the birds out of the trees. When people meet you for the first time, they are instantly drawn to you, entertained by your amusing tales and charisma. You listen to their problems and give them lots of attention; however, once you get to know them, they will have your loyalty but not your initial softness.

life path ★ You make friends quickly and easily and are forever faithful once you have given your heart. However, you can take the people you love for granted. You expect them to have the same value system as you and to love you unconditionally, but others may need more time to become so absolute.

love ★ When you love, you love deeply and romantically; you want a relationship that is for life. You are good at showing affection, but you can forget that a relationship needs work. Try an Aquarius whose ruling planet is your birth date ruler, Uranus.

best present ★ Quad bike, games console.

birthday share ★ 1939 Harvey Keitel, actor; 1944 Armistead Maupin, author; 1950 Stevie Wonder, singer and pianist; 1961 Dennis Rodman, basketball player.

on this day ★ In 1981, Pope John Paul II was shot four times by a Turkish gunman in St. Peter's Square, Rome, but survived.

color blue ★ **number** 5, 14, 23 ★ **stone** rutilated quartz—fires you up and gives you direction ★ **flora** peace lily ★ **animal** monkey ★ **occupation** taxi driver, publisher, historian ★ **key features** studious, articulate, inventive ★ **naturally good at** all aspects of studying

character ★ You have a passion for knowledge and will often have a consuming hobby or interest that is separate from your job. You are a deep thinker and attracted to people who have an agile mind. You can be a little insecure about your intellectual ability but you are generally brighter than most.

life path ★ It is important for you to succeed but you're not in any rush. You have big plans for the future and think about issues, such as retirement, years before you get there. You may want to do something radical in the future, maybe moving to another country, but whatever it is you will work toward it with determination.

love ★ You tend to get into relationships that began as friendships. You find yourself easing into this, as you are a little lazy in this area. Have a more passionate love affair with a Gemini, whose ruling planet, Mercury, is your birth date ruler.

best present ★ Wok, foot spa.

birthday share ★ 1944 George Lucas, film producer; 1952 David Byrne, singer; 1961 Tim Roth, actor; 1969 Cate Blanchett, actress.

on this day ★ In 1948, Israel declared itself an independent nation.

may 15

character ★ Love is the focus of your life and it can take you over. When you are in a relationship, it always comes first and you never fail to give your partner what they desire. You can suffer from jealous rages and issues of control within the relationship, but you have great friends, whom you adore, who give you balance.

life path ★ Learn to deal with your obsessive nature and you will be left with an abundance of pure love. You have more love within you than most people, but your insecurity can lead this to be destructive if you're not careful. Build up your relationship with yourself and your independent side.

love ★ Relationships have a huge effect on you, and you need to be aware of how you respond to them. Your birth date ruler is Venus, planet of love, so perhaps go for another Taurus or a Libra, whose ruling planet is also Venus.

best present ★ Rose-quartz heart, a dozen red roses.

birthday share ★ 1909 James Mason, actor; 1914 Tenzing Norgay, mountaineer; 1923 Richard Avedon, photographer; 1937 Madeleine Albright, politician.

on this day ★ In 1990, *Portrait of Doctor Gachet* by Vincent van Gogh sold for $82.5 million at Christies in New York, smashing the world record of $53.9 million for a painting.

color sea green ★ number 7, 16, 34 ★ stone moss agate—this little gem looks as if it has moss growing inside, so it connects you to the earth and removes stress ★ flora fern ★ animal wild deer ★ occupation headhunter, sailor, lifeguard ★ key features imaginative, sensitive, earthy ★ naturally good at getting yourself into sticky situations

may 16

character ★ You love security but can rock your own boat by being over the top. Because you can be ruled by your imagination and spontaneous feelings you often behave impulsively. You like to test your friends and family but are so adorable that you get away with it.

life path ★ Use some of that wild energy to go after your dreams. You tend to spend a lot of time dreaming up wonderful and often impossible plans but then become bored in your real life. This energy block makes you get into mischief because your life doesn't feel interesting enough; you're always sorry afterward, but loved ones need to be treated with a little more respect.

love ★ Difficult but delightful, you are a challenging but exciting partner. Your heart is in the right place and ultimately you do want to settle down. Choose a Pisces whose ruling planet is also your birth date ruler, Neptune.

best present ★ Boat trip, diary.

birthday share ★ 1919 Walter Valentino Liberace, pianist; 1953 Pierce Brosnan, actor; 1955 Debra Winger, actress; 1966 Janet Jackson, singer.

on this day ★ In 1929, the first Academy Awards ceremony was held in Hollywood to focus attention on the achievements of actors, actresses, and filmmakers.

color hunter green ★ **number** 8, 35, 44 ★ **stone** malachite—gives you power and protects against negativity ★ **flora** petunia ★ **animal** meerkat ★ **occupation** minister, policeman, truck driver ★ **key features** judgmental, opinionated, trustworthy ★ **naturally good at** sticking to an opinion

may 17

character ★ You have a fixed view on things but this could hold you back—life is not as black and white as you think it is. Some people will not bother to argue with you because you dig your heels in and refuse to budge, but you do have friends who like this solid side of you. What you see is what you get.

life path ★ Underneath that hard exterior beats a heart of gold. Fairness is important to you and you like everyone to know exactly where they stand with you. Your romantic drive is voracious but you may try to suppress it. Release some of that sensuality because it will mellow you.

love ★ You will never leave a loved one once you have committed, unless they are unfaithful or lie to you. You like devoted relationships and are happiest when in one. Why not try a Capricorn, whose ruling planet is also your birth date ruler, Saturn?

best present ★ Gold chain, roulette wheel.

birthday share ★ 1936 Dennis Hopper, actor; 1955 Bill Paxton, actor; 1956 Sugar Ray Leonard, boxer; 1961 Enya, singer.

on this day ★ In 1792, the New York Stock Exchange was founded at 70 Wall Street, New York.

color red ★ **number** 9, 36, 45 ★ **stone** bloodstone—grounds you and gives you drive ★
flora foxglove ★ **animal** wolf ★ **occupation** soldier, martial artist, archaeologist ★
key features zealous, steadfast, politically active ★ **naturally good at** implementing
social reform

may 18

character ★ As well as caring about the state of the world you have a passion that rules your life; this can take any form from pigeon racing to religion. Whatever your passion is you will give it far too much time! You tend to choose a partner and friends who share your interests, but perhaps you need to meet people with differing tastes to broaden your horizons?

life path ★ You have stupendous stamina and strength. You love a good argument and don't take offense if people disagree with you, unless they are rude—you despise impoliteness and will not tolerate anyone disrespecting you, no matter what their position. This may have got you in hot water in the past and you need to quell your warlike nature.

love ★ A tender, loving massage or a cuddle on the sofa is a great mental release for you and turns you from a ferocious lion to a little kitten. Make sure you make enough time for love because it is your personal tonic. Try an Aries, whose ruling planet is also your birth date ruler, Mars.

best present ★ Hi-fi system, DVD player.

birthday share ★ 1868 Nicholas II, czar of Russia; 1872 Bertrand Russell, philosopher; 1897 Frank Capra, film director; 1919 Dame Margot Fonteyn, ballerina.

on this day ★ In 1980, Mount St. Helens in the state of Washington erupted after lying dormant for 123 years.

color orange, yellow ★ number 1, 11, 22 ★ stone tiger's eye—for spiritual protection and to spark ideas ★ flora primula ★ animal lion ★ occupation salesperson, veterinarian, television host ★ key features articulate, serious, confident ★ naturally good at convincing others of the truth of your argument

may 19

character ★ You do not take hassling from anyone and are extremely proud, which may be mistaken for pomposity. You need to learn how to show your strong sense of self in a more charming manner if you are to avoid regular power struggles. Whether you are male or female you are considered stunning and attract lots of hangers-on.

life path ★ You have a great deal of personal power but crave external power. Perhaps you should examine your motives for this, as beneath that self-assurance is a nagging feeling of insecurity, although no one would guess this. You will go far in life and achieve more than your peers.

love ★ You seek the ideal lover, who, ironically, is usually the boy or girl next door. You like sweet, kind people, and this is one area of your life that brings you peace and harmony. Choose a Leo, whose ruling planet is your birth date ruler, the Sun.

best present ★ Walkman, houseplant.

birthday share ★ 1925 Malcolm X (Malcolm Little), civil rights campaigner; 1939 James Fox, actor; 1951 Joey Ramone, singer; 1952 Grace Jones, model, singer, and actress.

on this day ★ In 1935, T. E. (Thomas Edward) Lawrence, known as Lawrence of Arabia, died five days after a motorcycle crash in England. He described his military exploits during World War I in *Seven Pillars of Wisdom*.

character ★ You often spend your time talking to others about what is going on in their lives. You have a strong connection to your own family, and you give off very loving, warm vibes. You love to be surrounded by the people you love, enjoying simple things like a picnic.

life path ★ Needy people are drawn to you. You developed your nurturing skills at a very early age and have always been a giver. You tend to be overprotective with your family, which can cause resentment, but you are also deeply loved.

love ★ Relationships are your foundations in life and you tend to give all of yourself, but when a relationship fails, you can be devastated. You must be sure to keep back some time and space for yourself to cope with such trauma. Try a Cancer with the same priorities, as Cancer's ruling planet, the intuitive Moon, is also your birth date ruler.

best present ★ Scented candles, dining-room furniture.

birthday share ★ 1908 James Stewart, actor; 1944 Joe Cocker, singer; 1946 Cher, singer and actress; 1972 Busta Rhymes, rap artist.

on this day ★ In 1774, Britain's Parliament passed the Coercive Acts to punish American colonists for their increasingly anti-British behavior.

may 21

character ★ You feel connected to your higher self and are good at listening to your inner voice. This connection to your spirit has led you to some very lucky experiences. You have managed to find your way in life, and by always paying attention to your intuition you will not go wrong.

life path ★ You have a low boredom threshold and get frustrated if things are not moving. Fortunately your life has quite a fast turnaround, so in times of frustration do things you enjoy, such as taking a vacation—when you return you will find everything back on track.

love ★ Love is a conundrum for you: you feel too busy for it, yet a part of you craves someone to adventure with. The right person will come or you will be able to commit to the right person after the age of 29. Try a Sagittarius, whose ruling planet, Jupiter, is your birth date ruler.

best present ★ Silver dice, trip to Mexico.

birthday share ★ 1844 Henri Rousseau, artist; 1904 Fats Waller, musician; 1917 Raymond Burr, actor; 1952 Mr. T, actor.

on this day ★ In 1932, Amelia Earhart became the first woman to fly solo across the Atlantic.

taurus

your ruling planet **Venus**, planet of love, is your ruler. Named after the Roman goddess of love, Venus is drawn to all things sensuous and beautiful. Actually Venus rotates backward, which is why you are attracted to the past—it feels like the right direction for you. Taurus's Venus moves very slowly; a single day on Venus equates to 243 Earth days. This can help you understand your desire to take life slowly and stay in one place longer than other signs. With Venus as your ruler you are given many blessings in the arena of passion. You have that Venus charm that attracts other people to you. Your life lessons are usually based on love and relationships, and you will also have the capacity to attract some fine-looking lovers. But remember that beauty is only skin deep! You can appear to blow hot or cold in love, but when you give your heart it tends to be for life. Even when a relationship is over you still carry a torch for those who have touched you.

your natural habitat You love luxury and the finer things in life. A house must be a home so you are more likely to be drawn to a place that feels very homey. You have a fridge full of food, cupboards brimming with herbs, spices, and preserves and a well-stocked wine rack or bar. You are an excellent cook, and you feed anyone who enters your domain. You adore clean sheets and towels and have comfortable seating and candles. Everyone who enters your habitat should feel at home there. You are a bit of a hoarder and can't throw things away, particularly if they have memories. You like to have photos of your loved ones in frames scattered about the place, mellow music in the background, and comfy chairs. If you have kids they may have toys scattered about, as you like your children to have freedom of expression. You love to entertain and should have a dining table that is well used. You love antiques, especially family pieces, but also quirky or functional objects.

are you a typical taurus?

You are loyal and love security. You have a big heart and will defend those you love with your very life. Relationships and family are hugely important to you, and your favorite pastime might be a massive dinner party for those you love with lots of indulgent food and drink. You can be a little controlling of those you care for and try to live their life for them, assuming that you know best. You find it difficult to let go of the past, and once you love someone they will always remain in your heart.

Why you're wonderful! You are funny and warm and will never let down someone you care about. If a friend is in trouble, you are there in a flash to pick up the pieces and cook a comforting meal to cheer them up. You have a nurturing spirit, and although you can be demanding and difficult, you tend to receive back the degree of love that you give. You are as solid as a rock, and that is a rare commodity.

Why you're impossible! Stubborn, sulky, and downright belligerent when you want to be, you never give in and you find it hard to apologize. You can be jealous and possessive and need constant reassurance from your partner; you don't ask for this in an obvious way but you soon let people know if you are not getting your fair share of pampering. You can also be lazy and expect others to wait on you hand and foot.

Your secret side You are totally dependable but fantasize about a life away from all the security that you have created. You may long for a romantic fling with no strings attached, and to explore your freedom. You have a vivid imagination and often daydream about ex-lovers, and are a great one for the phrase "what if?" These secret cravings can hold you back, but don't feel guilty—we all have a secret side.

taurus ▷ love compatibility chart

	aries	taurus	gemini	cancer	leo	virgo	
	🍾	🍾		🍾		🍾	
	💘	💘		💘	💘	💘	
	⭕	⭕		⭕	⭕	⭕	
	🎈	🎈	🎈	🎈	🎈	🎈	
	💋	💋		💋	💋	💋	
	🪑	🪑		🪑	🪑	🪑	
	👥	👥		👥	👥	👥	

	libra	scorpio	sagittarius	capricorn	aquarius	pisces
	✓	✓	✓	✓		✓
	✓	✓		✓		✓
		✓		✓		✓
	✓	✓	✓	✓		✓
	✓	✓		✓		✓
	✓	✓	✓	✓		✓
		✓		✓		✓

  passion chilling out spontaneity attentiveness

gemini

may 22–june 21

may 22

character ★ In numerology the number 22 is a master number, and this means that your life is bound to fate in some way. Those born on the 22nd certainly have an extra touch of magic about them. You are here for a deeper purpose, which may take years to fulfill but will usually be achieved. You have an exceptionally inquisitive mind and may end up inventing or discovering something unique.

life path ★ You have to decide what it is you want your life to represent. What is it you want to build? The main problem with the birth number 22 is that it sometimes takes the person years to decide what they want to create. As a Gemini you have an advantage because your thoughts are sharp. When you reach a conclusion, back it up with action.

love ★ You are very enthusiastic about relationships in the beginning but can get confused if your partner does not follow your philosophy of life. You like unique lovers, so don't try to change them when you capture their heart. Your birth date ruler is Uranus, so try a free-spirited Aquarius, who will relate well to you.

best present ★ Gift certificate from a bookstore, ticket to a poetry reading.

birthday share ★ 1813 Richard Wagner, composer; 1907 Laurence Olivier, actor; 1946 George Best, soccer player; 1970 Naomi Campbell, supermodel.

on this day ★ In 1908 U.S. aviators Orville and Wilbur Wright patented their flying machine.

color violet ★ **number** 5, 14, 32 ★ **stone** amethyst—the wisdom and sobriety stone ★
flora sunflower ★ **animal** spaniel ★ **occupation** entertainer, escort, writer ★ **key
features** mentally agile, energetic, articulate ★ **naturally good at** journalism and writing

may 23

character ★ You love communication and could talk forever but can make yourself dizzy with all the different things you are thinking at once. You need to calm your mind—perhaps take up a physical activity to burn off some of that mental energy. When faced with a dilemma you have brilliant eureka moments when the answer just pops up, but ironically this is usually when you are not focused on the problem at hand.

life path ★ Not only are you, as a Gemini, ruled by Mercury, planet of communication, but your birth number also resonates to Mercury, making you a natural communicator. You have a natural flair for all things imaginative but sometimes need to stop thinking about creating and get on and do it! Writing is an ideal activity for you, so let your spirit out through your inventiveness.

love ★ You need a partner who will turn you on intellectually. Nothing is worse for you than intimacy without communication. Your mind needs to be seduced, and who better to do that than another Gemini, who is also ruled by Mercury and therefore needs that stimulation, too?

best present ★ Leather-bound diary with blank pages, laptop computer.

birthday share ★ 1928 Rosemary Clooney, singer; 1933 Joan Collins, actress; 1958 Drew Carey, comedian; 1974 Jewel, singer, actress, and poet.

on this day ★ In 1934, the infamous outlaws Bonnie and Clyde were caught in their final shootout in Ruston, Louisiana.

may 24

character ★ You can be obsessed with talking about relationships—others as well as your own—but you mean no harm. You would make a great gossip columnist. Your friends love to have you over for a meal because you crack them up with your latest side-splitting tales of emotional gaffes.

life path ★ You have a gift of expressing what others feel but can become oddly detached if someone comes on too heavy with you. You like to explore the inner recesses of your partner's mind and should think about writing down all the revelations of human nature that you gather—you could write an excellent self-help book. Do be careful not to betray these intimate confidences, though; always change names and places if you discuss them!

love ★ Your lover may be totally worn out by your endless discussions about trivia. Don't just talk about life and love—act it, live it, feel it! Your birth date is ruled by Venus, planet of love, so go for a Taurus or Libra who will understand your enchantment.

best present ★ Ylang ylang massage oil, rosebush.

birthday share ★ 1819 Queen Victoria of Britain; 1941 Bob Dylan, singer; 1945 Priscilla Presley, actress; 1955 Roseanne Cash, singer and author.

on this day ★ In 1844, inventor Samuel F. B. Morse transmitted his first telegraph message from Washington, D.C. to a friend 40 miles away in Baltimore. The message read "What hath God wrought!"

color sapphire blue ★ **number** 7, 16, 34 ★ **stone** lapis lazuli—a sacred stone symbolizing heaven and sky ★ **flora** orchid ★ **animal** tropical fish ★ **occupation** philosopher, boxer, race-car driver ★ **key features** valiant, dreamy, psychic ★ **naturally good at** predicting the future

may 25

character ★ You have the unusual ability to be able to predict the future or pick up on people's secrets, and your hunches are usually right. This may be an unconscious gift or something you have developed. You may talk about situations, particularly with lovers, and before you know it your words are coming true.

life path ★ Your birth number resonates to Neptune, the planet of intuition and visions. As this is coupled with your Sun sign ruler, Mercury, you can sense the future—not only that, you can express it well. You need to make the most of this unusual ability. Keep a dream diary to record your visions. If you use this unique skill, you will be one step ahead of the game throughout your life.

love ★ You have good instincts about partners—sometimes too good! They may find that you are too deep and perceptive,

as you can practically read their minds. Choose a spiritual and profound Pisces who will love this ability in you and whose ruling planet is the same as your birth date ruler, the watery Neptune.

best present ★ Astrological chart, tarot reading.

birthday share ★ 1803 Ralph Waldo Emerson, poet and essayist; 1939 Sir Ian McKellen, actor; 1963 Mike Myers, actor; 1975 Lauryn Hill, singer.

on this day ★ In 1989, Mikhail Gorbachev was elected executive president of the USSR.

color navy ★ **number** 8, 17, 35 ★ **stone** red jasper—this earthy stone grounds you and gives you a sense of security ★ **flora** bonsai tree ★ **animal** boxer dog ★ **occupation** political activist, tailor, commando ★ **key features** powerful, stubborn, opinionated ★ **naturally good at** giving orders

may 26

character ★ You have a potent charisma and very firm views on everyone and everything, but you may have a tendency to be too single-minded and intense about specific topics or people. You also love to talk about your views and would make an excellent, if extreme, politician.

life path ★ Saturn, your birth number ruler, and Mercury, your own ruler, give you the ability to express yourself with conviction. Perhaps you were a preacher in a past existence! Life is not as black and white as you may think, and you have trouble living up to your own expectations sometimes. Remember that "to err is human, to forgive divine."

love ★ You need a partner who is as hardworking as you but ideally one with the gentleness to bring out that loving heart. You hate to show vulnerability but vulnerability will, ironically, give you strength. Your birth date ruler, Saturn, is the ruling planet for powerful Capricorns, so perhaps one of those will be strong enough to handle you.

best present ★ Autobiography of a politician, tickets to a baseball game.

birthday share ★ 1907 John Wayne, actor; 1920 Peggy Lee, singer; 1951 Sally Ride, astronaut; 1964 Lenny Kravitz, singer.

on this day ★ In 1868, President Andrew Johnson was acquitted of impeachment charges of "high crimes and misdemeanors."

color red, maroon ★ **number** 9, 18, 36 ★ **stone** carnelian—a roman good luck talisman to bring you encouragement and support ★ **flora** wallflower ★ **animal** german shepherd dog ★ **occupation** dancer, researcher, spiritual teacher ★ **key features** energetic, ardent, bouncy ★ **naturally good at** all forms of physical activity

may 27

character ★ You have more energy than a roadrunner and are always whizzing around, never settling down for more than a minute at a time. You're such a dynamo that people marvel at how you pack so much into your life, but for you it's easy because your birth number ruler is powerful and energetic Mars.

life path ★ Clever, bright, and passionate, you are capable of seeing through several major projects at the same time. Most people would burn out doing all that you do but you have the vitality of 10 people. You love life and are generally cheerful but woe betide anyone who makes you lose that volcanic temper.

love ★ You are an excellent lover and have a very persuasive seduction technique. You can talk your partners into your embrace and then keep them entertained with your fantastic tales. Because Mars is your birth

date ruler you should search for a fiery Aries, also ruled by Mars, who will be able to match your vigor.

best present ★ Pogo stick, Rollerblades.

birthday share ★ 1911 Vincent Price, actor; 1922 Christopher Lee, actor; 1923 Henry Kissinger, politician; 1965 Pat Cash, tennis player.

on this day ★ In 1937, the Golden Gate Bridge was officially opened in San Francisco.

color orange, sunshine yellow ★ **number** 1, 11, 22 ★ **stone** sandstone—this glittering jewel brings you optimism and vitality ★ **flora** fennel ★ **animal** pekinese dog ★ **occupation** ice-hockey player, bar owner, train engineer ★ **key features** charming, warm, self-centered ★ **naturally good at** starting new projects with eagerness

may 28

character ★ You are appealing and funny and have a large array of friends. You love to be the center of attention and you usually are; your dress sense is individual and makes you stand out from the crowd. You believe that people create their own destiny and you intend to make yours magnificent.

life path ★ Your birth number is 1, which relates to the Sun, and in numerological terms this means that not only do you like to be No. 1, but you are also a rather magical creature. You have stunning persuasive skills, and can solve problems and create miracles with nothing more than your quick-witted Gemini mind. Mercury is your Sun sign ruler.

love ★ You are searching for someone who will be proud of and adore you, but they must never try to control you because you are too much of a free spirit. Your birth date ruler, the Sun, is also the ruling planet of Leo, so a Leo would be a good choice. You

should get on like a house on fire and share moments of great passion.

best present ★ Camera, DVD player.

birthday share ★ 1738 Joseph Guillotin, inventor of the guillotine; 1908 Ian Fleming, author and creator of James Bond; 1944 Rudolph Giuliani, former mayor of New York; 1968 Kylie Minogue, singer and actress.

on this day ★ In 1987, a 19-year-old West German, Mathias Rust, flew a plane from Helsinki to Moscow, passing through Soviet airspace unchallenged and eventually landing on Red Square.

color ocean blue at dusk ★ **number** 11, 22, 37 ★ **stone** green topaz—represents love and affection ★ **flora** allium ★ **animal** tabby cat ★ **occupation** writer, actor, charity worker ★ **key features** honest, stunning, vibrant ★ **naturally good at** being all things to all people

may 29

character ★ You juggle more things at once than a plate-spinner and need to get to the bottom of what you really want. You care so much about doing the right thing that you can easily forget what is right for you. However, you are foxy, charismatic, and wholly unique, so you deserve to love yourself enough to relax and just be you.

life path ★ In some ways you are a typical Gemini and can crave two lives. You have a well-developed conscience and need to learn you cannot please all of the people all of the time—be true to yourself. You are incredibly creative, and if you make use of this gift, life will get smoother. You are capable of great things, so don't make excuses and shy away from them. Your birth number is 11, a master number, which enhances your genius and sheer magic.

love ★ You are a stunning and magnificent lover and put your heart and soul into your romantic relationships, but you are careful in your choice of who you will open up to. You are as rare and passionate as a phoenix and need a wolfish Aries to match your fire.

best present ★ Book of Shakespeare's sonnets, antique chair.

birthday share ★ 1903 Bob Hope, actor and comedian; 1917 John F. Kennedy, 35th U.S. president; 1958 Annette Bening, actress; 1959 Rupert Everett, actor.

on this day ★ In 1953, Edmund Hillary and Tenzing Norgay became the first people to conquer the summit of Mount Everest.

color deep purple ★ number 3, 12, 33 ★ stone pink topaz—opens the heart and brings delight ★ flora rose ★ animal parrot ★ occupation entrepreneur, football player, hairdresser ★ key features unrestrained, fast, foolhardy ★ naturally good at leaping into the unknown

may 30

character ★ Wildly free spirited, you are difficult to keep up with. You are a fast learner and love to consume knowledge and experiences. You were born lucky but your reckless nature may lead you to feel that at times your life is like a roller coaster. You need to learn to look before you leap and slow that va-va-voom personality down a fraction!

life path ★ You may often find yourself in unexplored territory because you are fearless about making sweeping changes. But you should remember that you can handle any situation you get yourself into. Your life was not meant to be mundane—it is exciting and unusual, so enjoy it!

love ★ You are looking for an enthusiastic and adventurous lover that you can discuss your many plans with—a fellow seeker of life lived to the fullest. Jupiter, planet of expansion, is your birth date ruler, so why not search for a wacky Sagittarius, whose ruling planet is also Jupiter?

best present ★ Trip to the races, go-kart.

birthday share ★ 1846 Peter Carl Fabergé, jeweler; 1908 Mel Blanc, the voice of Bugs Bunny and Daffy Duck; 1909 Benny Goodman, musician and bandleader; 1964 Wynonna Judd, country singer.

on this day ★ In 1431, French martyr and saint, Joan of Arc, was burned at the stake as a heretic in Rouen, France.

color gray, silver ★ **number** 4, 31, 44 ★ **stone** fluorite—a magical stone said to foretell the future and increase intuition ★ **flora** snapdragon ★ **animal** doberman dog ★ **occupation** statesman/woman, director, lawyer ★ **key features** stern, opinionated, strong ★ **naturally good at** keeping order

may 31

character ★ Some people see you as a bit of a tough cookie because of your very strong views. You have a seriousness about you that was probably there from birth, and you would benefit from letting your hair down a little occasionally. However, if you direct your brilliant and serious mind to being expansive rather than single-minded, you can achieve star status and possibly fame.

life path ★ Your overpowering mind rules your life and it would be wise to get in touch with your feelings as well as your mind. You have a tendency to quash any sign of weakness and always be strong. We are all a combination of the two, and expressing this will make your loved ones feel closer to you.

love ★ You are determined to make love work and believe that you will fall in love once forever. Do not let past heartache hold you back or put you off. Love is downright

good for you! Your birth date relates to Uranus, so choose an Aquarius, whose ruling planet is also Uranus.

best present ★ Sunglasses, tickets to the opera.

birthday share ★ 1819 Walt Whitman, poet; 1930 Clint Eastwood, actor and director; 1943 Sharon Gless, actress; 1965 Brooke Shields, actress.

on this day ★ In 1927, the last Model T Ford (No. 15,007,003) rolled off the assembly line.

color burnt orange, sunflower yellow ★ **number** 1, 11, 22 ★ **stone** citrine—increases self-esteem and brings courage ★ **flora** feverfew ★ **animal** lion ★ **occupation** singer, performer, boss of your own business ★ **key features** warm, spontaneous, talkative ★ **naturally good at** arranging social events

june 1

character ★ You love to be the center of attention, and people adore your wit and humor. You always look good even if you are not conventionally attractive—maybe it is that mischievous sparkle in your eye. You can be tempted to flit from friend to friend, depending on who flatters you the most.

life path ★ You have a natural ability to bring happiness to other people, leaving them feeling uplifted after they have met you. Consider building on this to become a performer or writer so that you can radiate that positive vibe to more people.

love ★ Love comes easily to you but it can also slip away because you get bored and you do have a tendency to be fickle. Funnily enough, the more difficult your partner, the more likely you are to stay with them! Your birth date resonates to the Sun, so go for a proud and captivating Leo, whose ruling planet is also the Sun.

best present ★ Diamond watch, hip designer clothes.

birthday share ★ 1926 Marilyn Monroe, actress; 1930 Edward Woodward, actor; 1937 Morgan Freeman, actor; 1974 Alanis Morissette, singer.

on this day ★ In 1938, the first issue of *Action Comics*, featuring Superman, was published.

color pearl, silver ★ **number** 11, 22, 101 ★ **stone** spectrolite—a magical stone that imparts inspiration ★ **flora** rosemary ★ **animal** canary ★ **occupation** psychotherapist, poet, artist ★ **key features** reflective, emotional, caring ★ **naturally good at** helping people emotionally

june 2

character ★ Analytical and intense, you are fascinated by the way the mind and emotions are linked. You spend hours analyzing your emotions and those of others, but this can be to such an extent that you go around in circles and end up with no answers.

life path ★ This attraction to how the mind works could lead to a career helping others. Whatever you study you will excel in, but you need to have a little more belief in yourself. Your mind is a rapier sword, so be careful how you wield it.

love ★ Avoid the temptation to become your partner's counselor, as sometimes you delve too deeply and can end up becoming a mother or father figure. Your birth date relates to the Moon, and as the Moon is also the ruling planet of Cancer, a Cancer will have a natural affinity with you.

best present ★ Book on Carl Jung, moonlight trip to the beach.

birthday share ★ 1840 Thomas Hardy, author and poet; 1857 Sir Edward Elgar, composer; 1904 Johnny Weissmuller, Olympic swimmer and actor; 1941 Stacey Keach Jr., actor.

on this day ★ In 1924, the U.S. Congress granted citizenship to all native Americans.

june 3

character ★ You have a strong belief in the equality of all and hate to see injustice. You tend to be unconventional and are not afraid to speak your mind. You will not tolerate prejudice of any kind and would love to live in a world with no social divisions. The air of peace and love you exude affects everyone around you.

life path ★ You were born to express yourself and fight for the rights of others. You have plenty of important things to say and get frustrated if boxed in or imprisoned in any situation. As a free spirit you need to express your individuality. You are slightly eccentric, but so what? When you are true to yourself, rewards will follow.

love ★ You tend to draw people to you who want to mother you in some way, or partners who try to dampen your unique spirit. Your birth date ruler is Jupiter, planet of expansion, so why not try a Sagittarius whose ruling planet is also Jupiter and who will allow you to be free?

best present ★ CD of protest songs, laptop computer.

birthday share ★ 1906 Josephine Baker, entertainer; 1911 Paulette Goddard, actress; 1925 Tony Curtis, actor; 1926 Allen Ginsberg, poet.

on this day ★ In 1968, pop-art creator Andy Warhol was shot and badly wounded at his studio in New York City by radical feminist Valerie Solanas.

color lavender ★ **number** 13, 22, 44 ★ **stone** moss agate—this gorgeous stone looks like it has captured plants within it and connects you to nature ★ **flora** apple blossom ★ **animal** turtle ★ **occupation** public speaker, astronaut, doctor ★ **key features** eccentric genius ★ **naturally good at** having flashes of inspiration

june 4

character ★ You have an unusual and interesting character. You may have chosen a very conventional profession, but you have an edge of eccentricity about you that makes you stand out from the crowd. Your taste in clothes is often flamboyant and you have a more personal manner with your clients than is usual, but the secret of your success is knowing when to temper your eccentricity with a little conservatism.

life path ★ You are programmed to be a little bit different. You will never conform all the way but will do a darn fine job of whatever career you take up—just not in the conventional way.

love ★ You are naturally adored for being special. There is nothing run of the mill about you, and you can keep a partner constantly stimulated, mentally, physically, and even spiritually. Your birth date ruler is

Uranus, so why not try an Aquarius, whose ruling planet is also Uranus and has the same free spirit?

best present ★ Book of poetry, tickets to the theater.

birthday share ★ 1910 Sir Christopher Cockerell, inventor of hovercraft; 1924 Dennis Weaver, actor; 1971 Noah Wyle, actor; 1975 Angelina Jolie, actress.

on this day ★ In 1989, Chinese soldiers opened fire on student protesters in Tiananmen Square, Beijing, killing more than 2,500 people and injuring thousands more.

june 5

character ★ You love to read and are a naturally skilled writer. You delight in long conversations, which often stretch into the night. You play with words and could be a brilliant songwriter or poet. Don't ignore this ability, but put your heart into it and allow it to develop fully.

life path ★ You are born to stimulate others to think. You have a questioning mind and are always seeking to unearth some great mystery or another. You would make a good stand-up comic because you have a great talent for using language to make others laugh as well as reflect.

love ★ You play the fool in love and find it difficult to reveal how you feel, possibly because you overanalyze your emotions. You are turned on by people's minds rather than their bodies. Because both your birth date ruler and your Sun sign ruler is Mercury, another Gemini would be perfect for you.

best present ★ Journal, fountain pen.

birthday share ★ 1878 Pancho Villa, revolutionary; 1898 Federico Garcia Lorca, poet and playwright; 1941 Spalding Gray, actor, screenwriter, and monologue artist; 1971 Mark (Marky Mark) Wahlberg, actor and singer.

on this day ★ In 1968, U.S. Senator Robert Kennedy was shot in Los Angeles by Palestinian Arab Sirhan Sirhan. Kennedy died the following day.

color blossom pink ★ **number** 15, 33, 42 ★ **stone** pink tourmaline—a heart stone that brings unconditional love ★ **flora** jasmine ★ **animal** chicken ★ **occupation** advice columnist, radio show host, party planner ★ **key features** loving, passionate, eloquent ★ **naturally good at** talking about love

june 6

character ★ You're passionate and feisty. You always make your friends laugh with your madcap adventures and strange friendships. You collect people in the same way others collect beer mats. All your friends are different and you thrive on diversity. You are the queen of advice-giving and usually the first port of call for friends who have a problem.

life path ★ You can be a social butterfly who travels from party to party or meeting to meeting, never staying very long because you are easily bored. However, you are a loyal friend with a huge heart and you would never walk away from someone in need.

love ★ You love to love, and love comes easily to you. Your birth date ruler is Venus, planet of love, so you are assured many adventures in this area. Don't forget that this is where you will grow the most. Try a partner who is a Libra, whose ruling planet is Venus.

best present ★ Satin underwear, exotic body lotion.

birthday share ★ 1875 Thomas Mann, writer and Nobel Prize winner; 1935 Dalai Lama, Buddhist leader; 1955 Sandra Bernhard, actress; 1956 Bjorn Borg, tennis player.

on this day ★ In 1925, Walter Percy Chrysler founded the Chrysler Corporation.

june 7

character ★ You tend to live in your head and are often so deep in your thoughts that you are unaware that someone is talking to you. Many people think you live in a land of make-believe. However, what is stirring inside you is an amazing inner world full of potential. Realize some of those great ideas and you could make a fortune.

life path ★ You could be a songwriter or design web sites, but whatever you do will be slightly ahead of its time. You know how to touch people with your creative energy and, more important, you have the capacity to make other people think. Your rich inner landscape is normal for you but others may find it hard to understand; this occasionally makes you feel you are odd, but you're not—you're just special!

love ★ You love to swim in the depths of your emotions and constantly fantasize about love. Fathomless Neptune is your birth date ruler, and this dreamy, romantic side of you would be well suited to a Pisces whose ruling planet is also Neptune.

best present ★ Boat trip to see dolphins, guitar.

birthday share ★ 1917 Dean Martin, actor; 1952 Liam Neeson, actor; 1958 Prince, singer; 1981 Anna Kournikova, tennis player.

on this day ★ In 1939, King George VI and Queen Elizabeth crossed from Canada to the United States to become the first British monarchs to visit the United States.

color hunter green ★ number 17, 35, 62 ★ stone garnet—this stone is said to be an aphrodisiac ★ flora red-hot poker ★ animal doberman dog ★ occupation lawyer, civil engineer, architect ★ key features straightforward, tough, honest ★ naturally good at creating order

june 8

character ★ You speak your mind, calling a spade a spade, and have a very strong sense of fair play, but this may not be as free and liberal as other people's. You are an early riser, despise laziness in any form, and have certain expectations of yourself and other people.

life path ★ You are often put in the position of having power or control over other people. You don't like it if the situation is reversed because you were born to be a leader, not a follower. When you are young you adhere to the rules of others but in maturity you are too powerful to allow others to rule you. You would probably be best suited to working for yourself.

love ★ You want a partner who is hardworking and traditional but may find it difficult to express your emotions or show affection. However, in your own way you do tell your partner how much you value them,

and as your birth date is ruled by Saturn, you may get along best with a Capricorn, who also has Saturn as their ruling planet.

best present ★ Briefcase, ride in a horse and carriage.

birthday share ★ 1867 Frank Lloyd Wright, architect; 1933 Joan Rivers, comedienne; 1940 Nancy Sinatra, singer; 1953 Bonnie Tyler, singer.

on this day ★ In A.D. 632, Mohammed, prophet and founder of Islam, died.

color crimson ★ number 18, 27, 63 ★ stone carnelian—linked to the goddess isis, who used it to protect; it is also said to stimulate energy ★ flora red rose ★ animal husky dog ★ occupation mountaineer, athlete, events organizer ★ key features fiery, adoring, energetic ★ naturally good at most sports

june 9

character ★ You have a real verve for life. You are always on the go and have limitless energy. You talk rather quickly and it is sometimes difficult for others to keep up with your ever-changing thoughts, feelings, and emotions. You can have a bad temper but are also quick to forgive.

life path ★ *Action* is a key word for you; you thrive on challenges and it is hard for your friends and partners to keep track of you. Life is a mad dash from one commitment to another. You have very little spare time because you love to feast on everything life has to offer. Slow down sometimes to catch your breath.

love ★ Stamina is your middle name but you may lack gentleness. As with everything else, you rush love and can make rash promises in the heat of passion. Your birth date ruler is fiery Mars, so why not hook up with an Aries, who can match that ardor?

best present ★ Day at a spa, parachute jump.

birthday share ★ 1891 Cole Porter, composer and lyricist; 1961 Michael J. Fox, actor; 1963 Johnny Depp, actor; 1981 Natalie Portman, actress.

on this day ★ In 1959 the first ballistic missile submarine, the USS *George Washington*, was launched.

color silver, white ★ **number** 1, 11, 22 ★ **stone** onyx—releases the past and any ties to former lovers ★ **flora** wild garlic ★ **animal** jack russell dog ★ **occupation** gardener, stockbroker, radio commentator ★ **key features** gifted, friendly, sturdy ★ **naturally good at** showing off

june 10

character ★ You have an extreme nature and are a firecracker. You sizzle and pop and bounce around the place but underneath have a serious and intense mind. Although you appear extremely confident, behind that positive aura you suffer from bouts of self-doubt. Rest assured that no one else knows!

life path ★ You have a highly physical nature and can often be led astray if someone panders to your ego. You don't like to hurt people, but you find yourself in complex emotional dramas as you leap in and out of people's lives at will. Put your boundless energy into your work and you will make a fortune!

love ★ You love to flirt and schmooze. You often have more than one love interest hanging around and find it hard to make up your mind. Your birth date is ruled by the Sun, so choose a Sun-ruled Leo who will live up to your expectations.

best present ★ Membership at an elegant nightclub, trip to Las Vegas.

birthday share ★ 1915 Saul Bellow, author; 1922 Judy Garland, singer and actress; 1965 Elizabeth Hurley, model and actress, and Linda Evangelista, supermodel and actress.

on this day ★ In 1909, a Morse code SOS signal was transmitted for the first time in an emergency by the Cunard liner *Slavonia*, wrecked off the Azores.

june 11

character ★ You have a wonderful aura about you that relaxes people. They feel they can trust you and often share their secrets or problems with you. You love to look after others, but do make sure that you also take time out for yourself. You are a stunning homemaker wherever you live and love to have company to spoil.

life path ★ You have a gift for helping others talk about their emotions. You work well in a team and people love you, but you can get caught up in your own emotions and ironically sometimes feel unlovable. Work on that self-esteem, because you give so much of yourself to others.

love ★ What a fantastic partner you make! You are very loving and giving and make your loved ones feel like a million dollars. Your birth date is ruled by the Moon, so why not choose a Cancer, whose ruling planet is also the Moon, and who will love your style?

best present ★ Vintage wine, cookbook.

birthday share ★ 1933 Gene Wilder, actor; 1939 Jackie Stewart, race-car driver; 1956 Joe Montana, football player; 1978 Joshua Jackson, actor.

on this day ★ In 1963, Governor George Wallace allowed the enrollment of two black students at the University of Alabama after he had first blocked their entry by standing in front of the door.

color mauve, lilac ★ **number** 3, 21, 33 ★ **stone** topaz—a protective stone also said to encourage unconditional love ★ **flora** cherry blossom ★ **animal** siamese cat ★ **occupation** humanitarian, teacher, personal coach ★ **key features** thoughtful, lucky, buoyant ★ **naturally good at** cheering people up

june 12

character ★ You always see your glass as half full rather than half empty. So even though you are quite lucky, you count your blessings and believe in the power of positive thought. Other people can become irritated by this sunny disposition, but it serves you well and you do help those around you to change, so keep it up.

life path ★ Your strong belief in the power of good can have a big effect on those around you. You would make a good motivational speaker or personal coach, so think about heading in this direction. You are a tonic to most people, so don't let grinches rain on your parade.

love ★ Sizzling and sassy, you are usually lucky in love as long as you love yourself. You are adorable and positive and anyone would be happy to be your lover. Avoid cynical people and all should be well. Your birth date numerology is linked to lucky

Jupiter, so choose a cheerful Sagittarius, who also has the spark of Jupiter.

best present ★ Ride in a hot-air balloon, bunch of sunflowers.

birthday share ★ 1915 David Rockefeller, banker; 1924 George Bush, 41st U.S. president; 1929 Anne Frank, diarist; 1977 Kenny Wayne Shepherd, singer.

on this day ★ In 1839, a new ball game, known as *baseball*, was played for the first time at Cooperstown, New York.

june 13

character ★ Wacky and weird to some, you are ahead of your time. Frustrated by the mundane and everyday, you live life according to your own rules and morals. Others may think the phrase "mad, bad, and dangerous to know" captures you exactly, but they are just very conservative and you like only unusual, interesting people anyway.

life path ★ You have your own code of honor and a unique and special way of viewing the world. You may be fascinated by the occult or UFOs; in any case, you feel that there are secrets in life to be unearthed and that you are the one to expose them. Sometimes you keep your wackiness to yourself, but as you get older you will meet others on your wavelength.

love ★ You are very easily bored in relationships and hate to be trapped in a suburban lifestyle. If you do find yourself in too secure a relationship, you are capable of bolting quite out of the blue, so you need to find someone unusual who will keep surprising you. Try a free-spirited Aquarius, whose ruling planet Uranus is also your birth date ruler.

best present ★ Telescope, digital camera.

birthday share ★ 1865 W. B. Yeats, poet and playwright; 1893 Dorothy L. Sayers, author; 1943 Malcolm McDowell, actor; 1953 Tim Allen, comedian and actor.

on this day ★ In 1990, East Germany began the final demolition of the Berlin Wall, knocking out concrete slabs all over the city to reopen streets sealed off since the Cold War barrier was built in 1961.

june 14

character ★ You are at home with the written word and love to watch television and listen to the radio. You can be critical and creative and want to communicate with everyone. You make friends with the homeless and those in need of a listening ear and are an all-around good sort. However, less well-disposed types may say you talk too much and have an opinion on everything.

life path ★ Reading books is a passion and you devise plots for soap operas or movies in your spare time. Why not try to get all this great material down on paper? You also love to hoard things. A big decluttering would help clear your mind.

love ★ You can be a loner, and because you have so much junk stored in your apartment there may not be space for a lover. Try another Gemini, also ruled by your double ruler, Mercury. The very least they can do is persuade you to ditch some of your stuff.

best present ★ Storage units, screenwriting software.

birthday share ★ 1928 Ernesto (Che) Guevara, revolutionary hero; 1946 Donald Trump, multimillionaire; 1961 Boy George, singer and dj; 1969 Steffi Graf, tennis player.

on this day ★ In 1777, the Continental Congress adopted the Stars and Stripes as the official flag of the United States.

june 15

character ★ No matter what your physical form, you have the voice of an angel. People just stop and listen to you and are soothed. There is magic in those dulcet tones and a sense of the dramatic. You have an aura of sensuality that is breathtaking.

life path ★ A living, breathing love machine, you send out vibes of love, yet you are strangely detached from your own sensuality. Don't put yourself down—rejoice in your loveliness. Maybe try a holistic approach and explore your spirituality.

love ★ You're a lover not a fighter, yet you can spend many years on your own. "What is going on in the love stakes?" you may ask yourself. Well, let me tell you. You have to believe the reality that you're desireable. Once you really believe this, your ideal lover will come. Try a secure Taurus, whose ruling planet is also your birth date ruler, Venus, planet of love.

best present ★ Karaoke machine, surprise party.

birthday share ★ 1923 Erroll Garner, jazz pianist; 1963 Helen Hunt, actress; 1964 Courteney Cox Arquette, actress; 1969 Ice Cube, rapper and actor.

on this day ★ In 1978, King Hussein of Jordan married his U.S. bride, 26-year-old Elizabeth Halaby, who became Queen Noor of Jordan.

color blue ★ **number** 7, 25, 70 ★ **stone** aquamarine—to help you express yourself ★ **flora** waterlily ★ **animal** crocodile ★ **occupation** crime writer, journalist, doctor ★ **key features** articulate, imaginative, anxious ★ **naturally good at** writing poetry

june 16

character ★ You have a vivid imagination and a complex emotional life. You swing between being demonstrative and being detached, which can drive your partners crazy because they never know where they stand. You have big plans and an uncanny ability to pick up lifestyle trends before they happen.

life path ★ Despite being inventive and original, you can be caught up in self-doubt or become overanalytical and talk yourself out of expressing your ideas. You are good at communicating with people unless you are in a love relationship, as you then get confused between what you think and what you feel. You have a talent for writing and need to nurture this.

love ★ You can be considered fickle but are really quite vulnerable and just can't handle emotional pressure. Try not to run away from emotions but open up slowly

and build solid foundations. Why not try a Pisces whose ruling planet, Neptune, is also your birth date ruler?

best present ★ Skateboard, digital radio.

birthday share ★ 1890 Stan Laurel, actor; 1917 Katharine Graham, *Washington Post* publisher; 1937 Erich Segal, author; 1971 Tupac Shakur, rap singer.

on this day ★ In 1884, the first roller coaster in the United States began operating at Coney Island, New York.

june 17

character ★ Strong and inspirational, you amaze your friends by being able to work 9-to-5 but also have a wild social life. You need to be around wealthy people to inspire you, but you are not judgmental and believe we all have it within to follow our dreams.

life path ★ You are a fascinating combination of creative soul and business-person. You know how to conform but also have a vivid imagination that you want to plunder and profit from. Great! Get on with it and know that this is what you were born to do.

love ★ You have diverse tastes when it comes to lovers and may get involved with someone who drives you crazy because they are successful or living their dream, even if they are married or already taken. But there is someone out there just for you—try a Capricorn, whose ruling planet is also your birth number ruler, Saturn.

best present ★ Newspaper published on the day of your birth, classic jewelry.

birthday share ★ 1882 Igor Stravinsky, classical composer; 1935 Donald Sutherland, actor; 1943 Barry Manilow, singer; 1980 Venus Williams, tennis player.

on this day ★ In 1994, U.S. football star OJ Simpson, accused of killing his ex-wife and a male friend, was arrested after a dramatic car chase and a 90-minute standoff in the driveway of his estate.

color red ★ **number** 9, 72, 90 ★ **stone** fire opal—sparks your passion ★ **flora** buttercup ★ **animal** german shepherd ★ **occupation** environmental campaigner, drummer, stunt man/woman ★ **key features** humorous, reckless, vivacious ★ **naturally good at** learning circus tricks

june 18

character ★ You have a charming manner and zest for life, which is obvious to everyone at first glance. You bubble with a frenetic and zany energy, which is difficult to calm down. You love to laugh and are well known for your practical jokes, some of which do not go down too well. Learn who can handle your oddball sense of humor and those who need gentler handling.

life path ★ You are an adventurer and live life by the seat of your pants. Normality bores you and you want to explore the nooks and crannies of an alternative existence. You are likely to be a vegetarian and have a passion for saving the earth from global warming. You need others to understand your passion if you are close to them, but you don't give two figs for acceptance from anyone else.

love ★ You have definite phases in love. Sometimes you are highly focused and passionate, whereas at other times you just spin off into a world of your own and need to hang out with your friends. This can be confusing to your partner, so give them lots of reassurance. Choose an Aries, whose ruling planet, Mars, is your birth date ruler.

best present ★ Trip to Sedona on a Harley-Davidson, surfboard.

birthday share ★ 1937 John D. Rockefeller IV, millionaire; 1939 Lou Brock, baseball player; 1942 Paul McCartney, singer; 1952 Isabella Rossellini, actress.

on this day ★ In 1983, Dr. Sally Ride became the first U.S. woman in space in the space shuttle *Challenger*.

june 19

character ★ Bright but boisterous, you have half the people you meet worshiping at your feet and the other half running for the hills. Your huge and affable personality can intimidate lesser folk at first, but don't take their alarm too seriously—they will get used to you.

life path ★ You are inquisitive and love to be at the heart of a scandal. People like to gossip about you, and most of the time you enjoy this. You want to be noticed and are quite a snazzy dresser. If you took up meditation or some spiritual path to balance your bustle, you would be unbeatable.

love ★ You will have many great loves in your life, but be careful you don't love yourself too much! You are so preoccupied with how you look that you don't realize that others could see this as vanity. Try a Leo, whose ruling planet is also the glowing Sun, your birth date ruler—they think all that mirror worship is normal.

best present ★ Video camera, expensive beauty products.

birthday share ★ 1623 Blaise Pascal, mathematician; 1897 Moe Howard, actor; 1947 Salman Rushdie, author; 1954 Kathleen Turner, actress.

on this day ★ In 1910, Father's Day was celebrated for the first time, in Spokane, Washington, under the guidance of Mrs. John B. Dodd.

color milky white ★ **number** 2, 11, 22 ★ **stone** rainbow moonstone—connected to your ruler, the moon, this tunes you into your emotions and grants wishes ★ **flora** digitalis ★ **animal** labrador retriever ★ **occupation** teacher, nurse, aid worker ★ **key features** generous, giving, engaging ★ **naturally good at** giving hugs

june 20

character ★ Lovable and genuine, you are affectionate and tender with everyone you meet. Sometimes this makes cynics suspicious, imagining you must have something sinister to hide beneath that sugary veneer. But no—it's all above board. You just love to love with your huge heart.

life path ★ You may run off to be a nun in Outer Mongolia or want to feed the poor in Afghanistan, but even if you don't pursue these lofty goals you will always be around for your friends. You have a few hangers-on because of this, so consider the recipient well before you give so unconditionally.

love ★ You feel that you don't have time for love because your social life is packed to the rafters. However, when you do find The One, your life will take on a new dimension, so be open to love, and if you have found it,

cherish it. A Cancer will understand you because their ruling planet, the Moon, is also your birth date ruler.

best present ★ Moonstone necklace/cufflinks, cooking course.

birthday share ★ 1909 Errol Flynn, actor; 1949 Lionel Richie, singer; 1952 John Goodman, actor; 1967 Nicole Kidman, actress.

on this day ★ In 1819, the 320-ton paddle-wheel steamship *Savannah* became the first steamship to cross the Atlantic. It arrived in Liverpool, England, after a journey from Savannah, Georgia, of 27 days and 11 hours.

color lilac, purple ★ number 3, 30, 33 ★ stone sugilite—opens you up spiritually and liberates you physically ★ flora delphinium ★ animal iguana ★ occupation designer, entrepreneur, critic ★ key features persuasive, critical, stunning ★ naturally good at examining others' mistakes

june 21

character ★ You are always one step ahead of the game when it comes to work. Your career is important to you, perhaps too important. Your self-esteem needs to come from who you are, not what you do in the world. Having said that, this determination makes you succeed.

life path ★ You have an uncanny ability to get whatever you desire in life, but remember that old adage "be careful what you ask for." Because of this easy success you are sometimes dissatisfied with your lot when others would gnaw off their right hand for what you have. Count your blessings— you have done well!

love ★ You are very choosy in the love stakes but you tend to be able to captivate most people. You get bored quickly and want a partner who is above you materially or educationally. If they give in to your demands too soon, you're off, as you like a challenge. Your birth date is ruled by expansive and generous Jupiter, so choose a Sagittarius, whose ruling planet is Jupiter, and you may have met your match.

best present ★ Trip to the ocean, designer watch.

birthday share ★ 1905 Jean-Paul Sartre, philosopher; 1921 Jane Russell, actress; 1973 Juliette Lewis, actress; 1982 Prince William, second in line to the British throne.

on this day ★ In 2003, after a three-year wait, the fifth Harry Potter book, *Harry Potter and the Order of the Phoenix*, went on sale at one minute past midnight with a record print run of about 8.5 million copies, becoming the fastest-selling book in history.

gemini

your ruling planet Mercury, planet of communication and messenger of the gods, makes you a good communicator; learning and expressing are your greatest passions. Mercury gives you an air of androgyny and you can flit between your masculine and feminine sides. You like to be free of the constraints of gender and can relate to both sexes equally well. Your thoughts rule you but it is difficult for you to hold any particular one for more than a few hours because Mercury has an erratic and eccentric orbit; if it were habitable the residents would see the Sun changing shape and expanding and contracting in a haphazard fashion. You too are able to see life from differing perspectives. Your mercurial mind does not always know what is true and what is illusion. Mercury was named after the messenger of the gods because when seen from Earth it appears to move faster than any other planet; you have this natural swiftness and hate to be tied down or held back. You would benefit from sitting still occasionally to get some perspective on your life.

your natural habitat You need a large, light, and airy space with room to spread out in. A loft-style apartment would suit you. You love new technology and like to update your computer, telephone, and gadgets with the latest versions. You would adore a state-of-the-art kitchen. You like to keep things simple so your mind doesn't get cluttered. White linen sheets and neutral colors grace your bed, which you rarely make because you are too busy leaping up in the morning and hurrying to get things done. An open-plan environment would be best for you, big enough for you to rush about amid books and newspapers containing all those valuable facts you want at your fingertips. If you have more traditional tastes, you will surround yourself with antiques, your prize possessions being a writing desk and a library of rare books. You like to escape to an outdoor space, so a garden is essential. If you have a conservatory, this would be one of your favorite rooms.

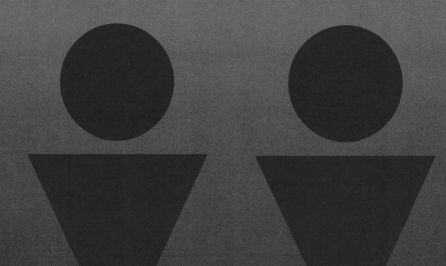

are you a typical gemini?

You are kind, entertaining, and supremely intelligent. Energetic but indecisive, you like to keep all your options open. You flit from idea to idea and are always on the move. Inspired by life, you have a hunger for knowledge. You have a bouncy personality but can seem shallow, mostly because you don't stand still long enough for other people to sound your emotional depths.

Why you're wonderful! Effervescent, bright, and witty, you are the life and soul of your social circle. You're also a creative genius with a real writing ability—go look for it! You can tell a funny story well and have a wicked sense of humor; your excellent one-liners have your friends in stitches. This is balanced by an analytical approach to things, and you can spend hours analyzing your emotions and people close to you.

Why you're impossible! You tend to run around like a headless chicken, making it hard for others to relax around you. You need to take time just to be still. You can also contradict yourself and change your mind within the blink of an eye. Promises are made but it's difficult for you to stick to them, not because you don't mean to but because you never know what you're feeling from one minute to the next.

Your secret side You can be neurotic and isolated. You sometimes feel the need for a deep and intense emotional or physical relationship, which will sweep away everything else. You know that to a certain degree you are self-constructed and would like the layers to be stripped away to reveal what lies beneath. You long to have absolute truths in your life, but deep down you know that these probably don't exist for you. Occasionally you may tell white lies or exaggerate in your enthusiasm to communicate.

gemini love compatibility chart

aries	taurus	gemini	cancer	leo	virgo	
🍾		🍾	🍾	🍾	🍾	
💘		💘	💘	💘	💘	
🎈	🎈	🎈	🎈	🎈	🎈	
		💋	💋	💋	💋	
🪑		🪑	🪑	🪑	🪑	
💡		💡	💡	💡	💡	
		👥				

	libra	scorpio	sagittarius	capricorn	aquarius	pisces
	🍾		🍾		🍾	🍾
	💘		💘		💘	💘
	💍				💍	
	🎈		🎈		🎈	🎈
	👄		👄		👄	👄
	🪑		🪑		🪑	🪑
	💡		💡		💡	💡
	👥				👥	

  passion chilling out spontaneity attentiveness

cancer

june 22–july 22

color silver, chrome ★ **number** 4, 11, 22 ★ **stone** opal—a powerful stone that magnifies your emotions and draws love to you ★ **flora** busy lizzie ★ **animal** rabbit ★ **occupation** caterer, dj, nurse ★ **key features** idealistic, tender, insecure ★ **naturally good at** sensing other people's pain

june 22

character ★ You have a very unusual view of love and are sometimes led by your heart without using your common sense. Love is a drug to you and you sometimes pick unusual partners. Nothing but the soul matters, which means that you don't always see the true personality of your conquests. Look at the surface as well as the depths of the people you are attracted to.

life path ★ You can find it difficult to be practical because you are so consumed by your emotions. Having said that, you have a kind and open heart and are always tuning in to the vulnerability or pain of others. A job as a nurse or counselor will appeal to you, but try not to get overburdened by the needs of others.

love ★ You may have a complicated love life. Things that seem to be too good to be true often are, and you make rash choices. However, when you find The One, you will have the secure family you desire. Try an Aquarius, who has Uranus, your birth date ruler, as their ruling planet, which should give you freedom and love.

best present ★ Trip to the lake, hand-written love letter.

birthday share ★ 1906 Billy Wilder, film director; 1936 Kris Kristofferson, singer and actor; 1949 Meryl Streep, actress; 1953 Cyndi Lauper, singer.

on this day ★ In 1941, Nazi Germany invaded the Soviet Union, in one of the most dramatic turning points of World War II.

june 23

character ★ You are a lively, lovely, and loving creature. The truth is everything to you, and you are very aware of the way others communicate. You may have had an interest in philosophy or literature and may secretly want to be a writer yourself. You will be drawn to all areas connected to the media or the written word.

life path ★ You are an excellent mimic and can pick up accents just from being in a different state or country for a few hours. You love to chat with people, appreciating their diversity without being judgmental, and you adapt your own personality to get along with them. Sometimes this chameleon habit makes you forget your own path.

love ★ You can be a love junkie—you love to love and you love to talk about your liaisons. You see love as an adventure, and entering the heart of another person is like an epic journey through a strange land. You could find a Gemini to love because their ruling planet is the same as your birth date ruler, Mercury, planet of communication.

best present ★ Vacation on an exotic island, soft toy.

birthday share ★ 1912 Alan Turing, mathematician; 1927 Bob Fosse, dancer and choreographer; 1940 Adam Faith, singer and actor; 1972 Selma Blair, actress.

on this day ★ In 1868, Christopher Latham Sholes was granted a patent for an invention he called the *Type-Writer*.

color pink, light green ★ **number** 6, 7, 33 ★ **stone** rhodochrosite—the pink "rescue remedy" stone that brings calm to the one who holds it ★ **flora** sweet pea ★ **animal** any—you adore all animals ★ **occupation** magician, poet, nun ★ **key features** profound, sensitive, vulnerable ★ **naturally good at** drowning in your emotions

june 24

character ★ Often you feel you are not waving but drowning because you feel things so deeply. It is essential to ground yourself and perhaps take up a spiritual practice to help you find emotional balance. You are like a crab with no shell, so you sometimes feel stabbed when people say the slightest thing to you. Learn to take things a little less personally.

life path ★ You can swing from being wild to being judgmental. Find the middle ground. Life is not about extremes, and you will never feel comfortable with either of these approaches. Embrace your sexuality but see it as sacred.

love ★ Relationships can be tough for you because you crave love desperately and want to believe it exists in perfect form, but a part of you is terrified that it is all a myth. Find yourself a Libra, whose ruling planet is

Venus—your birth date ruler—as love is what both of you are here to learn

best present ★ Yoga classes, weekend in a hotel with a fireplace and sheepskin rug.

birthday share ★ 1813 Henry Ward Beecher, clergyman and orator; 1895 Jack Dempsey, boxer; 1942 Mick Fleetwood, musician; 1944 Jeff Beck, musician.

on this day ★ In 1947, an American pilot reported seeing strange objects in the sky looking like "saucers skipping across the water." The incident led to the first use of the term "flying saucers."

color marine blue ★ **number** 7, 12, 61 ★ **stone** seashells—not strictly gemstones, but they give you great self-confidence ★ **flora** swan river daisy ★ **animal** whale or dolphin ★ **occupation** scuba diver, designer, marine biologist ★ **key features** emotional, original, sympathetic ★ **naturally good at** interior design

character ★ You have an eye for detail and a real creative flair. You love blues and purples and rooms with a spiritual or romantic theme. You see your home as a living extension of yourself and express your quirky nature there. You are also very sensitive to smell and surround yourself with aromatic fragrances to soothe your responsive spirit.

life path ★ You are drawn to water, which has a particularly calming effect on your mind. This is because Neptune is your birth number ruler, coupled with the emotional Moon of your Sun sign, making you sensitive and dreamy. Whenever you are stressed just take yourself to the sea and feel all your worries ebb away with the tide.

love ★ You often have crushes, even when in a committed relationship, because you relish fantasy and romance. This is fine unless it disrupts your security; remember that a fantasy is sometimes better left in your head. Find a good old romantic Pisces, whose ruling planet is the same as your birth date ruler Neptune, and who can indulge your sensitivity.

best present ★ Cruise, trip to an ice rink.

birthday share ★ 1903 George Orwell, author; 1925 June Lockhart, actress; 1945 Carly Simon, singer; 1963 George Michael, singer.

on this day ★ In 1993, Kim Campbell was the first woman to be elected prime minister of Canada.

june 26

character ★ You have a solid and reliable personality. You want those you love to be able to lean on you, and you show great concern if they have any problems—they can rely on you totally. You are great at taking control of the family home.

life path ★ You put others before yourself and tend not to ask for help when you need it, so beware of becoming too selfless. You can be too bound by duty and honor instead of what is real and in the present. Try to live in the moment and go with the flow.

love ★ Committed and steadfast, you tend to have long-term relationships that you take very seriously. You have strict Saturn as your birth date ruler, and as this is coupled with your ruling planet, the sensitive Moon, you need someone who is equally loyal. Try a Capricorn, whose ruling planet is Saturn.

best present ★ Set of golf clubs, picture of your family tree.

birthday share ★ 1914 Laurie Lee, author; 1955 Mick Jones, musician; 1956 Chris Isaak, singer and actor; 1970 Chris O'Donnell, actor.

on this day ★ In 1906, the first Grand Prix motor race was held in Le Mans, France. It was won by the Hungarian, Ferenc Szisz, in a Renault.

color volcanic red ★ **number** 1, 9, 18 ★ **stone** ruby—the ancient egyptians loved this stone and believed that it warned of danger when the color paled ★ **flora** viola ★ **animal** border collie ★ **occupation** marine, boxer, saxophone player ★ **key features** volatile reactions, self-protective, warlike ★ **naturally good at** defending your position

june 27

character ★ You have a rugged character, but you tend to overreact and be explosive. No one had better mess with you and yours. This is because your birth date ruler is Mars, fiery planet of war. Relax—you are safe and so are those you love.

life path ★ Perhaps you need to trust in the universe a little more; your tendency to overreact in various situations can get you into trouble. You like to feel emotions surging through you, but you need to resist giving in to insecurity, fear, and doubt. Confidence building and some anger management wouldn't go amiss.

love ★ Once you love you are like a volcano, all fierce passion and protection for your partner, but you had your fingers burned in the past. You may spend months or even years of your life alone out of fear,

but you should get back on the love train, because you are a brilliant lover. Why not try an Aries, whose ruling planet is the same as your birth date ruler, hot and fiery Mars?

best present ★ CD of chill-out music, night at a jazz club.

birthday share ★ 1880 Helen Keller, author and teacher; 1938 Shirley Ann Field, actress; 1942 Bruce Johnston, singer; 1975 Tobey Maguire, actor.

on this day ★ In 1893, the New York stock market crashed leaving the nation in panic. By the end of the year, 600 banks and 74 railroads had gone out of business.

june 28

character ★ Wild and free, you hate to be put in a box. Even if you have a normal job you will often have a sideline in acting or performing. You have your finger in many pies and want to show the world what you can do. As you are such a likeable character, you will no doubt succeed.

life path ★ Follow your heart. You pretend sometimes that you don't know what your dreams are but could this be an excuse? You may fear that if you try and fail, you couldn't live with yourself, but you have it within you to succeed beyond your wildest dreams— so go for it!

love ★ You are irresistible, but you often choose lovers whom you don't consider to be your equal. Could this be because of a fear of intimacy? You can have any lover you desire, so choose an equal—your relationships will be so much more

rewarding. A Leo whose ruling planet is also your birth date ruler, the Sun, would give you a run for your money.

best present ★ Mirror, trip to somewhere hot.

birthday share ★ 1926 Mel Brooks, actor and director; 1948 Kathy Bates, actress; 1966 John Cusack, actor, and Mary Stuart Masterson, actress.

on this day ★ In 1919, the Treaty of Versailles was signed by Germany and the Allies, officially ending World War I.

color silver, white ★ **number** 2, 11, 22 ★ **stone** pearls—calming and centering, they attune you to the ebb and flow of life ★ **flora** angels' trumpets ★ **animal** owl ★ **occupation** psychic, full-time parent, midwife ★ **key features** nurturing, maternal, intuitive ★ **naturally good at** sensing emotions in others

character ★ You're a bit of a magical, spooky one, very tuned in to the moods of others and your own spiritual journey. You live life on a deeper level than most of us do. The good news is that your intuition, sensitivity, and strong inner voice will serve you well.

life path ★ Because you have an inescapable sixth sense you often know where your life is heading six months in advance. However, this can make you seem moody to others who don't understand the depth of your perception. Meditating on the full Moon will increase these intrinsic powers.

love ★ You need someone who can understand your ultrafeminine nature if you are a woman and your gentle, feminine side if you are a man. Men and women born on this date have strong parental instincts. As your birth date and Sun sign share the same ruler—the Moon—another Cancer may understand your openness.

best present ★ Gold candleholder, trip to the beach.

birthday share ★ 1901 Nelson Eddy, actor and singer; 1944 Gary Busey, actor; 1947 Richard Lewis, comedian; 1962 Amanda Donohoe, actress.

on this day ★ In 1956, playwright Arthur Miller married actress Marilyn Monroe.

color purple, lilac ★ **number** 3, 13, 33 ★ **stone** emerald—said to soothe your heart and bond loved ones together ★ **flora** aquilegia ★ **animal** tarantula ★ **occupation** cashier, hotel manager, retailer ★ **key features** money minded, seeking good fortune, ambitious ★ **naturally good at** gaining unexpected money

june 30

character ★ You see your fate as being very tied up with love and security and can make the mistake of measuring happiness by how much financial security you have. You will not rest until you have a home you can be proud of, and this can put a strain on less motivated partners. Wherever you are, you want to take the next step up.

life path ★ You're very loving and kind but get caught up in the process of trying to succeed. Learn to be in the present moment and enjoy what you have right now. You will get what you deserve and the universe loves you, so allow your energy to flow rather than getting stressed and controlling.

love ★ Love is a huge issue in your life; you seek a partner who is very solid and secure and of whom you can be proud. In your youth you may have settled down with someone who was familiar and safe but whom you did not respect. Try a Sagittarius, whose ruling planet is also your birth date ruler, Jupiter.

best present ★ Leather bag, white-gold bracelet.

birthday share ★ 1917 Lena Horne, singer and actress; 1918 Susan Hayward, actress; 1943 Florence Ballard, singer; 1966 Mike Tyson, boxer.

on this day ★ In 1936, Margaret Mitchell's novel *Gone With the Wind* was published.

color ginger, gold ★ **number** 1, 11, 22 ★ **stone** malachite—promotes peace and tranquility and helps you face your fears ★ **flora** pansy ★ **animal** rooster ★ **occupation** yoga teacher, healer, sprinter ★ **key features** balanced, extreme, warm ★ **naturally good at** balancing male and female energies

character ★ You have the ability to be an extrovert, but can be more touchy than people realize because you tend to take things very personally and can get annoyed if people don't sense this. You have one or two friends you can share everything with, but you never reveal your true identity to people in general.

life path ★ You have been born to balance the yin and yang within you. You are equally solitary and gregarious. It is important for you to learn to give *and* receive or you could get trapped in only one half of your true self. When you reach this balance, you will be blessed by a rare and exquisite magic that enhances your love life.

love ★ Your perfect partner is someone who can see the whole of you, and not simply fall for your outgoing charm but understand your need to be cared for as well. As your birth date ruler is the Sun, find a sun-ruled Leo to shine their light on you.

best present ★ Circus-skills workshop, Harley-Davidson motorcycle.

birthday share ★ 1934 Sydney Pollack, director; 1952 Dan Ackroyd, actor; 1961 Diana, Princess of Wales; 1977 Liv Tyler, actress.

on this day ★ In 1903, the first Tour de France bicycle race began.

color silver, rose ★ number 2, 11, 22 ★ stone moonstone—to balance your double-moon energy ★ flora dahlia ★ animal shetland pony ★ occupation illusionist, comedian, cook ★ key features mood swings, vivid imagination, originality ★ naturally good at making people laugh

july 2

character ★ You're brilliant at making people laugh, and your observations are hilarious and outrageous. This eccentric sense of humor comes from understanding the height and depth of emotions. You have often been overwhelmed by your own emotional range and have developed an inspired way to deal with it by making yourself and others laugh at misfortune.

life path ★ Your gift is emotional intensity, but you must master your emotions. You can be carried away by big ideas that sometimes don't come to fruition, but if you can put that vivid imagination to good use, your life will be much smoother. Work on what you are good at.

love ★ Your heart has been broken a number of times but you don't give up; you may have a friend you are obsessed with but this is more a safe option than what you really want. Both your Sun sign and your birth date are ruled by the Moon, so go for another Cancer who will understand your emotional depth.

best present ★ Tickets to a vaudeville show, Italian meal.

birthday share ★ 1877 Hermann Hesse, writer; 1929 Imelda Marcos, former first lady of the Philippines; 1939 Paul Williams, singer; 1956 Jerry Hall, model and actress.

on this day ★ In 1976, North and South Vietnam were reunited as one country with Hanoi as the capital following the Vietnam War. It had been divided since 1954.

july 3

character ★ You have a very rational mind, and this orders your strong emotions. You want the world to be a better place and you may get involved in political or charitable causes. You have a tendency to hide your passionate emotions and are extremely self-effacing.

life path ★ You are very intellectual and have an unusual way of convincing people you are right. You can charm with your mild manner and rarely show offense if people don't agree with you. When you believe in a cause, you are capable of great acts of courage.

love ★ Love is not a big issue. You expect it will come along at the right time when all will be rosy, and you are probably right. Your birth date ruler is Jupiter, and a forward-thinking Sagittarius, whose ruling planet is also Jupiter, will have the same values as you.

best present ★ Complete works of Karl Marx, slippers.

birthday share ★ 1883 Franz Kafka, author; 1946 Johnny Lee, country singer; 1956 Montel Williams, talk show host; 1962 Tom Cruise, actor.

on this day ★ In 1608, French explorer Samuel de Champlain founded the Canadian city of Quebec.

color cobalt blue, lavender ★ **number** 16, 31, 44 ★ **stone** turquoise—a protective truth stone of the native americans ★ **flora** heliotrope ★ **animal** eagle ★ **occupation** zookeeper, firefighter, bar owner ★ **key features** stubborn, thoughtful, sympathetic ★ **naturally good at** remaining objective in an argument and winning it

july 4

character ★ You love to banter and argue but do not take things as personally as most Cancers. In fact, you are quite stubborn and thick-skinned. You would thrive in any job that involves people, risk, and an element of heroism. Being a firefighter would give you a buzz as well as fulfill your desire for danger and serving mankind.

life path ★ It is not a coincidence that you were born on Independence Day. You have a courageous spirit and like to fight the good fight if someone needs defending or protecting. However, you are not at all aggressive and can often get out of any difficulties by means of your inspired conversation skills.

love ★ Again, you are unusual for a Cancer in that you don't like to be pinned down or possessed by your lover. Although you like to recharge about once a week by doing homey things, you are always gallivanting about. Find yourself a free-spirited Aquarius, whose ruling planet is the same as your birth date ruler, Uranus.

best present ★ Day at the races, stockcar racing.

birthday share ★ 1804 Nathaniel Hawthorne, author; 1927 Gina Lollobrigida, actress; 1938 Bill Withers, singer; 1962 Pam Shriver, tennis player.

on this day ★ In 1976, the United States of America celebrated its 200th anniversary.

color indigo blue, silver ★ **number** 2, 14, 32 ★ **stone** sapphire—buddhists believe this is a devotional stone signifying spiritual purity ★ **flora** orchid ★ **animal** siamese cat ★ **occupation** train engineer, mail carrier, speechwriter ★ **key features** literary, clever, sharp ★ **naturally good at** analyzing world events

character ★ You are too clever for your own good! You get lost in the power of your own intellect as you juggle thought and feeling. You are always aware of your surroundings, but you lose sight of your emotions. You may decide to take a job in which you have to communicate or assist someone else, possibly someone more powerful.

life path ★ You may well be the next Carl Jung, but in the meantime sort out your own emotional life. It's time, perhaps, to put more effort into your home and environment. Order makes you feel safe, as do comfortable surroundings, so you should give this matter more priority.

love ★ You can be a loner but have loads of friends and colleagues you spend time with. However, you need to make more space in your life for a lover, or if you have one you should give them more quality time. Your birth date ruler is Mercury, so try a chatty Gemini, whose ruling planet is Mercury, and who will engage your mind.

best present ★ One year's free dry-cleaning, date to see a movie.

birthday share ★ 1810 Phineas T. Barnum, circus entrepreneur; 1853 Sir Cecil Rhodes, founder of Rhodesia (now Zimbabwe); 1936 Shirley Knight, actress; 1950 Huey Lewis, singer.

on this day ★ In 1975, Arthur Ashe beat fellow American Jimmy Connors to become the first black tennis player to win the Wimbledon men's singles title.

color pink, crimson ★ number 6, 15, 42 ★ stone rose-quartz—the love stone, to balance your turbulent emotions ★ flora begonia ★ animal poodle ★ occupation actor, marriage counselor, painter ★ key features obsessive, lustful, emotional ★ naturally good at getting caught in complicated relationships

july 6

character ★ Love makes your world go round. You are obsessed with relationships but rarely have one that is stable. Perhaps you prefer the adventurous ups and downs of grand passion? Your life is like a 1950s melodrama, but you wouldn't have it any other way.

life path ★ You are the high priest or priestess of love. You tend to give all of yourself away and project your fantasy onto the object of your desire. In reality you are the one in control, if only you could realize it.

love ★ You love the trials and tribulations of a tempestuous affair and will go to the ends of the earth for a romantic dream. Try a Libra, whose ruling planet is the same as your birth date ruler Venus, planet of love.

best present ★ A dozen red roses, book of love poems.

birthday share ★ 1921 Nancy Reagan, former first lady; 1925 Bill Haley, singer; 1935 Dalai Lama, Tibetan spiritual leader; 1946 Sylvester Stallone, actor.

on this day ★ In 1785, the dollar was unanimously chosen as the money unit for the United States. It was the first time a nation had adopted a decimal coinage system.

color sea green, emerald ★ **number** 25, 34, 61 ★ **stone** sodalite—which the ancient egyptians used to dispel fear and build confidence ★ **flora** evening primrose ★ **animal** shark ★ **occupation** professional jockey, football coach, sailor ★ **key features** perceptive, sympathetic, distant ★ **naturally good at** being at home in the water

character ★ Honesty is very important to you, yet you have a habit of changing your mind. Even those close to you can accuse you of being deceptive, although this could not be further from the truth. You love people and give a lot of yourself, but you should hold your tongue until you are 100 percent committed to something or someone, because your good intentions could get you into trouble.

life path ★ You can be gullible, so make sure that people don't take advantage of you, particularly concerning money—your trusting nature makes you a con man's dream. The good news is that you have very protective friends.

love ★ You fall in and out of love quickly and need romance to maintain your interest but also a partner who is grounded and secure. Choose a Pisces, whose ruling planet, Neptune, is your birth date ruler.

best present ★ Deep-sea fishing trip, day at the beach.

birthday share ★ 1860 Gustav Mahler, composer; 1922 Pierre Cardin, fashion designer; 1940 Ringo Starr, musician; 1949 Shelley Duvall, actress.

on this day ★ In 1981, President Reagan nominated Sandra Day O'Connor to become a Supreme Court justice. She became the first woman member of the Supreme Court in September of that year.

july 8

character ★ Bold and determined, you can be a little naughty when you want something, and will stop at nothing to achieve it. If you want something badly enough you can be tempted to cross the boundaries of what is legal or honorable. Decide what your personal morals are and stick to them.

life path ★ You may have grown up with a feeling that you were not good enough. Because of this you are doubly determined to achieve the pinnacle of success in both your career and your relationships. You need to get in touch with your soft side, which is one of the most gorgeous things about you.

love ★ You have had challenges in this area and maybe had a partner who would not fully commit to you. It may have been a grand passion, but love is not about force of will and control. If it isn't working, let it go.

Harsh Saturn is your birth date ruler, so try a Capricorn, whose ruling planet is also Saturn—you will have a natural affinity with each other.

best present ★ Expensive fragrance, crystal glasses.

birthday share ★ 1839 John D. Rockefeller, entrepreneur; 1914 Billy Eckstine, singer; 1951 Anjelica Huston, actress; 1958 Kevin Bacon, actor.

on this day ★ In 1889, the first issue of *The Wall Street Journal* was published.

color cherry red ★ **number** 18, 36, 72 ★ **stone** ruby—a stone of passion ★ **flora** bird of paradise ★ **animal** german shepherd dog ★ **occupation** engineer, composer, opera singer ★ **key features** passionate, energetic, powerful ★ **naturally good at** achieving your goal

character ★ You are a powerhouse of energy most of the time, but you may find that your energy dips and you become exhausted regularly, because you don't pace yourself. Whether it is work or a romantic liaison you put your heart and soul into everything you do. Always make sure you get enough sleep and eat a nutritious diet to fuel that volcanic energy.

life path ★ You are a high achiever in all areas but also need periods of solitary meditation. You may not like to spend time alone but the need to recharge is an essential part of your nature and you will suffer if you neglect this. Have a date with yourself once a month and do all your favorite things.

love ★ You enjoy passion and are highly imaginative as a lover, but you should remember that you have nothing to prove and that the more you relax, the better love will be. Your birth date ruler, Mars, is also the ruling planet of Aries, a good choice to match that amorous spark.

best present ★ Ruby ring, copy of a passionate novel, such as Emily Brontë's *Wuthering Heights*.

birthday share ★ 1901 Barbara Cartland, author; 1947 OJ Simpson, football player and actor; 1956 Tom Hanks, actor; 1964 Courtney Love, actress and singer.

on this day ★ In 1922, swimmer Johnny Weissmuller (who later starred in the movie *Tarzan*) became the first man to swim 109.36 yards (100 meters) in less than a minute, clocking 58.6 seconds.

color orange, yellow ★ **number** 1, 11, 22 ★ **stone** fire opal—stirs you into action and fans the flames of your lust for life ★ **flora** black-eyed susan ★ **animal** lion ★ **occupation** entertainment agent, acupuncturist, yoga instructor ★ **key features** sunny, charismatic, insecure ★ **naturally good at** bringing fame to others

july 10

character ★ You have a sunny personality that radiates wherever you go. However, you are also quite shy and insecure, and may often feel that your function in life is to be in the background boosting someone else, be that in your work or in relationships.

life path ★ You know that if you put your mind to it you could be in the limelight, so why not go for it? Some are born for greatness, and with your charismatic personality you could be one of them. You simply have to invest the effort in your own journey. You are truly scrumptious and many people adore you.

love ★ Because you are so giving in relationships you are usually in one. However, you can easily become a doormat and need to learn to respect yourself and the wonderful gifts you offer as a lover. Perhaps

a Leo whose ruling planet is the dazzling Sun, your birth date ruler, would be a good match for you.

best present ★ Silver ring, framed photograph.

birthday share ★ 1834 James McNeill Whistler, artist; 1871 Marcel Proust, writer; 1943 Arthur Ashe, tennis player; 1980 Jessica Simpson, actress and singer.

on this day ★ In 1992, former Panamanian dictator Manuel Noriega was sentenced to 40 years in jail in the United States on drug-trafficking charges.

color silver, white ★ **number** 2, 11, 22 ★ **stone** diamond—the strongest stone in the world will give you courage ★ **flora** osteospermum ★ **animal** llama ★ **occupation** psychiatric nurse, clairvoyant, ice-skater ★ **key features** gentle, vulnerable, emotional ★ **naturally good at** soothing other people's emotions

character ★ You have the energy of an elf, gentle and kind but with a dash of mischief thrown in for good measure. You have a delightful childlike quality coupled with delicacy and compassion, and you sometimes find the world too harsh a place. Learn to build up your defenses and protect that pure spirit.

life path ★ You would prefer to live in a land of make-believe, but as you are here you might as well make the most of it. You have a strong sense of justice and protect others who are vulnerable or weak. You are one of the good guys so should value yourself more highly and not become disillusioned—the universe loves you.

love ★ Love scares you a little and you have an almost adolescent attitude toward it, which allows you to be taken over and rendered helpless. Take your time, go slowly, and it will be easier. Your birth date ruler, the Moon, is the same as your ruling planet, so look for love with another Cancer.

best present ★ Pearl earrings or cufflinks, scented candles.

birthday share ★ 1899 E. B. White, author; 1934 Giorgio Armani, designer; 1953 Leon Spinks, boxer; 1959 Suzanne Vega, singer.

on this day ★ In 1979, the Skylab space station fell out of orbit, making a dazzling display as it burned up in the Earth's atmosphere.

color imperial purple ★ **number** 3, 21, 33 ★ **stone** amethyst—known as the sobriety stone, the romans used this to prevent overindulgence ★ **flora** lavender ★ **animal** guinea pig ★ **occupation** aerobics instructor, drama teacher, gambler ★ **key features** patient, spontaneous, lucky ★ **naturally good at** successful gambling

july 12

character ★ You are incredibly lucky, but may take this luck for granted. You are very patient and have a relaxed attitude toward life, but then what you wait for nearly always comes eventually. You have the gift of gab and can make people sit up and take notice of your ideas.

life path ★ Planning ahead is what you were born to do and you will achieve great things every year. However, you should also look around you and count your blessings occasionally. You were born fortunate, so you should make the most of it. You like the good things in life, but be careful not to squander cash on a lavish lifestyle if money is yet to arrive.

love ★ You may end up having two great loves in life, one you meet very early and one who takes you by surprise in your fifties. These loves will be equal, but different. Search for a madcap Sagittarius, as your birth date is ruled by their ruling planet, Jupiter, planet of good fortune.

best present ★ Champagne, silver dice.

birthday share ★ 1895 Oscar Hammerstein II, songwriter; 1904 Pablo Neruda, poet; 1908 Milton Berle, actor and comedian; 1937 Bill Cosby, actor.

on this day ★ In 1982, *E.T.: The Extra-Terrestrial* broke all box-office records by surpassing the $100 million mark in its first month of ticket sales.

color light blue, silvery white ★ **number** 4, 13, 22 ★ **stone** fluorite—opens your mind to your highest truth and knowledge ★ **flora** bluebell ★ **animal** newt ★ **occupation** rocket scientist, physics teacher, entertainer ★ **key features** erratic, mad genius, serious ★ **naturally good at** understanding scientific theories

july 13

character ★ You have a touch of the mad professor about you. Your thoughts are jumbled and changeable but strangely they reap rewards for you. This is because your unusual mind was built to solve problems and perhaps invent new concepts. However, some people think you're simply crazy.

life path ★ Even if you live a conventional life you have periods of transformation. You may suddenly change career or lover, but these dramatic changes always work to your greater good. Don't be afraid to embrace those times when everything disintegrates, because they make way for a better life.

love ★ You never really feel understood and can suddenly cut yourself off from loved ones. Decide what it is you want from a partner and you will find it. Try a free-spirited Aquarius, whose ruling planet is your birth date ruler, Uranus.

best present ★ Telescope, book on astronomy.

birthday share ★ 1940 Patrick Stewart, actor; 1942 Harrison Ford, actor; 1944 Erno Rubik, inventor; 1954 David Thompson, basketball player.

on this day ★ In 1985, two Live Aid concerts were held in London and Philadelphia to benefit African famine relief; nearly $100 million was raised by the televised events.

july 14

character ★ People are drawn toward you like moths to a flame, and you are immersed in a social life that consumes most of your time. You tend to have intense friendships and love affairs, but this can lead to battles and jealousy between people vying for your attention.

life path ★ Perhaps you need more boundaries in your friendships, as you are never off the telephone and have very little time to yourself. Take the time to think about your career. If you can have such an effect on your friends, perhaps you should think about how your natural charm and influence could benefit you in a career in the entertainment industry.

love ★ Love comes easily to you, and your deep and melodic voice persuades even the most cautious of lovers to give you their heart. Why not try a Gemini, who loves to converse and will fascinate your mind?

best present ★ Video of an old movie, digital radio.

birthday share ★ 1858 Emmeline Pankhurst, suffragette; 1912 Woody Guthrie, singer; 1913 Gerald Ford, 38th U.S. president; 1918 Ingmar Bergman, director.

on this day ★ In 1789, an angry mob stormed the Bastille prison in Paris, marking the start of the French Revolution.

color pink, light green ★ **number** 6, 33, 42 ★ **stone** rose-quartz—a stone that brings unconditional love ★ **flora** larkspur ★ **animal** tiger ★ **occupation** relationship counselor, matchmaker, speech therapist ★ **key features** romantic, sensual, dreamy ★ **naturally good at** sorting out your friends' emotional problems

character ★ Sweet and loving, you care about everyone and give out good vibes. You can be a love junkie and you read too many romantic stories. Life is not a movie, but somehow you make it so. Guard your heart and try not to say "I love you" after the first date.

life path ★ You are here to give some sort of service to mankind, usually involving emotional well-being, but you aren't very good at sorting out your own life and relationships. Read some books on unconditional and spiritual love to balance out your extreme infatuations. Don't let one bad experience color your whole life.

love ★ Love is a compulsion for you—you feel that you need it like a drug. Chill out, back off, and trust that things will get smoother; otherwise you will set yourself up with unrealistic expectations. Try a Libra, whose ruling planet is your birth date ruler, Venus.

best present ★ Tickets for a sentimental movie, box of chocolates.

birthday share ★ 1606 Rembrandt van Rijn, artist; 1931 Clive Cussler, author; 1961 Forest Whitaker, actor; 1963 Brigitte Nielsen, actress.

on this day ★ In 1997, Italian fashion designer Gianni Versace was shot and killed outside his mansion in Miami Beach by serial killer Andrew Phillip Cunanan.

color lagoon blue ★ number 7, 52, 70 ★ stone blue lace agate—a stone that helps you communicate clearly ★ flora lobelia ★ animal hamster ★ occupation preacher, dolphin trainer, author ★ key features unrealistic, compulsive, imaginative ★ naturally good at telling a great story

july 16

character ★ You have to watch out for your addictive nature and avoid going to extremes. You may love to drink and party or spend all your time on the golf course, but whatever your passion you tend to do it all the time. This can really annoy those close to you.

life path ★ You have a vivid imagination and can be prone to dangerous exaggeration, which could get you into trouble. People find you unreliable and you are then hurt by their disbelief. Take a good look deep within and examine your motives when telling a story or recounting an experience. Honesty is the best policy.

love ★ You can be an addict in this area, too, and find it hard to be faithful. You do love your partner, but you can't resist temptation. Your birth date is ruled by Neptune, so go fishing for a dreamy Pisces, who can swim in the depths of your soul.

best present ★ Bottle of whiskey, backgammon set.

birthday share ★ 1872 Roald Amundsen, explorer; 1911 Ginger Rogers, actress and dancer; 1952 Stewart Copeland, musician; 1971 Corey Feldman, actor.

on this day ★ In 1969, *Apollo 11*, the rocket that made the first manned Moon landing, was launched.

july 17

character ★ You are diligent, hardworking, and determined, and you know exactly where you are going in life, which could well be into the realms of power and influence. Your family helps to keep you grounded, although you may have had problems with your father in the past.

life path ★ You have a keen interest in politics and may join a campaign trail. You know that you should try to keep your personal life inscrutable in case you are ever involved in something secret. You also love to hold things back from others and appear enigmatic.

love ★ You are quite traditional and a solid family life is your aim, but you may also be tempted to have a secret love affair. Try a Capricorn if you want to settle down, as they are ruled by your birth date ruler, strict and sensible Saturn.

best present ★ Gold watch, cell phone.

birthday share ★ 1889 Erle Stanley Gardner, author; 1899 James Cagney, actor; 1934 Donald Sutherland, actor; 1952 David Hasselhoff, actor.

on this day ★ In 1953, Disneyland, in California, opened its gates to the public for the first time.

july 18

character ★ You seize life and enjoy the ride. Throwing yourself body and soul into all that you do, you seem to have limitless energy and enthusiasm. You can sometimes feel taken for granted, but you need to look at your own contribution to this—you do everything for everyone even when they don't need you to, so you can't complain about it afterward!

life path ★ You are very loyal and support your friends and colleagues in difficult situations. You're a legend in your own lifetime, but you are also human and need quiet times like the rest of us. Take up some de-stressing activities and have regular massages to relax that overworked body.

love ★ You are passionate and a good kisser, and you love being adventurous with your partner—when you have the time for it in your busy schedule. You need an ardent lover who can keep up, so try an Aries, whose ruling planet is Mars, your birth date ruler.

best present ★ Gym membership, relaxation tape.

birthday share ★ 1811 William Makepeace Thackeray, author; 1918 Nelson Mandela, former president of South Africa; 1921 John Glenn, astronaut; 1967 Vin Diesel, actor.

on this day ★ In 1925, Adolf Hitler published the first volume of his personal manifesto, *Mein Kampf* (*My Struggle*).

color orange, yellow ★ **number** 1, 11, 22 ★ **stone** carnelian—prized by the romans as a good luck charm, this stone will energize you ★ **flora** morning glory ★ **animal** iguana ★ **occupation** tennis coach, ballet dancer, bodybuilder ★ **key features** eye-catching, fit, energetic ★ **naturally good at** expressing yourself

july 19

character ★ You love your body and like other people to admire it as well, although you may have been overweight at certain times in your life and hated it then. Love your body as it is now and it will love you back. You do have the capacity to be fit and powerful, but this needs to be nurtured from within.

life path ★ You can be a little superficial and judge others the way you judge yourself. Remember that your body is only a vehicle for the soul's journey on earth, so don't get too addicted to body perfection.

love ★ You love to be admired but can get embroiled in power struggles in your relationships. Lovers worship you at first, but it is hard not to fall off the pedestal. The key is not to get up there in the first place! Try a warm Leo, whose ruling planet, the Sun, is also your birth date ruler.

best present ★ Sneakers, trampoline.

birthday share ★ 1834 Edgar Degas, painter and sculptor; 1941 Vikki Carr, singer; 1946 Ilie Nastase, tennis player; 1947 Brian May, guitarist.

on this day ★ In 1941, Winston Churchill introduced his "V for Victory" campaign which rapidly spread through Europe. The BBC took the first four notes of Beethoven's Fifth Symphony, which matched the dot-dot-dot-dash Morse code for the letter V, and played it before news bulletins.

color silvery white ★ **number** 2, 11, 22 ★ **stone** smoky quartz—helps you overcome your fears ★ **flora** geranium ★ **animal** mynah bird ★ **occupation** therapist, bird handler, dog trainer ★ **key features** sweet, open, manipulative ★ **naturally good at** creating harmony in all environments

july 20

character ★ You long to be accepted and needed and can sometimes go to extremes to get this reassurance. You often work overtime and put in extra effort because of your insecurity. Your intuitive skills are refined, so you are instantly aware of what others are feeling and often comfort them if they have problems.

life path ★ Your strongly empathetic nature is great, but try not to be manipulative and control those you help. It is essential that you remain objective when listening to others or you will end up caught in many tangled webs of emotional intrigue.

love ★ You may have wrestled with issues of control in past relationships. You require a partner who is stable and reliable and lets you go off into your wild imagination without stifling you. Why not try finding love with another Cancer, as you are both ruled by the Moon, which is also your birth date ruler?

best present ★ Candy, meal in a five-star restaurant.

birthday share ★ 1919 Edmund Hillary, mountaineer; 1938 Natalie Wood, actress, and Diana Rigg, actress; 1947 Carlos Santana, guitarist.

on this day ★ In 1881, the Sioux Indian chief Sitting Bull surrendered to the U.S. Army at Fort Buford, Canada.

color green ★ **number** 3, 12, 33 ★ **stone** clear quartz—the magic wand of crystals, which clarifies and amplifies your thoughts and energies ★ **flora** gladioli ★ **animal** cougar ★ **occupation** party planner, filmmaker, designer ★ **key features** lucky, successful, wacky ★ **naturally good at** securing your dreams

july 21

character ★ Your nature is charming if a little oddball, and your unique personality helps you succeed. Never run of the mill, you can choose any career you desire, as you are something of a magician and what you truly desire will be pulled toward you like iron to a magnet.

life path ★ Create your own destiny and rule your own fate. You have a magical existence that resembles a Hollywood film script—it might be a rags-to-riches story or feature an unlikely love affair. But remember, you write the script, so think big!

love ★ You are lovable and affectionate and in some ways childlike and innocent in the ways of love. This leads other people to open up to you emotionally in a way they would not normally. Try a Sagittarius whose ruling planet is also your birth date ruler, Jupiter.

best present ★ Horseback-riding lessons, kite.

birthday share ★ 1816 Paul von Reuter, founder of Reuters news agency; 1899 Ernest Hemingway, author; 1948 Cat Stevens, musician; 1952 Robin Williams, actor.

on this day ★ In 1873, Jesse James pulled off the first train robbery in the United States, stealing more than $3,000 from the express delivery car's safe and robbing the train's passengers of hundreds of dollars and some jewelry.

july 22

character ★ Up and down, flying around, your moods shift faster than the Concorde. You are greatly influenced by your surroundings, and if you are in a place you feel is ugly or confined, your mood becomes heavy. This chameleon approach to your environment can have its plus points, though, as you shine when you are in places that you adore.

life path ★ You have an overwhelming desire to create a masterpiece but are unsure of the form it should take. It may be an acclaimed play or a fantastic themed room, but you are determined to make a statement with your life. However, you must stop flitting from idea to idea and ground your artistic thoughts if you want to achieve your goals.

love ★ You are cranky and changeable if you are tied down and may prefer to have your own space to live in, even in long-term relationships. Partners must accept your free spirit. Why not try an Aquarius, whose ruling planet is your birth date ruler, Uranus?

best present ★ Model of a Ferrari, roller coaster ride.

birthday share ★ 1923 Bob Dole, U.S. senator and presidential candidate; 1947 Don Henley, musician, and Danny Glover, actor; 1964 John Leguizamo, actor.

on this day ★ In 1933, U.S. pioneer aviator Wiley Post became the first person to fly solo around the world, in seven days, 18 hours, and 49 minutes.

cancer

your ruling planet **The moon**, planet of emotions, is your ruler. It has a weighty effect on Earth, and greatly affects the tides of your emotions. The changing shape of the Moon, the dark and light, the hidden and the bright, is all expressed in your character. You can be outgoing, cheerful, and bright, but then become secretive, silent, and unavailable. Your lovers have a hard time getting to the bottom of you and your inscrutability. You behave in ways understandable only to you because you are so sensitive—even the raising of an eyebrow can inflict a deep wound. Like the Moon, you can light someone's way or plunge them into darkness—the choice is yours. Meditating and tuning in to the rhythms of the Moon will greatly support you and give you a more thorough understanding of yourself.

your natural habitat You would ideally like a home like the Waltons', rambling and filled with family and the smell of home cooking. You love to have people around and the kitchen is the central room of your house. Even if you are young and trendy, if you're honest you prefer a dinner party at your place to a club. You like a house to be clean but lived in, a place where people feel comfortable and relaxed. You would have a massive dinner table and fireplace in the kitchen, a multitude of saucepans hanging from the ceiling, and a vegetable rack overflowing with fresh, organic produce. With a glass of wine in hand and laid-back music playing in the background, you are content and at peace. You dream of a home on the beach so that you could stroll along at night gazing up at the Moon, with the sound of the waves soothing your mind.

are you a typical cancer?

All those clichés about you being a **nurturing homebody** are usually true. You love to look after others and feed and nourish them. Your home is incredibly important to you, and if you are not comfortable there, you can become **unstable**. You are **maternal** even if you are male and love to be around children and adults who have a playful child within. You are **warm** and **affectionate** and very **sensitive**. You can be **moody** and retreat into a dream world.

Why you're wonderful! You're very giving of yourself. You listen to your partner's problems and are always there for those you love. You are kind and compassionate, which extends to humanity in general, and are very good at random acts of charity. You're supportive and sincere, and when you love, you love forever. You are quite traditional and like to have set rules for yourself and your family. You find it difficult to let people down.

Why you're impossible! If you feel taken for granted you can be scheming in order to have your needs met. You can also be moody, sulky, and crabby, withdrawing into your shell and fending off all incomers with those huge pincers. You must avoid getting bitter at all costs and keep that heart of yours open. You find change and disruption to your security almost life-threatening and need to feel safe inside yourself. Practice the art of trusting, and your experience of life will be far less alarming.

Your secret side You manipulate to cover up your profound vulnerability and rarely show your feelings even though you might appear to. You long to be swept off your feet. In your imagination you are quite bold when it comes to romance, but you really need someone confident and secure in their own identity to make the first move.

cancer love compatibility chart

	aries	taurus	gemini	cancer	leo	virgo
fun	🍾	🍾	🍾	🍾	🍾	🍾
romance	💘	💘	💘	💘	💘	💘
loyalty		🔗		🔗	🔗	🔗
adventure		🎈	🎈	🎈	🎈	🎈
kiss	💋	💋	💋	💋	💋	💋
relax		🪑		🪑	🪑	🪑
ideas			💡	💡	💡	💡
friends	👥	👥		👥	👥	👥

	libra	scorpio	sagittarius	capricorn	aquarius	pisces
		🍾	🍾	🍾		🍾
	💘	💘		💘		💘
	💍	💍		💍		💍
	🎈	🎈	🎈	🎈	🎈	🎈
	👄	👄		👄		👄
	🪑	🪑		🪑	🪑	🪑
	💡	💡	💡	💡	💡	💡
	👥	👥		👥		👥

 passion chilling out spontaneity attentiveness

leo

july 23–august 23

color blue ★ **number** 5, 14, 23 ★ **stone** green jasper—clears emotional stress and attracts prosperity ★ **flora** rosemary ★ **animal** manx cat ★ **occupation** entertainer, pr executive, racehorse trainer ★ **key features** vibrant, sparky, gorgeous ★ **naturally good at** turning business around

july 23

character ★ You are convincing and honest, and you exude a natural air of self-assurance that makes it easy for people to trust you. You don't take your good fortune for granted and are always willing to give others a helping hand up the ladder if you feel they have talent.

life path ★ When you give your word, you never break it. This is partly why you have achieved so much in your life. You have an innate winning way in all areas of business but you are particularly drawn to a showbiz lifestyle. You never give in when you start a project and use all of your charisma to achieve whatever you set out to do.

love ★ Drop-dead gorgeous, you have no shortage of offers. You flirt and charm but are usually faithful. Watch overindulgence, as this can lead you to stray. Go for a

Gemini, whose ruling planet, Mercury, planet of communication, is also your birth date ruler.

best present ★ Antique typewriter, basketball hoop.

birthday share ★ 1888 Raymond Chandler, author; 1961 Woody Harrelson, actor; 1965 Slash, guitarist; 1973 Monica Lewinsky, former White House intern.

on this day ★ In 1864, Dr. David Livingstone, the missionary and explorer, returned to England from Africa.

color pink ★ number 6, 15, 33 ★ stone pink quartz—to heal your heart and soothe your mind ★ flora red currant ★ animal lovebird ★ occupation adventurer, tightrope walker, explorer ★ key features daring, impulsive, loyal ★ naturally good at leaping in where angels fear to tread

july 24

character ★ Excitable and adventurous, you despise the mundane and are always seeking out your next escapade. You may express this somewhat dangerous side to your personality by taking up a dangerous sport or by dating someone entirely inappropriate. Whatever it is you fancy, you jump right in.

life path ★ You are unconcerned with the consequences of your actions while you pursue your interesting if challenging life. You are here to have a good time and you intend to do just that. The opinions of other people do not matter to you one bit. Sometimes it may be advisable for you to mull over what could happen if the parachute fails to open.

love ★ You often get involved in all sorts of questionable affairs of the heart—the riskier the better. It would take a god or a goddess to tie you down. Why not try a Libra, whose ruling planet is also your birth date ruler, Venus, planet of love?

best present ★ Helicopter ride, bungee jump.

birthday share ★ 1898 Amelia Earhart, aviator; 1951 Lynda Carter, actress; 1952 Gus Van Sant, director; 1970 Jennifer Lopez, singer and actress.

on this day ★ In 1974, the Supreme Court ruled that President Richard Nixon must obey a subpoena to hand over the Watergate tapes to a special investigation committee.

color ocean blue ★ **number** 7, 16, 34 ★ **stone** blue lace agate—said to help you be truthful and true to yourself ★ **flora** virginia creeper ★ **animal** seal ★ **occupation** private detective, pilot, captain ★ **key features** deep, daydreaming, changeable ★ **naturally good at** sensing others' frustration and helping them

july 25

character ★ Because you are consumed by your emotions you are easily confused. You tend to focus on your emotions before they settle and consequently keep changing your mind. This drives other people crazy because you say things with such typical Leo force, then contradict yourself minutes or seconds later. Allow your emotional process to complete itself before opening your mouth.

life path ★ You combine strength of character with sensitivity, which is a powerful mixture, and people love you for it. You frustrate yourself by always searching for the illusive meaning of life. You get bored easily and yearn for long, distant travel or exalted love to distract you.

love ★ When you really fall in love, you feel a spiritual and karmic connection with your partner. You love to look deep into their eyes and feel yourself merging into one with them. Focus on a Pisces, whose ruling planet is also your birth date ruler, Neptune.

best present ★ Canoe trip, date next to a waterfall.

birthday share ★ 1894 Walter Brennan, actor; 1955 Iman, model; 1958 Thurston Moore, guitarist; 1967 Matt LeBlanc, actor.

on this day ★ In 1984, the Soviet cosmonaut Svetlana Savitskaya became the first woman to walk in space.

color maroon ★ **number** 8, 17, 44 ★ **stone** red jasper—said to ground you and make you secure ★ **flora** ivy ★ **animal** racehorse ★ **occupation** accountant, psychiatrist, director ★ **key features** self-critical, honest, strong ★ **naturally good at** self-restraint

july 26

character ★ You always strive to do the right thing and have very high principles. You have drive, ambition and the will to succeed. You are quick to act if you see an injustice, and you are honorable in all that you do, but you can be openly hostile to those you don't respect.

life path ★ You are charming and strong but can surround yourself with "yes" people. You tend to choose partners who can put you in your place, which keeps you from getting too big for your boots. You will give to those who deserve it but you need to come down off your high horse and be a little more lighthearted about life.

love ★ You need a partner as strong as you, but such a person is hard to find. You can argue and grumble in relationships but are faithful and loving in your own way. It would help to show your partner a little

more affection. Why not try a Capricorn, whose ruling planet is also your birth date ruler, Saturn?

best present ★ Leather wallet/purse, gold ring.

birthday share ★ 1875 Carl Jung, psychologist; 1943 Mick Jagger, singer; 1959 Kevin Spacey, actor; 1964 Sandra Bullock, actress.

on this day ★ In 1908, the Federal Bureau of Investigation was created in the United States and referred to as Office of the Chief Examiner. It became the FBI in 1935.

color red ★ **number** 9, 18, 72 ★ **stone** ruby—a stone that is powerful and passionate, just like you ★ **flora** inula ★ **animal** cougar ★ **occupation** weightlifter, firefighter, athlete ★ **key features** energetic, argumentative, stunning ★ **naturally good at** disagreeing with people

july 27

character ★ You're a fireball of activity and you hate to be in one place for too long. You need action and uncertainty in your life because you love to overcome it, but you can pick a quarrel over the color of oranges. You need to calm down and learn to release stress in constructive ways—try going hiking or jogging.

life path ★ You won't admit that you're a confrontational person because you always think it's the other person's fault! Passion is a great release for all that pent-up energy, so make sure you spend lots of high-quality time with your partner. You love to look good and can be rather controlling about what your partner wears as well. That's not good—so stop it!

love ★ You're a go-getter and have a limitless zest for new relationships. If things get stale you can get itchy feet, so you need

a firebrand like you as a mate. Why not choose an Aries, whose ruling planet, Mars, is also your birth date ruler?

best present ★ Mountain bike, skateboard.

birthday share ★ 1920 Homer (Henry D. Haynes), comedy singer; 1944 Bobbie Gentry, singer; 1948 Peggy Fleming, ice-skater; 1949 Maureen McGovern, singer.

on this day ★ In 1921, researchers at the University of Toronto led by biochemist Frederick Banting announced the discovery of the hormone insulin.

color orange ★ number 1, 11, 22 ★ stone fire opal—said to be a magical stone with as much charisma as you ★ flora bird of paradise ★ animal iguana ★ occupation movie star, drama teacher, performer ★ key features radiant, gorgeous, untouchable ★ naturally good at attracting admirers

july 28

character ★ You ooze charisma and magnetism, and when you walk into a room everyone turns around. You draw powerful lovers who want to possess you, but your independence and free spirit will prevent this. You were born to be appreciated, and even if you are not a traditional beauty, people find you attractive.

life path ★ Good looks and animal magnetism are not everything, but they can take you halfway there. You have the aura of a superstar whatever your profession, and should not settle for anything less than your ideal life. Go for it! The gods have given you something special you can believe in, so don't question or waste it.

love ★ You can have your pick of the pile and should never worry in this area. The more naturally confident you are, the more successful you will be. Why not try another Leo, as your ruling planet, the Sun, has a double placement, being your birth date ruler as well.

best present ★ Video camera, gold bracelet.

birthday share ★ 1866 Beatrix Potter, author and artist; 1915 Frankie Yankovic, musician and bandleader; 1929 Jacqueline Kennedy Onassis, former first lady; 1945 Jim Davis, cartoonist and creator of *Garfield*.

on this day ★ In 1914, Austria-Hungary declared war on Serbia, triggering the start of World War I.

july 29

character ★ You have a compassionate nature and like to help those around you. You are quite psychic and perhaps have dreams that end up being prophetic. You need to harness this intuition, as it will be of great benefit throughout your life. You share your ideas with others but are also a good listener and have a reassuring and encouraging manner.

life path ★ Well liked and well rounded, you manage to balance work and play. You tend to dress very differently when not at work and love natural fabrics and tasteful designers. You have style and class and always look attractive whatever you choose to wear.

love ★ Love is crucial to you and you are a lovely partner to have. You are giving, affectionate, and a brilliant homemaker. You will not tolerate infidelity and must never be with someone who does not commit to you.

Try a Cancer, whose ruling planet is also your birth date ruler, the Moon.

best present ★ Crystal glasses, moon pendant.

birthday share ★ 1883 Benito Mussolini, dictator; 1905 Dag Hammarskjöld, U.N. secretary general; 1946 Diane Keen, actress; 1966 Martina McBride, singer.

on this day ★ In 1958, the United States formally entered the space race as Congress established the National Aeronautics and Space Administration (NASA).

color purple ★ number 3, 12, 21 ★ stone azurite—to reduce stress and give you deeper insight ★ flora oriental poppy ★ animal llama ★ occupation computer expert, investor, beautician ★ key features fortunate, focused, energized ★ naturally good at making money through business

character ★ People are quick to lean on you and trust you, but you get bored with routine and can inadvertently let them down. You are something of a visionary when it comes to business and money; you know what works and are probably quite lucky at playing the stock market. You have a feel for success and always know which people will bring you good fortune.

life path ★ You tend to get rich quick but can lose money just as quickly if you're too greedy or rash. Take time to think what you are prepared to do and don't get tied down by too many unnecessary commitments. You will travel extensively, which always brings you luck.

love ★ You need a fellow explorer, not someone who is scared of change or too conventional. Why not try a Sagittarius, whose ruling planet is also your birth date ruler, Jupiter, planet of expansion?

best present ★ Romantic weekend in the mountains, Rollerblades.

birthday share ★ 1818 Emily Brontë, author; 1863 Henry Ford, engineer and founder of the Ford Motor Company; 1947 Arnold Schwarzenegger, actor; 1963 Lisa Kudrow, actress.

on this day ★ In 1935, the first Penguin paperback books went on sale, starting the paperback revolution. The idea came from Sir Allen Lane, who wanted to provide "a whole book for the price of 10 cigarettes." The first one to be issued was *Ariel* by Andre Maurois.

color purple ★ number 4, 13, 22 ★ stone tourmaline—to bring self-awareness and release the past ★ flora delphinium ★ animal jaguar ★ occupation inventor, internet designer, scientist ★ key features serious, curious, exceptional ★ naturally good at discovering new perspectives

july 31

character ★ You are always researching or digging around for further information. This need to have all the facts and to discover new frontiers makes it easy for you to invent something unique. You are a little eccentric, and quite self-absorbed for a Leo. Although usually attractive, you prefer to get attention for your ideas rather than your looks.

life path ★ You are a pioneer in whatever you focus on, and you need to be around others who are optimistic and forward thinking. It is difficult for the average Joe to understand you because you are a little too advanced. However, women are more likely to relate to you and encourage you.

love ★ You need an unusual but grounded partner who loves your vast mind and can take care of practicalities. You are never on time but are usually faithful. Look for an Aquarius, whose ruling planet is also your birth date ruler, Uranus.

best present ★ Telescope, atlas.

birthday share ★ 1911 George Liberace, musician; 1929 Lynne Reid Banks, writer; 1962 Wesley Snipes, actor; 1965 J. K. Rowling, author.

on this day ★ In 1498, the explorer Christopher Columbus, on his third voyage to the New World, landed on the Caribbean island of Trinidad.

color gold ★ number 1, 11, 22 ★ stone carnelian—used by the romans as a lucky amulet, it will protect you and fill you with passion ★ flora sunflower ★ animal gorilla ★ occupation retailer, fashion designer, model ★ key features unique, exceptional, individual ★ naturally good at knowing what the next trends will be and setting them

august 1

character ★ Individuality is important to you. You have exotic friends and are seen in all the right places. You like to stand out in the crowd with your style and flair. You are interested in fashion but add your own special twist. You do not look like anyone else, nor would you want to.

life path ★ Use that fabulous creative eye of yours in your career and do not be afraid to take risks. You were born with the ability to set trends, to be a leader not a follower, so don't hold back. You are unlikely to live where you were born and will find the place you call home after the age of 22.

love ★ You may end up in quite an unconventional relationship, but this suits you; you don't care what people think and have good self-esteem. Whatever floats your boat, go for it. Your ruling planet and birth date ruler are both the beaming Sun, so why not try another Leo?

best present ★ Retro sunglasses, disco mirror ball.

birthday share ★ 1819 Herman Melville, author; 1936 Yves Saint Laurent, designer; 1942 Jerry Garcia, musician; 1963 Coolio, singer.

on this day ★ In 1981, MTV made its first broadcast. The first video played was "Video Killed The Radio Star" by Buggles.

color white ★ number 2, 11, 22 ★ stone lunar quartz—to increase your intuition ★ flora white tulip ★ animal polar bear ★ occupation snake charmer, ballet dancer, pr consultant ★ key features telepathic, perceptive, instinctive ★ naturally good at glimpsing the future

august 2

character ★ You are sensitive to your environment and other people's moods. You may find that if you walk into a room and there is a bad atmosphere, you will take on this heavy feeling. Remember to protect yourself by visualizing a gold light around you. Meditating on a full Moon will also help.

life path ★ You have hypnotic eyes and people find it very difficult to lie to you, as your built-in lie detector helps you know instantly when they are not being honest. You always give money to the homeless and are a bit of a soft touch for a genuine sob story. You appear powerful and intense but are really a big old softie.

love ★ Because you get to the root of people and are also telepathic, it takes a brave and honest soul to live with you. You are likely to find stability in love after 30. Seek out a Cancer, whose ruling planet is also your birth date ruler, the Moon.

best present ★ Astrological chart, star named after you.

birthday share ★ 1891 Sir Arthur Bliss, composer; 1892 Jack Leonard Warner, co-founder of Warner Bros.; 1932 Peter O'Toole, actor; 1939 Wes Craven, director and scriptwriter.

on this day ★ In 1876, legendary gunfighter "Wild Bill" Hickok was killed by Jack McCall while playing poker in Deadwood, South Dakota.

color light green ★ **number** 9, 12, 21 ★ **stone** tiger's eye—for spiritual and emotional protection ★ **flora** sunflower ★ **animal** wolf ★ **occupation** hunter, truck driver, pr consultant ★ **key features** spirited, fearless, rash ★ **naturally good at** confronting issues most people ignore

character ★ You are not one to let sleeping dogs lie. If something is bothering you, you have to clear the air or you get consumed with the problem. Some would describe you as argumentative, and you are used to getting your own way. You have had some stunning good luck in your time and do not take failure lightly.

life path ★ It's great that you expect to succeed and you certainly like to win, but perhaps try to wield your charismatic power with a little more gentleness. Following a spiritual path or attending some form of relaxation class will be beneficial. You're a kitten, really, so remember to play.

love ★ You have had some absolutely gorgeous lovers and others have been quite envious of you. You often seem to stumble on the right person at the right time. You love to be adored and worshiped, and luckily you seem to inspire this! Why not try a

Sagittarius, whose ruling planet is Jupiter, which is also your birth date ruler?

best present ★ Tai-chi class, white-water rafting adventure.

birthday share ★ 1926 Tony Bennett, singer; 1940 Martin Sheen, actor; 1941 Martha Stewart, lifestyle guru; 1950 John Landis, film director.

on this day ★ In 1492, Christopher Columbus left Spain on a voyage that would lead him to the discovery of the Americas.

august 4

character ★ You would like to be a free spirit but you stick to the rules of life. You have a powerful aura and will never allow anyone to tell you what to do; it's your way or the highway. This uncompromising attitude can cause conflict in your life, particularly where work is concerned.

life path ★ You have quite a wacky mind underneath that conventional exterior. People are very drawn to you but feel they can never get right inside your mind. You also like your own company and need space alone sometimes. You can think laterally and have some amazing ideas that you should follow through. It may be a good idea to start your own business, as you will be determined to succeed at all costs.

love ★ You love ardently but almost from a distance. You hate to be tied down or controlled. You will commit yourself but on your terms. You need a free-spirited Aquarius, whose ruling planet is also your birth date ruler, Uranus.

best present ★ Trip to a science museum, ticket to a UFO convention.

birthday share ★ 1792 Percy Bysshe Shelley, poet; 1900 Queen Elizabeth, the Queen Mother; 1901 Louis Armstrong, musician and singer; 1955 Billy Bob Thornton, actor.

on this day ★ In 1914, Britain declared war on Germany and so became embroiled in World War I.

color sapphire blue ★ **number** 14, 23, 50 ★ **stone** turquoise—sacred to native americans, it brings truth and protection ★ **flora** delphinium ★ **animal** cheetah ★ **occupation** media worker, teacher, author ★ **key features** articulate, sophisticated, sexy ★ **naturally good at** causing a stir

character ★ You are noticed wherever you go because you have great presence. However, you don't realize this, and even though you are generally adored you still feel that you have never experienced total love. In your career you soar ahead and have the ability to persuade people.

life path ★ You should think about working on your self-esteem. You are beautiful inside and out but feel unlovable. This holds you back emotionally but can push you on to achieve incredible results in your career. However, this pattern will ultimately cause you a lot of unnecessary pain. You inspire love, so try turning this within.

love ★ You may be attracted to people who can't or won't commit to you, or who perhaps live in another city or country. Bear in mind that this is your choice and that you can change the situation if you want to. You are in control of your destiny. Why not try a Gemini, whose ruling planet, Mercury, is also your birth date ruler?

best present ★ New Age book on confidence, scented candles.

birthday share ★ 1906 John Huston, director, producer, and actor; 1930 Neil Armstrong, astronaut; 1946 Loni Anderson, actress; 1968 Terri Clark, country singer.

on this day ★ In 1962, legendary film actress and sex symbol Marilyn Monroe died from an apparent drug overdose in Los Angeles at the age of 36.

august 6

character ★ Amusing and engaging, you can capture an audience with your compelling banter. You love to make others smile and are always trying to cheer up your friends when they are down. You look on the bright side of everything and have a passionate and warm nature.

life path ★ You're a giver and a healer of the human spirit. This comes partly from your good nature and lightheartedness, although underneath you are a deep and worthy spirit who seeks to bring joy to others. You may have a talent for writing and be able to capture the answers to human sadness in written form.

love ★ You always seem to be helping others out with their love life and are rarely off the telephone giving advice. Your own love life is sometimes kept on the back burner, but a loving soul like you deserves the best partner. Search for a Libra, whose ruling planet is also your birth date ruler, Venus, planet of love.

best present ★ Romantic meal for two, relaxing massage.

birthday share ★ 1809 Alfred, Lord Tennyson, poet; 1911 Lucille Ball, actress; 1917 Robert Mitchum, actor; 1928 Andy Warhol, artist and director.

on this day ★ In 1945, the first atomic bomb of World War II was dropped on the Japanese city of Hiroshima by the U.S. B-29 bomber Enola Gay.

color sea blue ★ **number** 7, 25, 43 ★ **stone** chrysocolla—to ease stress and bring you back down to earth ★ **flora** bluebell ★ **animal** penguin ★ **occupation** detective, dancer, swimmer ★ **key features** dramatic, passionate, imaginative ★ **naturally good at** spinning a great tale

character ★ Your life can often get out of control because you have a vivid and sometimes dangerous imagination. Your impulsive nature leads you to one adventure after another. You get a sudden emotion that you feel is fate or destiny and you run wild with it. It may be better to stand still and wait 24 hours before you rush off on a madcap, rash journey.

life path ★ You do not like to stand still, and have a thirst for knowledge and experience. You cannot bear a normal 9-to-5 existence and would need to become lost in an inner world if you were subjected to such normality. You like to have separate friends and lovers who never meet, so that you can express different sides of your complex personality.

love ★ You find it difficult to express your vulnerability so it's hard for you to commit, and when you do, you always seem to have one eye out for the ultimate fantasy relationship. This will spoil your closeness to your current partner. Why not try a Pisces, whose ruling planet, Neptune, is also your birth date ruler?

best present ★ Surveillance equipment, digital camera.

birthday share ★ 1876 Mata Hari, dancer and spy; 1942 Garrison Keillor, radio host and author; 1960 David Duchovny, actor; 1975 Charlize Theron, actress.

on this day ★ In 1974, French stuntman Philippe Petit walked on a tightrope strung between the twin towers of New York's World Trade Center.

august 8

character ★ You have a sturdy feel about you, strong and solid. You take yourself and life very seriously and are dedicated in all that you do; you make an excellent employee or lover because of this. People know they can rely on you. Of course, you can have a laugh, but only after you have finished your work or commitments.

life path ★ You may find it difficult to admit mistakes or accept when you are in the wrong. This is only because you try so hard not to be wrong! However, we are all human and mistakes happen, so accept that you cannot be perfect. Others will always forgive you because of your loyalty and your honorable personality.

love ★ If you make a commitment you stick to it and will love your partner with all your passion and protect them with your life. You can be a little controlling, but hey,

we all have our faults. A Capricorn whose ruling planet is your birth date ruler, Saturn, would complement you.

best present ★ Compass, silver pen.

birthday share ★ 1922 Esther Williams, swimmer and actress; 1937 Dustin Hoffman, actor; 1944 Peter Weir, film director; 1949 Keith Carradine, actor.

on this day ★ In 1974, President Richard Nixon announced his resignation over his involvement in the Watergate cover-up.

color red ★ **number** 36, 45, 72 ★ **stone** ruby—said to be regal and passionate, just like you ★ **flora** lupine ★ **animal** leopard ★ **occupation** singer, marine, athlete ★ **key features** energetic, egoistic, insecure ★ **naturally good at** all kinds of physical activities

august 9

character ★ You have a huge appetite for life that sometimes gets you into hot water. You are wild and spontaneous, will go to extremes, and sometimes don't know when to stop. You love having a good time and can party harder than anyone. You are also very entertaining, relish being the center of attention, and find that people are instinctively infatuated with you.

life path ★ Your life is something of a carousel. You hardly ever have a mundane existence; it is always on a high or a low. Balance is an important lesson for you to learn. If you can harness that passion and tame it a little, life for you will be sweet.

love ★ You love the thrill of the hunt and the high drama at the beginning of relationships; you may pretend this is not the case, but you seek out tempestuous partnerships with much breaking of plates and passionate making up. Your birth date ruler is Mars so why not search for an Aries, whose ruling planet is also Mars?

best present ★ Trip to a carnival, horseback-riding boots.

birthday share ★ 1918 Robert Aldrich, director; 1957 Melanie Griffith, actress; 1963 Whitney Houston, singer and actress; 1968 Gillian Anderson, actress.

on this day ★ In 1974, Gerald Ford became the 38th president of the United States after Richard Nixon formally resigned from the presidency.

august 10

character ★ Sweet-natured, you have a warm and generous spirit and a giving nature, and always have a glow about you. You are affable and loving and like to help others. You may be very attractive but you don't let this go to your head. You also have a creative streak and with enough confidence could succeed in a field that required it.

life path ★ Your life may have been marked with strange twists of fate for good or bad. This has disturbed you a little, making you feel that life is like a wild, untamed beast that could bite you at any moment. Luck can be variable, but the more you trust and believe that you are the magician and not the apprentice, the more you can turn things around and feel safe.

love ★ The old adage that it is better to have loved and lost than never to have loved at all could be your motto. When you love, you love totally and rarely forget those who have touched your heart. Why not try another Leo, as their ruling planet, the vibrant Sun, is both your ruling planet and your birth date ruler?

best present ★ Tickets to a music festival, singing lessons.

birthday share ★ 1874 Herbert Hoover, 31st U.S. president; 1928 Eddie Fisher, singer; 1959 Rosanna Arquette, actress; 1960 Antonio Banderas, actor.

on this day ★ In 1966, *Orbiter 1* was launched from Cape Kennedy and became the first spacecraft to transmit lunar photographs of possible landing sites.

color silvery white ★ number 2, 11, 22 ★ stone lunar quartz—to protect and inspire you ★ flora peruvian lily ★ animal whale ★ occupation personal aide, therapist, astrologer ★ key features giving, talented, sensitive ★ naturally good at using your intuition

august 11

character ★ You come across as supremely confident and organized, but you are more sensitive than you seem. You were born on the day of a master number, and this gives you a deeper destiny than most. It is essential that you discover what you desire for your life, because when you do, it will happen quite easily.

life path ★ People born on the 11th of any month have special gifts of magic. You can create your reality far more easily than most people, so pay attention to what you believe. Whatever you think and feel will probably happen, so make your thoughts fantastic and inspiring.

love ★ If you want love, it will come to you. You are more shy than you let on, but once you are secure in a relationship it is smooth sailing. You have a lot to give another person. You love to nurture and spoil your partner and are very affectionate.

You may like to try a Cancer, whose ruling planet is the Moon, your birth date ruler.

best present ★ Meditation tape, trip to a natural history museum.

birthday share ★ 1949 Eric Carmen, musician and singer; 1950 Steve Wozniak, founder of Apple Computers; 1953 Hulk Hogan, wrestler and actor; 1954 Joe Jackson, singer.

on this day ★ In 1877, U.S. astronomer Asaph Hall discovered the two satellites of Mars (Phobos and Deimos) at the Naval Observatory in Washington, D.C.

august 12

character ★ You generally have a happy-go-lucky air about you and feel comfortable in your own skin. You like who you are and have made the best of your life. You're likable and generous and always have a wide circle of friends. You have plenty of admirers but tend to look before you leap into relationships.

life path ★ You have the capacity to live for the moment and are well balanced. You can flirt like a gold medalist, but it is all harmless fun. Jupiter, planet of good fortune, is your birth date ruler, and occasionally you experience bouts of supreme good fortune.

love ★ Loyal and big-hearted in a relationship, you enjoy being in love. You tend to share your money and shower your lover with presents. You build solid foundations and enjoy the whole experience. Why not find a Sagittarius, whose ruling planet is Jupiter?

best present ★ Twister game, decanter.

birthday share ★ 1881 Cecil B. DeMille, director; 1939 George Hamilton, actor; 1949 Mark Knopfler, guitarist and singer; 1971 Pete Sampras, tennis player.

on this day ★ In 1908, the first Model T cars (colloquially known as the Tin Lizzie and the Flivver) rolled out of the Ford Motor Company factory in Detroit, Michigan.

color purple ★ **number** 13, 22, 31 ★ **stone** amethyst—a favorite of the romans for sobriety and wisdom ★ **flora** magnolia ★ **animal** lynx ★ **occupation** producer, stage manager, inventor ★ **key features** imaginative, eccentric, strong ★ **naturally good at** harnessing your creativity

august 13

character ★ You have a delightfully quirky nature that fascinates people. You can make chairs out of bottle tops or invent a remote control to open your curtains. You are a sophisticated mad professor. You don't look eccentric—in fact, you can be quite tailored and well groomed—but you give off a vibe of unpredictable excellence.

life path ★ Follow some of your crazy inventive thoughts and you may make your fortune. You are a mini Isaac Newton and have a profound insight into things that other people take for granted. There's genius in them there bones, so live it!

love ★ When it comes to lovers you have wildly varying tastes and want someone as unusual as you. It may be wiser to find someone more practical and stable—but what the heck! You would get on well with a wacky Aquarius, whose ruling planet, Uranus, is also your birth date ruler.

best present ★ Chemistry set, book about famous inventors.

birthday share ★ 1422 William Caxton, printer; 1860 Annie Oakley, sharpshooter; 1899 Alfred Hitchcock, director; 1926 Fidel Castro, Cuban leader.

on this day ★ In 1972, the last U.S. troops left Vietnam.

august 14

character ★ You have something to say and will let nothing stop you. You believe in the power of peaceful resistance and would love to live in a society where all people are equal. You retain facts and information and use them as a weapon. Nothing gets by you; you love language and can be quite pedantic if people use the wrong words. You need to remember that communication is not just about words or language, but also about connection.

life path ★ Your addiction to knowledge could come from a feeling of inadequacy when, ironically, you are brighter than most. You may go into politics or journalism to have an effect on this far-from-perfect world, but if you ignore this higher calling you could end up being rather superficial.

love ★ You generally have good relationships but can often get caught up in overanalyzing your partner or your relationship. Let yourself go a little and allow that Leo passion to come out. A Gemini would suit you, as their ruling planet, Mercury, is also your birth date ruler.

best present ★ Radio, bottle of tequila.

birthday share ★ 1945 Steve Martin, actor; 1947 Danielle Steel, author; 1950 Gary Larson, cartoonist and creator of *The Far Side*; 1966 Halle Berry, actress.

on this day ★ In 1900, the Boxer Rebellion in China was ended by an international force.

august 15

character ★ You're a wild one; you go to extremes and have a huge personality. You need to be loved and adored and can be obsessive and excessive in relationships. You will pursue a love interest to the end of the earth, but, ironically, if you catch them you may lose interest.

life path ★ All the world's a stage, and you're darn sure you're going to get a leading role. You adore dressing up, love to party, and exude enthusiasm. Your friends admire your zeal and sheer stamina. You refuse to lead a sensible existence and are a legend in your own lifetime.

love ★ Love is a drug to you and you just can't get enough. You hunt, you chase, you pounce, and if you're interested it is virtually impossible for your prey to get away. You may like to try a Libra, who has your birth date ruler, Venus, as their ruling planet.

best present ★ Tiara, stage makeup.

birthday share ★ 1769 Napoleon Bonaparte, emperor of France; 1771 Sir Walter Scott, author; 1950 Princess Anne (Mountbatten), British royalty; 1972 Ben Affleck, actor.

on this day ★ In 1969, the Woodstock Festival opened to 400,000 festival goers in Bethel, New York.

august 16

character ★ You have charm and you know how to use it. You sense what others think of you and can be a little manipulative to get them to adore you. You have an awesome presence that makes people nervous when they meet you. You cannot bear being disrespected or—even worse—ignored.

life path ★ You are unique. Whatever your profession, you stand out from the crowd and people always talk about you—you wouldn't have it any other way. You like to make an impact and you sure do. Try not to be so invincible and omnipotent that you alienate yourself from real affection.

love ★ You can get involved with some lovers for the wrong reasons. Perhaps they are powerful or can help you in some way. Friends have a habit of falling in love with you, but even though you may string them along you prefer to chase than be chased. Perhaps choose a Pisces, whose ruling planet, Neptune, is also your birth date ruler.

best present ★ Tickets to the theater, karaoke machine.

birthday share ★ 1923 Shimon Peres, Nobel Peace Prize winner; 1954 James Cameron, director; 1958 Madonna, singer and actress; 1960 Timothy Hutton, actor.

on this day ★ In 1977, rock 'n' roll legend Elvis Presley died of heart failure at the age of 42, in his home in Memphis, Tennessee.

color hunter green ★ **number** 8, 44, 80 ★ **stone** hematite—to protect your self-image ★
flora fern ★ **animal** pitbull terrier ★ **occupation** agent, movie executive, stockbroker ★
key features affluent, canny, controlling ★ **naturally good at** making money

august 17

character ★ You are very focused on your career and will no doubt make loads of money. Power and influence surround you and you were born to lead. You want it all and will work 24/7 to get it. You are steadfast and forceful and probably have an interest in celebrity.

life path ★ Be careful that you don't burn yourself out with your relentless quest for success. You need harmony and relaxation in your life as much as anything else but you often forget this. Learn how to chill out and, paradoxically, your goals will be achieved faster. Make sure you open up to at least one other person or you will feel lonely in the crowd.

love ★ Love takes a backseat for you, but when you find it you demand total loyalty and commitment. You are rather a good judge of lovers and will tend to have long-term relationships after the age of 28. Why not try a Capricorn, whose ruling planet Saturn is your birth date ruler?

best present ★ Jewelry box, engraved key ring.

birthday share ★ 1786 Davy Crockett, frontiersman; 1893 Mae West, actress; 1943 Robert De Niro, actor; 1960 Sean Penn, actor.

on this day ★ In 1978, Double Eagle II became the first hot-air balloon to cross the Atlantic Ocean when it landed in Miserey near Paris, 137 hours after leaving Preque Isle, Maine.

color bright red ★ **number** 9, 36, 54 ★ **stone** amber—to soak up negativity ★
flora red-hot poker ★ **animal** bear ★ **occupation** mountaineer, dancer, driving instructor
★ **key features** tenacious, powerful, alluring ★ **naturally good at** battling to win

august 18

character ★ You often choose a difficult path because you have the heart of an adventurer and love the adrenaline rush of a good battle. You will fight to the end to get what you want and, although you may not want to admit this, if you look at the choices you have made in life, you rarely choose the safe option.

life path ★ You are a little bit special, like a good pirate in a classic movie—slightly impudent, slightly wicked, but irresistible and convincing. You want to live life to the fullest and get depressed if the real world and its realities catch up with you. You will set about creating chaos if things are going too smoothly, and you have a habit of being very mischievous.

love ★ You love passionately in the moment but can be swept away by the next challenge or eye-candy in a second. You don't mean to be unfaithful, but it would take someone quite incredible to pin you down. Look for an Aries whose ruling planet, Mars, is also your birth date ruler.

best present ★ Expensive underwear, heart-shaped lollipop.

birthday share ★ 1922 Shelley Winters, actress; 1933 Roman Polanski, director; 1937 Robert Redford, actor; 1952 Patrick Swayze, actor.

on this day ★ In 1587, Virginia Dare became the first child of English parents to be born in the United States. She, along with the rest of the early settlement at Roanoke, later disappeared without a trace.

color orange ★ **number** 1, 11, 22 ★ **stone** carnelian—a roman amulet said to draw energy to you ★ **flora** poppy ★ **animal** coyote ★ **occupation** horseback rider, designer, model ★ **key features** optimistic, alluring, classy ★ **naturally good at** moving to positions of power

august 19

character ★ You are a flame to many moths; once met, never forgotten. People will often go against their better judgment to give you what you want. Fortunately, you don't let your magnetic charm go to your head, which is why it is so effective.

life path ★ Sometimes you can let your lazy side stop you from reaching your full potential. You love to bask in success but really need to move forward. You have a cheerful and warm persona that is very attractive to other people. You love romance and can get yourself into compromising situations, as you lose your judgment when presented with an amorous possibility.

love ★ You may have lovers who have influence or are involved in the media. You mix with the movers and shakers and are cautious of commitment. Your ruling planet and birth date ruler is the Sun, so another Leo would be a perfect match.

best present ★ Red Ferrari (toy or real), diamond earrings/cufflinks.

birthday share ★ 1871 Orville Wright, aviator; 1883 Coco Chanel, designer; 1965 Kyra Sedgwick, actress; 1969 Matthew Perry, actor.

on this day ★ In 1960, the Soviet satellite Sputnik V was launched into the Earth's orbit carrying two dogs named Belka and Strelka.

august 20

character ★ You have a kind and magnanimous nature. You will always try to be polite and kind to those you meet. You are regal and alluring but not arrogant. Others may see you as cocky but that is their own insecurity; you represent power, which others may find alarming, but you use your power only for good.

life path ★ Your genuine love of people shines through and helps you carve out a successful career path. People are more than happy for you to be the boss or the team leader because you have the air of a benevolent ruler. You make friends with people less fortunate than yourself and seem to bring them luck.

love ★ All right, you're not a saint, but you do your darnedest to be the best person you can be. You have strong empathy and would not intentionally hurt a loved one. You're also a considerate and giving lover. Why not try a Cancer, whose ruling planet, the Moon, is also your birth date ruler?

best present ★ Diary, simple gold ring.

birthday share ★ 1906 Henry (Bunny) Austin, tennis player; 1942 Isaac Hayes, actor; 1946 Connie Chung, broadcast journalist; 1949 Phil Lynott, singer and guitarist.

on this day ★ In 1980, Italian mountaineer Reinhold Messner made the first successful solo ascent of Mount Everest.

color green ★ **number** 3, 12, 21 ★ **stone** jade—sacred to the chinese for good fortune ★
flora bluebell ★ **animal** kangaroo ★ **occupation** basketball player, financier, sky-diver ★
key features daring, lucky, maverick ★ **naturally good at** taking risks

character ★ You have a talent for taking a gamble on life. More than half the time it pays off, but you have also had your fingers burned on wild schemes. Nothing seems to deter you. You have a feeling in your soul that one day you will make it big—and you may just be right.

life path ★ You have a certain amount of spiritual protection around you. You may have found in the past that uncanny coincidences saved you from disaster. Don't take this divine intervention for granted, though, and try to think a little before you leap into your next unmanageable situation. You do have the Midas touch and will no doubt hit the jackpot one day.

love ★ Love comes and goes but you always have a ball with your lovers. You are generous and you also inspire generosity. Your best bet is a Sagittarius, whose ruling planet, Jupiter, is also your birth date ruler.

best present ★ Trip to the desert, giant hop ball.

birthday share ★ 1904 Count Basie, bandleader; 1936 Wilt Chamberlain, basketball player; 1938 Kenny Rogers, singer and actor; 1956 Kim Cattrall, actress.

on this day ★ In 1959, Hawaii became the 50th state admitted into the United States.

color lavender ★ number 4, 13, 22 ★ stone obsidian—to help you face your fears ★
flora jasmine ★ animal rhinoceros ★ occupation critic, columnist, pool player ★
key features forward, cutting, jovial ★ naturally good at witty one-liners

august 22

character ★ You have a sharp tongue but put down only people who are arrogant. You use humor as a weapon and wield your wit wildly. You prize yourself on your intellectual abilities and always have your head in a book. Alternatively, you get obsessed with television and can recite lines from famous movies as a party trick.

life path ★ You are amusing and have an enormous personality. You try hard to fulfill your commitments but actually prefer to be out having a good time socializing or partying with friends. Unless you work in a creative field you find work tedious, but you persevere with it.

love ★ You dip in and out of relationships but will only really settle with someone who allows you a certain amount of freedom. You may like to pair up with an Aquarius, whose ruling planet, Uranus, is also your birth date ruler.

best present ★ Antique print, orchid tree.

birthday share ★ 1893 Dorothy Parker, author; 1917 John Lee Hooker, blues singer; 1920 Ray Bradbury, author; 1963 Tori Amos, singer and songwriter.

on this day ★ In 1911, Leonardo da Vinci's *Mona Lisa* was stolen from the Louvre museum in Paris by an Italian waiter, Vincenzo Perruggia.

color blue ★ **number** 23, 14, 50 ★ **stone** lapis lazuli—to bring you wisdom and clarity ★ **flora** blue salvia ★ **animal** sloth ★ **occupation** drummer, computer expert, editor ★ **key features** conventional, adept, strong ★ **naturally good at** achieving results

august 23

character ★ You're hardworking but still fun to be around. You make your working environment a better place because you're affable and good natured. It is important for you to give 110 percent to your job and you're very ambitious. You may have a flair for music, which you love and should be serious about. You have the heart of a musician.

life path ★ You want a life that is well balanced and complete. Family is important to you and so are your friends. You manage to balance work, friendships, love, and family and deserve a pat on the back for this, as most mortals never achieve it.

love ★ You have great communication skills in relationships and inspire loyalty, but you can be a little argumentative. You respect and value your partner, but over time you can be less charming to them than to anyone else. Why not try a Gemini, whose ruling planet, Mercury, is your birth date ruler?

best present ★ Aromatherapy body lotion, CD of relaxing music.

birthday share ★ 1912 Gene Kelly, dancer, singer, producer, and director; 1949 Shelley Long, actress; 1951 Queen Noor of Jordan; 1970 River Phoenix, actor.

on this day ★ In 1979, the Soviet Bolshoi Ballet dancer Alexander Godunov defected to the United States while performing in New York City.

leo

your ruling planet **The sun** represents the ego and the surface personality. It emanates warmth just like you, searing passion, and a golden, bright glow. The Sun can light your way or burn you to a cinder. It gives you personal power and magnetism and makes others view you as individual and unique. The whole emphasis of the Sun is the personality. Your life lessons revolve around how you perceive yourself and how others perceive you. Ultimately it is about the surrender of the personality and the understanding that although we are all different we are a part of the whole. None of us is more spectacular or better than anyone else, but this is a challenging lesson for you to learn because you believe in greatness. Combining love with that huge personality and giving yourself to your fellow travelers will free you from the confines of your superficial side, which occasionally threatens to take over.

your natural habitat In your head your natural habitat is probably a palace or a castle, as you love luxury and opulence. You need an environment in which to shine. You have very expensive tastes, and your home is probably decked out in expensive and glamorous furniture. You may go for the latest decor, and you have an almost magical sixth sense of what is in and what is out of fashion. No gimmicky knick-knacks for you or deeply unfashionable color schemes—you are style personified. Your house is designed to impress and is an extension of your personality. You may have an abundance of mirrors in each room, especially the bedroom. You can be attracted to classical prints and statues, and your home may have the feel of an ancient Greek temple. It is essential to you that it is original and enables others to see how together you are. You loathe disorder and ideally would have someone to dust every corner on a daily basis!

are you a typical leo?

You are magnificent! When you walk into a room all heads turn in your direction because they sense your leonine majesty. You have charisma and you usually have fantastic hair. You hold your head high when you walk, or should I say sashay? Your energy is proud and regal, and you like to be adored and worshiped. Others may see you as arrogant, but you don't generally care what other people think of you and would never show it if you did. You may saunter around appearing rather self-important, but you do make an effort to be humble and cannot abide arrogance in anyone else.

Why you're wonderful! You have such magnetism that people love to be given your attention. You're a born entertainer and hold court very well. You dress immaculately and always look fantastic, even first thing in the morning. You light up your surroundings and seize life with both hands. You're an excellent and caring lover, who will always make sure that your partner is taken care of.

Why you're impossible! Egotistical and a little conceited, you can be obsessed with yourself and unkind to anyone you don't respect. You like to be king of the jungle, and woe to anyone who tries to step on your toes. You can come across as big-headed and selfish and need to keep this shadow side of yourself in check. It is essential that you respect your lovers—if you don't, you must move on before you totally destroy their confidence. This impossible side does not need to rear its ugly head, though. If you are an evolved Leo you will have reflected on what true power is and be able to handle your life with compassion, humility, and love.

Your secret side You're a big kitten, really—you can give away your power in relationships, although you hate to lose face. If someone gives you a run for your money in the love stakes you can go to pieces and become quite subservient. You may despise this part of your personality but the weakness is there. You thrive on love but wither with coldness or neglect. Because you are so powerful you hate the idea of someone not loving you, and your pride will not let you walk away when you have given your heart to someone.

leo love compatibility chart

aries	taurus	gemini	cancer	leo	virgo
🍾		🍾	🍾	🍾	🍾
💘	💘	💘	💘	💘	💘
🔗	🔗		🔗	🔗	🔗
🎈	🎈	🎈	🎈	🎈	🎈
💋	💋	💋	💋	💋	💋
🪑	🪑	🪑	🪑	🪑	🪑
💡		💡	💡	💡	💡
👥	👥		👥	👥	👥

KEY ▷   fun   romance   loyalty   adventure

	libra	scorpio	sagittarius	capricorn	aquarius	pisces
champagne	✓		✓	✓	✓	✓
heart	✓	✓	✓	✓	✓	✓
rings		✓		✓	✓	✓
balloon	✓		✓	✓	✓	✓
passion	✓	✓	✓	✓	✓	✓
chilling out	✓		✓		✓	
spontaneity	✓		✓		✓	✓
attentiveness	✓		✓		✓	

 passion chilling out spontaneity attentiveness

virgo

august 24–september 22

august 24

character ★ Deeply compassionate, you want the best for everyone around you. You have an intense desire to help and to please. Always fascinated to know what your partner or friends are thinking, you can't be quite as open with your own emotions as you would like. You are constantly thinking of ways to make other people's lives easier.

life path ★ You tend to take on other people's responsibilities and problems. This is great if you can find a balance and maintain good boundaries; if not you will be swept into a sea of confusion. You are uncertain whether you're a sinner or a saint, but the truth is that you're a wonderful person who is imperfect like the rest of us, so try to accept both sides of yourself.

love ★ You were born to love as your birth date ruler is Venus, planet and goddess of love. You seek the perfect soul mate who will fulfill all of your fantasies and practical needs. Why not search for a Taurus, whose ruling planet is also Venus?

best present ★ Poetry book, romantic meal for two.

birthday share ★ 1894 Jean Rhys, author; 1899 Jorge Luis Borges, author; 1948 Jean Michel Jarre, musician; 1958 Steve Guttenberg, actor.

on this day ★ In A.D. 79, Mount Vesuvius erupted and buried the towns of Pompeii and Herculaneum in molten lava and ash.

color jade green, blue ★ **number** 7, 14, 34 ★ **stone** blue topaz—the truth stone that leads you to your inner truth ★ **flora** lobelia ★ **animal** goldfish ★ **occupation** actor, photographer, model ★ **key features** stunning, charming, good natured ★ **naturally good at** seducing with just one glance

august 25

character ★ You have natural allure and an inner spark that draws people to you. Sometimes you are at a loss to know why you get yourself involved in complicated emotional situations; it is because you are ruled by the birth number 7, which means your life is guided more than most and has karmic undertones that make relationships a deeper growth experience.

life path ★ Strange coincidences and meaningful events occur regularly. You are here to learn and grow spiritually and no matter how hard you try to be superficial it just isn't in you! You are on an advanced knowledge course in the high school of life so just accept it and see the magic grow.

love ★ You are a babe or guy magnet and have huge physical charisma. The only problem is that you will always be susceptible to temptation no matter how settled you are.

You seek the perfect lover who can fulfill all your needs—an impossibility. Your birth date is ruled by Neptune, planet of dreams and illusions, so try a romantic Pisces whose ruling planet is Neptune.

best present ★ Silk shirt, meditation tape.

birthday share ★ 1918 Leonard Bernstein, composer and conductor; 1930 Sean Connery, actor; 1954 Elvis Costello, singer; 1970 Claudia Schiffer, model.

on this day ★ In 1978, the Turin shroud, once venerated as the burial cloth of Christ, went on public display for the first time in 45 years at the Cathedral of St. John the Baptist, Turin.

color hunter green, caramel ★ **number** 8, 17, 26 ★ **stone** obsidian or apache tears—will help you face your fears ★ **flora** jasmine ★ **animal** goldfish ★ **occupation** bank manager, accountant, police officer ★ **key features** controlling, disciplined, powerful ★ **naturally good at** maintaining control in all areas

august 26

character ★ Strong and rather domineering, you love the security of rules and regulations and are extremely loyal. You may stick to a set routine as well and dislike disorder intensely. You have an impeccably clean home and probably even iron your socks.

life path ★ Structure is important to you and you have a clear view of where you want to go in life. Your friendships tend to last forever but other people can find you far too uncompromising. You need to learn that you are not always right! Flexibility will make your life much smoother.

love ★ Chill out—you are loved for yourself, not what you do for others. You take your time with love, so when you do settle down, it is normally for life. Your birth date ruler is Saturn, so try a Capricorn, whose ruling planet is Saturn and who will understand your serious side.

best present ★ Wallet/purse, stock options.

birthday share ★ 1819 Prince Albert, consort to Queen Victoria; 1898 Peggy Guggenheim, art collector and patron; 1960 Branford Marsalis, musician; 1980 Macaulay Culkin, actor.

on this day ★ In 1920, the 19th Amendment to the U.S. Constitution was ratified, giving women the right to vote.

color scarlet, orange ★ **number** 9, 18, 27 ★ **stone** ruby—your lucky amulet, said to stoke passion ★ **flora** rock rose ★ **animal** stray cat ★ **occupation** politician, soldier, spiritual leader ★ **key features** self-sacrificing, generous, giving ★ **naturally good at** helping others

august 27

character ★ You have much to give and may do lots of charity work. You have a tendency to be easily disillusioned and may see the world as an unhappy place. Developing optimism and positive thinking will enable you to give and receive and turn your journey in life into an adventure.

life path ★ You have a huge humanitarian spirit and feel that you would like to heal the world, but you need to balance this with healing yourself and looking after your own needs. You deserve to be pampered and enjoy a little overindulgence occasionally. You are a special spirit with much to give. Let the universe give back to you as well.

love ★ Sometimes you feel like a loner, but this is only because you are looking too deeply within. When you pop out of your shell, you will find there are many people who will not only love you but have much to give you. Your passion is strong, so try an

Aries, whose ruling planet is also your birth date ruler, Mars, to show you some fireworks.

best present ★ Outdoor pursuits vacation, binoculars.

birthday share ★ 1770 Georg Wilhelm Friedrich Hegel, philosopher; 1890 Man Ray, photographer; 1910 Mother Teresa, Nobel Peace Prize winner; 1959 Jeanette Winterson, author.

on this day ★ In 1859, the world's first oil well was drilled in Titusville, Pennsylvania by Edwin L. Drake on property owned by the Pennsylvania Rock Oil Company.

color yellow, amber ★ **number** 1, 11, 22 ★ **stone** citrine—said to radiate confidence and dispel fear ★ **flora** daffodil ★ **animal** labrador retriever ★ **occupation** filmmaker, artist, writer ★ **key features** independent, original, willful ★ **naturally good at** being innovative

august 28

character ★ You are strongly individual and manage to create a happy marriage between your imagination and your practical side. You should be great at making projects successful. People are drawn to your witty and original mind, although you are actually quite conservative at heart. You love to listen to other people's ideas but always manage to steal the show by going one step further with your own thoughts.

life path ★ It is not only important that you create and communicate on a personal level, but you also need to allow your mind to enter the public domain in some way. You may end up making art or writing, but the gems you come up with in your mind deserve to be passed on somehow. Don't hide your light under a bushel!

love ★ You have an independent streak but tend to draw lovers to you with your magnetic personality. People love to hear you talk, and sometimes you may not realize they would like to do more than chat! Your birth date ruler is the Sun and you radiate warmth, so try a Leo for mutual adoration.

best present ★ Camera, tickets for a classic movie.

birthday share ★ 1943 David Soul, singer and actor; 1965 Shania Twain, singer; 1969 Jason Priestley, actor; 1982 LeAnn Rimes, singer.

on this day ★ In 1963, Dr. Martin Luther King Jr. gave his famous "I Have a Dream" speech to civil rights demonstrators at the Lincoln Memorial in Washington, D.C.

color pale blue, silver, white ★ **number** 2, 11, 22 ★ **stone** clear quartz—the magic wand of crystals that magnifies your thoughts ★ **flora** delphinium ★ **animal** pot-bellied pig ★ **occupation** nurse, teacher, singer ★ **key features** caring, sensitive, selfless ★ **naturally good at** helping others and transforming them with your kindness

august 29

character ★ You have a great capacity for empathy and are extremely sensitive, although you try to conceal it. You feel things deeply and think about your emotions a lot. Your family is your main commitment and you tend to put them first, but remember that if you block your own desires completely, you may feel an urge to rebel at a later date.

life path ★ You have a maternal nature and are very good at caring for others, especially children. People always feel better when they have been with you, and you should try to find a job that makes the most of these valuable qualities.

love ★ Love for you is very wrapped up in stability and the need for a secure family. Because this means so much to you, you may take your time when searching for a partner, as you tend to mate for life. Your birth date ruler is the Moon, so perhaps a Cancer, whose ruling planet is also the Moon, will give you the security you desire.

best present ★ Ring, moonlit boat trip.

birthday share ★ 1915 Ingrid Bergman, actress; 1920 Charlie Parker, jazz musician; 1923 Sir Richard Attenborough, actor and director; 1958 Michael Jackson, singer.

on this day ★ In 1949, the Soviet Union tested its first atomic bomb. The news of the test only emerged on September 22 when the United States, Britain, and Canada announced they had detected it.

color fire red ★ **number** 3, 9, 33 ★ **stone** turquoise—a native american protection stone ★ **flora** purple sage ★ **animal** lizard ★ **occupation** pr consultant, actor's agent, stockbroker ★ **key features** honest, trustworthy, firm ★ **naturally good at** making money for other people

august 30

character ★ You have a talent for helping other people achieve great heights, delighting in taking control of sticky situations and turning them around. You are a skilled troubleshooter and very lucky when dealing with people. It would benefit you, though, to devote some time to focusing on achieving your own dreams as well.

life path ★ Your life may seem to be nothing but hard work—too much to do, too little time—but it is up to you to step off the treadmill and balance work with nurturing your spirit. You have genius when it comes to your career, but you should put some more effort into your social life.

love ★ If you find time for love, you will find the right partner. You will have luck in this area if you pay more attention to it. A wacky Sagittarius—whose ruling planet is Jupiter, planet of good fortune and also your birth date ruler—will spur on your passion.

best present ★ Leather gloves, fine wine.

birthday share ★ 1797 Mary Wollstonecraft Shelley, author and creator of Frankenstein; 1896 Raymond Massey, actor; 1951 Dana, singer; 1972 Cameron Diaz, actress.

on this day ★ In 1963, a hot line to reduce the risk of accidental war was set up between the Kremlin and the White House.

color silver ★ **number** 4, 13, 22 ★ **stone** silver—although this is a metal it is said to give you protection and boost your energy ★ **flora** pansy ★ **animal** greyhound ★ **occupation** runner, scientist, computer analyst ★ **key features** analytical, quick-witted, detached ★ **naturally good at** finding solutions to technology problems

character ★ You have an analytical mind that chooses to focus on practical things. You should be very good with computers and all things technical, as you have a forward-thinking mind. You may invent something because your mind is always seeking solutions to make the practical aspects of life easier.

life path ★ Your mind is as sharp as a knife but it can easily grow bored. Male or female, you see things in a logical form and rarely let your emotions sway you. When you feel something, you look at the situation logically, and this can isolate those close to you, who would like you to express more feeling.

love ★ You're very giving of your time in a relationship but can appear somewhat aloof or detached. You need a partner who can accept this part of you and enable you to open up gently to your emotions. Try an

Aquarius, whose ruling planet is also your birth date ruler, wacky Uranus.

best present ★ Lego set, trip to a science museum.

birthday share ★ 1928 James Coburn, actor; 1945 Van Morrison, singer; 1949 Richard Gere, actor; 1955 Edwin Moses, athlete.

on this day ★ In 1997, Princess Diana and Dodi al-Fayed were killed in a car crash in Paris.

color orange ★ **number** 2, 5, 12 ★ **stone** sandstone—said to bring optimism ★
flora sunflower ★ **animal** flamingo ★ **occupation** hotelier, soldier, flight attendant ★
key features persistent, meticulous, strong ★ **naturally good at** organizing other people

september 1

character ★ Some people may find you a little uncompromising and stern, but underneath this hard exterior you have a very loving heart. However, you must avoid being judgmental, as you set yourself such high standards and can be disappointed if others don't share the same principles. You are great at taking responsibility and would do anything for those you love, but do take care to avoid being a martyr (a role you can all too easily slip into).

life path ★ You adore looking after people but need lots of space to indulge your individuality. It is hard for you to relax, which can become grating for those who love you, because they want to see you enjoying the quiet times rather than rushing around in an effort to get things done. When you are on your own is when you can stare into space and dream, but it would be even better if you could share these grand plans with your partner.

love ★ You are extremely passionate but you tend not to make your love life a priority; if you are not careful you could fill up your life with work and commitments, leaving no time for you to find a partner. A loyal Taurus would be ideal, but make sure you spend plenty of time with them on a one-to-one basis—then all that ardor within will blossom.

best present ★ Anything for the home, massage oil.

birthday share ★ 1875 Edgar Rice Burroughs, author; 1923 Rocky Marciano, boxer; 1946 Barry Gibb, singer; 1957 Gloria Estefan, singer.

on this day ★ In 1939, Germany invaded Poland, heralding the start of World War II.

color silvery blue ★ **number** 4, 22, 26 ★ **stone** moonstone—regulates your mood ★ **flora** daisy ★ **animal** border collie ★ **occupation** office worker, banker, antiques dealer ★ **key features** shy, earthy, dependable ★ **naturally good at** communication and practicalities

september 2

character ★ Intuitive but grounded, you hate to be misunderstood and tend to speak very plainly. You are efficient and clever and take your role in life seriously. Lucky in relationships, you can be very demanding and may see your partner as an extension of yourself. You should excel at sports but can be lazy when it comes to looking after your body; in contrast, you dress immaculately.

life path ★ You must learn to push yourself. You hate being stuck in a rut, but because you feel secure with what you already know, you sometimes try to avoid change. Allow yourself to dream big and then go for it; you have the wisdom to succeed if you can find the nerve.

love ★ You merge with your partner and expect them to be telepathic when dealing with you. You like to exercise a subtle control in your relationships and tend to feel that if anything needs doing you had better

do it yourself; this can disempower partners. If they slip up or do anything unexpected, you can get very annoyed and then sulk. Lighten up a little and have fun with your lover. Your birth date is ruled by the Moon, so Cancers, whose ruling planet is also the Moon, have an affinity with you.

best present ★ Stationery, watch.

birthday share ★ 1952 Jimmy Connors, tennis player; 1964 Keanu Reeves, actor; 1965 Lennox Lewis, heavyweight boxer; 1966 Salma Hayek, actress.

on this day ★ In 1789, U.S. Congress established the Department of the Treasury.

color jade green, silver ★ **number** 3, 6, 9 ★ **stone** hematite—gives you self-confidence ★
flora clover ★ **animal** parrot ★ **occupation** journalist, lawyer, lecturer ★ **key features**
individual, creative, vocal ★ **naturally good at** diplomacy and even-handedness

september 3

character ★ You are all things to all people and usually fight your natural Virgo tendency to be judgmental. You have a higher vision and want all people to be equal. Others are often surprised when you stand up boldly in defense of an underdog because you seem so mild-mannered on the surface. You have important things to say, so trust your intellect.

life path ★ You have a gift for words and explain things very easily. You find it hard, however, to express emotions and can be embarrassed about revealing the inner you. This will change with age—especially in relationships. Be aware that when you don't express yourself there is a danger of daydreaming about other lovers or becoming part of a love triangle.

love ★ You need a lover with a quick wit so would suit a Gemini. On the other hand, Jupiter, planet of good fortune, is your birth date ruler, so you may choose a free-spirited Sagittarius, whose ruling planet is Jupiter.

best present ★ Skipping rope, pair of Rollerblades.

birthday share ★ 1875 Ferdinand Porsche, automobile inventor; 1913 Alan Ladd, actor; 1940 Pauline Collins, actress; 1965 Charlie Sheen, actor.

on this day ★ In 1783, the War of Independence between the United States and Britain ended with the signing of the Treaty of Paris.

color white ★ **number** 3, 9, 12 ★ **stone** tiger's eye—the stone for protection ★ **flora** carnation ★ **animal** terrier dog ★ **occupation** real estate agent, builder, interior designer ★ **key features** grounded, virile, open ★ **naturally good at** property management

september 4

character ★ Other people would describe you as hardworking, albeit a little temperamental. You excel at building up business and contacts, but you are quite unpredictable at unexpected moments, which can confuse those you work with. You love your home but can get caught up in designing it simply to impress. Do not be seduced by materialism.

life path ★ You are here to learn to balance your love of material possessions and fine things with spirituality. People born on this day fall into two camps: those who prefer to follow a frugal life and those who adore excessive possessions and finery. Balance is the key.

love ★ You are drawn to partners who impress you. However, this is not the ideal basis for a relationship because you will often become disillusioned. Partners can feel that you don't open yourself up to them enough. Showing a little gentle affection will open your heart and improve your life. You are drawn to Aquarius, whose ruling planet, Uranus, is also your birth date ruler.

best present ★ Expensive fragrance, day at the races.

birthday share ★ 1931 Mitzi Gaynor, actress; 1949 Tom Watson, golfer; 1958 Dr. Drew Pinsky, counselor and radio show host; 1981 Beyoncé Knowles, singer.

on this day ★ In 1976, the unmanned U.S. spacecraft *Viking II* landed on Mars to take the first close-up, color photographs of the planet's surface.

color chrome ★ number 5, 14, 23 ★ stone calcite—calms you down and relieves stress ★ flora fern ★ animal fox ★ occupation advertising executive, party planner, fashion designer ★ key features impulsive, bright, imaginative ★ naturally good at convincing other people

september 5

character ★ You have a sharp wit and an extraordinary mind. You are always having new ideas of how you want your life to go or coming up with get-rich-quick schemes that you rarely follow through. Deep down you prefer security but you love to fantasize about what life would be like if you did throw caution to the wind and sail the stormy seas of your abundant imagination. Make your plans but follow them through for a change.

life path ★ Completion is an important issue with you: you are great at starting things, showing commitment and attention to detail, but somehow, halfway through, you get distracted by another brilliant idea or you lose interest in your initial plan. This is unusual for a Virgo, but as you *are* a Virgo you do tend to stick to your commitments even if you find them tedious. Look further within yourself and find your ultimate goal.

love ★ You can be quite sensual when you want to be and often sit and dream about passion. You tend to be drawn to lovers who are unobtainable or unavailable. This is not fate but your own way of thinking, so you do have the power to change it. Your birth date ruler is Mercury, so a Gemini, whose ruling planet is also Mercury, would love you.

best present ★ Day at a carnival, DVD of an old movie.

birthday share ★ 1847 Jesse James, outlaw; 1929 Bob Newhart, actor and comedian; 1940 Raquel Welch, model and actress; 1946 Freddie Mercury, singer.

on this day ★ In 1975, Lynette A. Frome, a follower of convicted murderer Charles Manson, attempted to shoot President Gerald Ford.

color pink ★ number 6, 24, 33 ★ stone quartz—the stone of love ★ flora lily ★ animal mongoose ★ occupation musician, psychologist, counselor ★ key features mercurial, loving, thoughtful ★ naturally good at seduction

character ★ Loving and passionate, you are great at communicating with other people about what they are feeling. People often turn to you with problems, and you are more than happy to sit down and be not only a listening ear but a wise adviser. You are cautious about life and hate the unexpected, but you just can't seem to avoid experiencing strange coincidences and fated meetings.

life path ★ What you need to do is not only sort out other people's problems but also learn to talk about your own inner feelings. All that wisdom that you apply to other people must be used to guide your own life as well.

love ★ You are very loving and eager to please your partner. You enjoy relationships but may have had your heart broken a few times because you are attracted to unpredictable people whose nature is often completely the opposite of yours. Why not seek a Libra, whose ruling planet, Venus, is also your birth date ruler?

best present ★ Weekend at an empowerment workshop, tickets to the ballet.

birthday share ★ 1964 Rosie Perez, actress; 1971 Dolores O'Riordan, singer; 1973 Greg Rusedski, tennis player; 1974 Tim Henman, tennis player.

on this day ★ In 1997, Princess Diana was buried in the grounds of her family home. The world-wide TV audience was estimated at over 2 billion.

september 7

character ★ You are a deep thinker with an uncanny ability to know what others are thinking and feeling. Although this is valuable, it can feel intrusive to those you probe, as you seem to get right into their minds. Hang back a little and ask people what they are thinking rather than trying to sense it, because sometimes you get it wrong or they can become paranoid.

life path ★ You have a vivid imagination and should write or paint in your spare time to ease tension. You may find you are exceptionally skilled in these areas and could pursue a career in them.

love ★ You need to boost your confidence in love because you often put your partner on a pedestal and think they are better than you … until they inevitably fall off. Your birth date ruler, Neptune, is also your ruling planet,

so a Pisces would be a perfect match for you, as long as you don't both drown in those watery depths of emotion.

best present ★ Computer, fishing rod.

birthday share ★ 1533 Queen Elizabeth I of England; 1909 Elia Kazan, director; 1936 Buddy Holly, singer; 1951 Julie Kavner, actress and voice of Marge Simpson.

on this day ★ In 1813, the term "Uncle Sam" was used for the first time to refer to the United States. The term appeared in an editorial in the *Troy Post*, an upstate New York daily newspaper.

color brown ★ **number** 5, 8, 12 ★ **stone** granite—helps to strengthen your will ★ **flora** snowdrop ★ **animal** poodle ★ **occupation** church minister, politician, newspaper columnist ★ **key features** stern, judgmental, decisive ★ **naturally good at** commanding respect

character ★ You are the least likely person to be reading this book because you have a very pragmatic and practical view of reality. You may be fervently religious or a fervent cynic, but whatever you believe, it is with passionate zeal. You stand by your convictions to the bitter end and can put ideology before people.

life path ★ One of your tasks on Earth is to overcome your seemingly inherent judgment of others. You can't seem to help comparing and judging those around you but this attitude holds up your personal growth. Live and let live, focus on being flexible, and occasionally be a little spontaneous.

love ★ Love is a serious business for you, and you have very high expectations of those with whom you become involved. However, try to be a little less controlling of your partner. Your birth date ruler is Saturn, so a Capricorn, whose ruling planet is Saturn, would give you a run for your money.

best present ★ Gold ring, book about the Dow Jones index.

birthday share ★ 1925 Peter Sellers, actor; 1932 Patsy Cline, country singer; 1971 David Arquette, actor; 1979 Pink, singer.

on this day ★ In 1974, President Gerald Ford pardoned Richard Nixon for his part in the Watergate scandal.

september 9

character ★ Strong-willed and full of energy, you love a good battle. You never give in and you never give up. You have a passionate nature but can be too extreme. All those roaring emotions may be kept under the surface … until you lose your temper. Channel that intense passion into avoiding conflict and skirting around obstacles—life will be much smoother.

life path ★ You are a real warrior and need to learn to be a little more serene and gentle. Try to accept yourself instead of always putting yourself down or thinking you should be doing more. You are lovable as you are, so put less emphasis on constant improvement.

love ★ You are passionate and insatiable, and as your birth date ruler is fiery Mars, you would benefit from a relationship with an Aries, whose ruling planet is also Mars. It would certainly be a challenging match but the flames of passion would burn bright.

best present ★ Go-kart racing, romantic weekend in the mountains.

birthday share ★ 1941 Otis Redding, singer; 1952 Dave Stewart, singer and guitarist; 1960 Hugh Grant, actor; 1966 Adam Sandler, actor.

on this day ★ In 1956, Elvis Presley made his first appearance on national U.S. television on *The Ed Sullivan Show*.

color yellow ★ **number** 1, 11, 22 ★ **stone** amber—dispels negativity ★ **flora** primrose ★ **animal** mynah bird ★ **occupation** billiards player, golfer, personal coach ★ **key features** charming, focused, inspirational ★ **naturally good at** responsibility and getting where you want to be

september 10

character ★ You are independent and focused on your goals. You take responsibility seriously but also value yourself. You're highly motivated and know where you want to get to and just how to do it. You have a warm and magnanimous personality but are aware when people try to take advantage of you and will put up with it only for so long before you put your foot down.

life path ★ You are aware that you need to be self-assured to get on, and although you may have problems with shyness when you are young, you develop confidence and radiate self-confidence as you get older. You are good at helping others become positive.

love ★ You are extremely loving and give your partner a deep sense of security. You have a huge heart and like nothing more than giving to your lover. Your birth date ruler is the Sun, so a dazzling Leo, whose ruling planet is also the Sun, will understand you—although you may both want to be in the limelight.

best present ★ Picnic by the sea or on a riverbank, engraved watch.

birthday share ★ 1907 Fay Wray, actress; 1929 Arnold Palmer, golfer; 1960 Colin Firth, actor; 1974 Ryan Phillippe, actor.

on this day ★ In 1950, Joe DiMaggio became the first player to hit three home runs in a baseball game.

color turquoise, sea green ★ **number** 1, 2, 22 ★ **stone** moonstone—said to be good for fertility and intuition ★ **flora** lavender ★ **animal** exotic fish ★ **occupation** lecturer, interior designer, creative director ★ **key features** extreme, intense, intuitive ★ **naturally good at** having big ideas or formulating ideologies

september 11

character ★ You may sit in a cocoon for many years, hatching plans of how you can transform yourself and the world at large. As long as you mix with people who don't have your depth or potential, you are lulled into the false idea that life just ticks along. At some point or another your life will suddenly take off in a way that exceeds even your own expectations, making you realize that you have wings and can indeed fly.

life path ★ You were born under a very special number, as 11 is a master number. This means that you are among a small percentage of people who have magic within them. You are capable of great deeds and will never really be totally happy until you do something magnificent with your life. Great things are so much easier for you to achieve than you realize. So dream it and do it!

love ★ The virgin and the temptress are the two parts of the whole that is Virgo, and you act out these two symbolic sides more than most Virgos. You are wild and free with passion, or restricted and celibate. Find balance, and spiritual and physical joy will come to you from love. Choose a sensitive Cancer, whose ruling planet, the Moon, is also your birth date ruler.

best present ★ Oils or watercolor paints, leather-bound journal.

birthday share ★ 1885 D. H. Lawrence, author; 1917 Herbert Lom, actor; 1965 Moby, singer; 1967 Harry Connick Jr., singer, jazz musician, and actor.

on this day ★ In 2001, terrorists hijacked airliners and flew two into the twin towers of New York's World Trade Center and one into the Pentagon.

color purple, violet ★ **number** 3, 6, 33 ★ **stone** amethyst—the romans thought this stone prevented excess and brought intuition and clarity to the wearer ★ **flora** petunia ★ **animal** chinchilla ★ **occupation** athlete, builder, investment banker ★ **key features** hardworking, warm, honest ★ **naturally good at** making money and building business

september 12

character ★ You are very focused on your work, and your career is especially important to you—that and security. You want to make it in the world but will do it your way with good, honest hard work. You don't like shortcuts and rarely take risks with money unless you are sure they will pay off. Make time for some social life or you could stagnate.

life path ★ What you think, you create, so make sure your mind creates a fabulous life for yourself. You tend to be a little cynical and need to learn about optimism, which doesn't come naturally to you. However, you have an expansive and warm nature that always brings you good fortune in the end.

love ★ Because you like to be in control it is difficult for you to trust people. Your birth date is ruled by Jupiter, planet of expansion, so do not limit yourself or your partner when you are in love—use the connection

for freedom and growth. Jupiter is also the ruling planet of eccentric and delightful Sagittarius, so find one and watch a perfect partnership unfold.

best present ★ Trip to Disneyland, membership to a gym.

birthday share ★ 1913 Jesse Owens, athlete; 1940 Linda Gray, actress; 1944 Barry White, singer; 1957 Rachel Ward, actress.

on this day ★ In 1953, Senator John F. Kennedy married Jacqueline Lee Bouvier in Newport, Rhode Island.

color electric blue, silver ★ **number** 4, 22, 44 ★ **stone** hematite—said to give self-confidence and increase self-esteem ★ **flora** bird of paradise ★ **animal** siamese cat ★ **occupation** inventor, jeweler, gardener ★ **key features** caring, responsible, dependable ★ **naturally good at** nurturing people and animals

september 13

character ★ You have a passionate, caring nature but need to believe in your own value, as you have a tendency to be self-deprecating. You are very generous with your time but commitments can mount up because you don't know when to say no. A little self-indulgence would not be a bad thing.

life path ★ You can become a bit resentful as a result of overcommitting to everything in life. Work on establishing boundaries. What you choose to take on is entirely up to you. If you do grow resentful, you can become manipulative to get your needs met. It is much better to be up front and express what you feel openly.

love ★ Your number, 4, means that you need security in relationships. You want to settle down but paradoxically often attract free-spirited partners, like an Aquarius, whose ruling planet is Uranus, your birth date ruler. Essentially you are more eccentric than you realize, and need to be individual in your relationship.

best present ★ Trip to the desert, turquoise ring.

birthday share ★ 1857 Milton Snaveley Hershey, chocolate manufacturer; 1916 Roald Dahl, author; 1944 Jacqueline Bisset, actress; 1980 Ben Savage, actor.

on this day ★ In 1788, New York City became the capital of the United States.

september 14

character ★ You like to do things perfectly and are vexed if others pay less attention to detail. You have very high moral values and strive to be the best person you can be. When you were young someone close to you may have let you down, and this experience has motivated you to fight for justice for others now.

life path ★ You are a very deep individual and tend to spend a lot of time thinking about things. This sometimes cuts you off from people. It is important for you to learn to bond and blend with those you love rather than just trying to solve their problems. You need to express affection as well as your thoughts.

love ★ You like to care for your partner and are quite good at commitment, but you can also be highly critical. Learn to be more easygoing with your lover and they will naturally want to please you; no one likes to be controlled. Your birth date ruler, Mercury, is also Gemini's ruling planet, so a Gemini would be a great match for you.

best present ★ Tickets to the theater, leather-bound novel.

birthday share ★ 1867 Charles Dana Gibson, artist; 1914 Clayton Moore, actor; 1934 Kate Millet, feminist and author; 1947 Sam Neill, actor.

on this day ★ In 1975, Elizabeth Ann Bayley Seton, founder of the Sisters of Charity of Emmitsburg, Maryland, was canonized, becoming the first U.S. Roman Catholic saint.

color baby pink ★ **number** 6, 24, 33 ★ **stone** rose quartz—to soothe a broken heart and draw unconditional love to you ★ **flora** daisy ★ **animal** west highland terrier ★ **occupation** store owner, private detective, teacher ★ **key features** loving, secretive, private ★ **naturally good at** nurturing a dream and bringing it to completion

september 15

character ★ You put a lot of effort into succeeding and doing a good job. You not only make an excellent employee but also have the potential to run your own business successfully. This may occur later on in life when your confidence has grown. You tend to put others on a pedestal and not know your own worth. Believe that you are great and your life could be even more bountiful.

life path ★ You will be drawn to helping others, but owing to lack of confidence you may feel you don't have the skills needed to follow this path. You are a marvelous listener and could take up healing or some kind of voluntary counseling work; it would reap rich emotional rewards for you.

love ★ Your birth date ruler is Venus, planet of love. Relationships can be very challenging for you but they always make you grow.

Because Venus is protecting you, it is safe for you to let yourself go and achieve the heights of passion. Stable and loving, Taurus is also ruled by Venus, so you two could have a marriage made in heaven.

best present ★ Romantic weekend for two, tickets to the opera.

birthday share ★ 1890 Agatha Christie, author; 1945 Jessye Norman, opera singer; 1946 Tommy Lee Jones, actor, and Oliver Stone, director.

on this day ★ In 1972, two former White House aides, Howard Hunt and Gordon Liddy, were added to the five men already charged with the break-in at the Watergate building.

color china blue ★ **number** 7, 25, 34 ★ **stone** aquamarine—guides you to your personal truth and helps you speak your mind ★ **flora** ivy ★ **animal** dolphin ★ **occupation** politician, doctor, fisherman/woman ★ **key features** unfathomable, profound, hardworking ★ **naturally good at** dramatic change

character ★ You are a dreamer who tries very hard to live in the real world. On the outside you project an image of respectability, but inside you are quite wild and have visions of rushing off on crazy adventures. You sometimes can change your life right out of the blue, shocking those around you. Perhaps more gentle transitions would make your life a little smoother, even though these upheavals happen only every few years.

life path ★ Your life task is to balance the tacit solidity that people generally assume is your nature with the longing to achieve more with your life. Balance adventure with security and you will have it all.

love ★ Your birth date ruler is Neptune, planet of dreams and dreamers. You can have very passionate affairs in your head but tend to be more conservative in real life.

Allow some of that intense passion to seep out and you will be happy. An emotional Pisces will help you to open up.

best present ★ Diving or water-skiing lessons, walking boots.

birthday share ★ 1924 Lauren Bacall, actress; 1927 Peter Falk, actor; 1956 Mickey Rourke, actor, and David Copperfield, magician.

on this day ★ In 1908, Buick Motor Company and Oldsmobile merged to form General Motors.

color ochre, brown ★ **number** 8, 17, 26 ★ **stone** tiger's eye— said to focus the mind, it is used as a protection stone and study aid ★ **flora** buttercup ★ **animal** alligator ★ **occupation** banker, lawyer, judge ★ **key features** solid as a rock, moral, strong ★ **naturally good at** looking after money and making investments

september 17

character ★ You are strong-willed and rather rigid in your thinking, with a clear-cut view of right and wrong. You have a heroic spirit, stamina, and impressive courage, but you are prone to being judgmental and restrictive with yourself as well as with other people.

life path ★ You do very well in all areas of finance and probably enjoy a high standard of living. You will achieve anything you set your heart on but may neglect your love life in the pursuit of your career goals. You would perhaps benefit from being a little less dogmatic and learning how to lighten up and have fun.

love ★ You have quite an old-fashioned idea of the ideal soul mate and very strong views on how your partner should be. You are rather conservative in this and need to practice sharing more of your vulnerability and affection. Your birth date ruler is stern

old Saturn, planet of hard lessons, most of which you bring on yourself! A Capricorn, whose ruling planet is also Saturn, could soften any blows.

best present ★ Expensive scent, fountain pen.

birthday share ★ 1883 William Carlos Williams, poet; 1929 Stirling Moss, race-car driver; 1931 Anne Bancroft, actress; 1934 Maureen Connolly, tennis player.

on this day ★ In 1787, the Constitution of the United States was signed in Philadelphia by 39 delegates.

color burnt orange ★ **number** 9, 27, 36 ★ **stone** moonstone—traditionally thought to bring fertility to mind and body ★ **flora** orange blossom ★ **animal** owl ★ **occupation** writer, researcher, athlete ★ **key features** mysterious, confusing, dramatic ★ **naturally good at** cracking mysteries in detective novels

september 18

character ★ You are a strange conundrum of contradictions. On the one hand you have a magnetic aura and love to attract attention, yet on the other hand you need privacy and seclusion. It is important for you to succeed but at times you wonder what life is all about, and you may take up a spiritual interest such as meditation or shamanism.

life path ★ You are an incredibly deep thinker and love nothing more than sitting down somewhere to ponder the meaning of life. It is important that you get enough exercise, as this brings instant relief from moodiness and really lifts your spirits. When you do, you should find that you have loads of stamina, and this will help you to succeed in any sport you take up.

love ★ You can blow hot and cold with your lover but you have a tremendously passionate vibe. You love physical intimacy but may alarm potential partners by coming on too strong too soon! Learn to take your time and add some romance. Your birth date ruler is fiery Mars, so an Aries, whose ruling planet is Mars, will ensure that sparks fly.

best present ★ Mountain bike, atlas.

birthday share ★ 1905 Greta Garbo, actress; 1939 Frankie Avalon, singer and actor; 1952 Dee Dee Ramone, singer; 1971 Jada Pinkett-Smith, actress.

on this day ★ In 1851, the *New York Times* began publication at 18 cents per copy.

color canary yellow ★ **number** 1, 10, 11 ★ **stone** fire opal—a powerful talisman to inspire passion and zest for life ★ **flora** daffodil ★ **animal** cat ★ **occupation** dancer, model, designer ★ **key features** warm, cheerful, outgoing ★ **naturally good at** dancing and looking good

september 19

character ★ You always look fabulous and radiate glowing warmth that brings a smile to the face of everyone you meet. You are a little less cheerful and charming with family members but nonetheless very lovable. Ironically, you can feel insecure about your looks and always want to change something about your body or personal style. You may spend an excessive amount of time on your appearance and need to realize that you are perfect just the way you are.

life path ★ You love to perform and be creative and should take up a job or pastime that enables you to express this lovely part of your character. You are a free spirit but often submit to restrictions put upon you by others. You have to practice being free like the social butterfly you truly are.

love ★ You are a firecracker but tend not to believe it and can give your power away in relationships. Practice loving yourself and surround yourself with friends who boost your ego rather than put you down. Your birth date ruler is the Sun, which gives you your natural charisma. A Leo, whose ruling planet is also the Sun, would complement you.

best present ★ Trip to Hollywood, CD of dance music.

birthday share ★ 1940 Zandra Rhodes, fashion designer; 1941 "Mama" Cass Elliot, singer; 1948 Jeremy Irons, actor; 1949 Twiggy, model and actress.

on this day ★ In 1928, Walt Disney released *Steamboat Willie*, the first cartoon film with sound, starring Mickey Mouse.

color silver, white, light blue ★ **number** 2, 11, 22 ★ **stone** pearls—said to open you up emotionally ★ **flora** magic carpet ★ **animal** parrot ★ **occupation** therapist, healer, telephone operator ★ **key features** emotional, intense, hopeful ★ **naturally good at** passionate affairs

september 20

character ★ You have great faith in your abilities and a burning desire to make it big time. You have high ideals and goals but you can be led astray by your emotions. You are attracted to powerful people and seek to attain power for yourself as well. Immaculate in your dress and personal taste, you like your home to be just as gorgeous.

life path ★ You want to make a mark on the world and become immortal through your achievements. Although this ambition is good, you can be easily disappointed if your grand plans are not immediately realized. The good news is that you will often find yourself in the right place at the right time and could well mix with the rich and famous in some way.

love ★ You are led by your emotions and can sometimes be totally carried away by desire. You are likely to have an affair or relationship that is part of a triangle. This may be morally questionable, but you could be consumed with desire and unable to resist. The Moon is your birth date ruler, which is why your emotions are often at a high pitch. A Cancer, whose ruling planet is also the Moon, will understand you.

best present ★ Ring with a white stone, silk scarf/tie.

birthday share ★ 356 B.C. Alexander the Great, King of Macedonia; 1890 Jelly Roll Morton, jazz musician; 1934 Sophia Loren, actress; 1956 Gary Cole, actor.

on this day ★ In 1973, Billie Jean King defeated Bobby Riggs in a tennis match in Houston, billed as the "Battle of the Sexes."

color red, indigo ★ **number** 3, 9, 33 ★ **stone** amethyst—the wisdom and sobriety stone ★ **flora** rose ★ **animal** husky ★ **occupation** comedian, tour guide, cyclist ★ **key features** adventurous, ahead of your time, entertaining ★ **naturally good at** having adventures and traveling

september 21

character ★ You are not an average Virgo, being born on the cusp, and tend to be a little more adventurous than most. You seek out the new and are usually ahead of the game in the creative stakes. You have a wonderful sense of humor and love to make people laugh, although sometimes you can be moody. The call to adventure is strong, and it is important for you to explore and discover life.

life path ★ You are sure to have some hidden genius inside you just waiting to be released, but the challenge for you will be to balance the creative with the practical. You are very lucky but you need to believe this to reap the full benefits from your numerological link with Jupiter, planet of abundance and good fortune.

love ★ You need a lover who accepts you as you are and can deal with your seemingly opposing sides of creative and practical. As

Jupiter is your birth date ruler, a dashing and adventurous Sagittarius could help you live out your dreams.

best present ★ Exotic holiday, tickets to a comedy show.

birthday share ★ 1866 H. G. Wells, author; 1931 Larry Hagman, actor; 1947 Stephen King, author; 1968 Ricki Lake, talk show host.

on this day ★ In 1903, *Kit Carson*, the first silent cowboy movie, was first shown.

color sky blue, silver ★ **number** 4, 11, 22 ★ **stone** amber—removes negativity and provides security ★ **flora** daffodil ★ **animal** snake ★ **occupation** stand-up comic, writer, charity worker ★ **key features** intense, gruff, charismatic ★ **naturally good at** leaping into the new

september 22

character ★ You are deep and very intense and do not suffer fools gladly, tending to be judgmental of people who are not as smart as you. You are hardworking, value intellectual communication, and are slightly eccentric in your personal style or dress sense. You get the feeling sometimes that your life is guided by the hand of fate, and indeed you are probably here for a higher purpose.

life path ★ The number 22 is a master number, which is very special and means you are here as a master builder. This can be manifested in many ways. You might build a career of great and unique creativity or work for a charitable organization and in some way help to change the world for the better. Whatever it is that your soul is called to do, you will follow the vision no matter how disruptive. Rest assured that when you do follow your path, amazing things will come your way.

love ★ It is essential for you to have personal space in a relationship or you will feel like a caged lion. You are likely to meet unconventional partners, and as your birth date ruler is the planet Uranus, a wacky and creative Aquarius would suit you.

best present ★ Tickets to a rock concert, contemporary painting.

birthday share ★ 1791 Michael Faraday, physicist; 1957 Nick Cave, singer, author, and actor; 1958 Joan Jett, singer; 1961 Scott Baio, actor.

on this day ★ In 1862, President Abraham Lincoln ordered all slaves in the South to be freed.

virgo

your ruling planet **Mercury** was the winged messenger of the gods. Unlike Gemini, also ruled by Mercury, you seem to lack the fast pace of your ruler, and also Mercury's mercurial, erratic nature. However, if you look at your moods and phases you will see that you can be a little inconsistent with your inner dialogue and desires. You tend to keep this changeable side well hidden. The main gift Mercury gives you is the ability to communicate precisely. You are obsessed with language and can be a little pedantic when it comes to the written and spoken word. You expect other people to communicate in exactly the same way, which can be unrealistic. You take every word literally and need to understand that people often communicate emotionally and that their tone is sometimes more relevant than the actual words. You can hold people ransom with their language, which can be annoying, but as a son or daughter of the planet of communication you cannot understand other people's irritation because you feel sure you are right. Technically you may be, but expanding your own ways of communicating will help you feel much freer.

your natural habitat You like to run a tight ship at home, being ordered and logical about the way you organize things. You may have your books and CDs arranged in alphabetical order or some other system that makes sense to you. You have a clean and tidy environment, and all food in the fridge is sealed and neat and never out of date. You never forget to iron your clothes and you have a regular day and time set aside to tackle each task. It is frustrating for you to live with someone less organized, but you generally have to because few others can keep up with your high standards. You are so fastidious that you won't even tolerate the top being left off the toothpaste! There are the odd Virgos who are completely the opposite, living in a pigsty and refusing to clean up, but that is not really their nature; they are just so sure that the house could never be totally perfect that they have given up and gone to the other extreme. Whether you are a tidy or a slovenly Virgo you'll always care what people think of your home and will be embarrassed if it isn't flawless.

are you a typical virgo?

Well turned out, with all your clothes neatly ironed and clean, you are the epitome of self-discipline. Any Virgo who is the opposite of this—careless, disheveled, and rumpled—is very much the exception to the rule. Virgos like to be in total control, and to lose control, particularly in work, makes you break out in a cold sweat. You are a perfectionist and this comes out in various ways. Being structured and in control is almost like a meditation for you and makes you feel secure.

Why you're wonderful! You pay close attention to detail and will make everything right in the home and for your loved one. You are loyal and committed in all that you do, and you love to serve and administer. It gives you real pleasure to provide care but you must be careful not to become too subservient. You weigh things before you speak and are kind and deliberate. You tend to take on the burdens of others and worry for them.

Why you're impossible! Pedantic and submissive, you wander around not asking for anything but are surprised when people take you for granted. You can be quite a martyr, often feeling that the whole world is against you even though you try to do your best. Unfortunately you tend to stay in this role because it is safer than risk and adventure. You are using others to keep yourself back when in reality they would probably support you if you did make changes and live a little more for yourself. Go for your dreams and know that you are free—in your case the need for responsibility is a self-constructed illusion 90 percent of the time.

Your secret side Virgo is the sign of the Virgin, but you long to be the opposite and can have some wild and jaw-dropping fantasies. On the surface you are a little prudish about physical intimacy, but underneath you're a wildcat with an appetite for adventure. You may live out this sultry side only in your very vivid imagination, but if you do let go, make sure you find balance or you will be plagued by that common Virgo emotion, guilt.

virgo love compatibility chart

	aries	taurus	gemini	cancer	leo	virgo
fun	✓	✓	✓	✓	✓	✓
romance	✓	✓	✓	✓	✓	✓
loyalty		✓		✓	✓	✓
adventure	✓	✓	✓	✓	✓	✓
lips	✓	✓	✓	✓	✓	✓
chairs	✓	✓	✓	✓	✓	✓
idea	✓		✓	✓	✓	✓
partnership		✓		✓	✓	✓

	libra	scorpio	sagittarius	capricorn	aquarius	pisces
	🍾	🍾	🍾	🍾	🍾	🍾
	❤	❤	❤	❤		❤
		⭕	⭕	⭕		⭕
	🎈	🎈	🎈	🎈	🎈	🎈
	💋	💋	💋	💋		💋
	🪑	🪑	🪑	🪑		🪑
	💡	💡	💡		💡	💡
	👥	👥	👥	👥		👥

 passion **chilling out** **spontaneity** **attentiveness**

libra

september 23–october 22

color sky blue ★ **number** 4, 22, 44 ★ **stone** blue lace agate—allows you to connect with your inner voice ★ **flora** asparagus ★ **animal** chinchilla ★ **occupation** musician, publisher, architect ★ **key features** tuneful, gentle, moody ★ **naturally good at** making beautiful music

september 23

character ★ You have a strong connection to music and love to listen to it. You may have musical talents and it is as if you become one with the sounds. Not all sounds, though—you have a sensitive disposition and any discordant or loud noise jangles your nerves, as does any form of aggression. You are a gentle soul who needs a peaceful and harmonious environment.

life path ★ If you are subjected to stressful situations or disharmony you can become very depressed and moody. You may go through periods of isolation when you hide yourself away and cut yourself off from loved ones. If you reconnect with things you love, like a walk in the park or a concert, your low mood should lift instantly.

love ★ You love relationships but are frightened of being hurt; fear and love are your two choices, so choose love! Also, in long-term relationships you may find you neglect physical affection; deal with this the moment it begins because hugs and kisses keep romance alive. You would be well suited to a Gemini, whose ruling planet is also your birth date ruler, Mercury.

best present ★ Tickets to a classical music concert, CD player.

birthday share ★ 1920 Mickey Rooney, actor; 1926 John Coltrane, saxophonist; 1930 Ray Charles, singer; 1949 Bruce Springsteen, singer.

on this day ★ In 1846, the planet Neptune was discovered by the German astronomers Johann Galle and Heinrich d'Arrest.

color baby pink ★ **number** 6, 33, 42 ★ **stone** rose-quartz—a stone that brings unconditional love ★ **flora** amaryllis ★ **animal** dove ★ **occupation** songwriter, entrepreneur, activist ★ **key features** wild, free, loving ★ **naturally good at** lobbying for change

september 24

character ★ You have a heart the size of the Empire State Building, and this sometimes causes you grief. You feel passionately about the state of the world and want to have some positive effect on it with your life. Ironically, wanting to do something this huge may make you feel impotent. Take it one step at a time and you may well achieve it.

life path ★ You have an optimistic vision of life. You just know that if we would only let our love out and wake up from our long sleep to realize how selfish we are, the world would be a better place. Don't let yourself be disappointed by the sloth of the rest of us. Keep pouring out that message of love, because that is the right path for you.

love ★ You adore your family and partner and want to live in the country enjoying a wholesome, back-to-basics lifestyle. If you're not living that dream already, go for it.

Remember that you are valued and adored. You may like to choose another Libra or a Taurus if you're single, as their ruling planet is also your birth date ruler, Venus.

best present ★ Walking book, hand-knitted scarf.

birthday share ★ 1896 F. Scott Fitzgerald, author; 1936 Jim Henson, creator of *The Muppet Show*; 1941 Linda Eastman McCartney, photographer and animal rights campaigner; 1948 Phil Hartman, comedian and actor.

on this day ★ In 1960, the USS *Enterprise*, the first nuclear-powered aircraft carrier, was launched at Newport News, Virginia.

september 25

character ★ Gentle yet powerful, you have a lovely aura that touches everyone you meet with a golden light. You like to enter into things deeply because your emotions and your dreams are very important to you. You can occasionally get carried away and head off down the wrong path, merrily led by your vivid imagination and romantic spirit.

life path ★ You will be firmly on your true path after the age of 31, but before that, unless you are very lucky, you may be tempted by some outrageous escapades. You are determined to feast on life but suffer when you are knocked back. Try to protect yourself and believe that you will find a pot of gold at the end of your rainbow.

love ★ Boy, have you made some big mistakes in this area. You like to find the best in people and often see qualities that aren't there. However, your quest for divine love will eventually be fulfilled, so keep going. Steer in the direction of a Pisces, whose ruling planet is also your birth date ruler, Neptune.

best present ★ Book on New Age philosophies, swimming with dolphins.

birthday share ★ 1944 Michael Douglas, actor; 1952 Christopher Reeve, actor; 1968 Will Smith, actor and singer; 1969 Catherine Zeta-Jones, actress.

on this day ★ In 1957, nine black children had to be escorted to class by U.S. Army troops at Central High School in Little Rock, Arkansas, because of racial unrest.

color burgundy ★ **number** 8, 4, 71 ★ **stone** copper—cheers you up and brings a sense of optimism ★ **flora** nicotiana ★ **animal** german shepherd dog ★ **occupation** scientist, researcher, private detective ★ **key features** analytical, hardworking, relentless ★ **naturally good at** carrying on when others have given up

september 26

character ★ Tenacity is your middle name. You demand excellence of yourself and others and cannot understand those with less drive. You are goal oriented and your career is of supreme importance. You never mix business with pleasure, but when you have time off you like to enjoy good food and fine wine and mix with intellectual company.

life path ★ You can make a rod for your own back and take on far too much. Nevertheless, you seem to thrive on pressure and achieve results that others would find impossible. You probably need to chill out a little more and ensure that you take regular vacations.

love ★ You have an old-fashioned approach to love no matter how young and trendy you may be. You expect and demand commitment, and once you give your heart, that's it. You need to open up more for love

to really work. Go on—show your soft side. A Capricorn whose ruling planet is also your birth date ruler, Saturn, would love to see it.

best present ★ Hand painted teapot, personal organizer.

birthday share ★ 1898 George Gershwin, composer; 1948 Olivia Newton-John, singer and actress; 1956 Linda Hamilton, actress; 1981 Serena Williams, tennis player.

on this day ★ In 1957, the musical *West Side Story* opened on Broadway.

color red ★ **number** 9, 36, 54 ★ **stone** red jasper—grounds you and makes you feel safe and snug ★ **flora** red-hot poker ★ **animal** lion ★ **occupation** ambulance driver, doctor, bullfighter ★ **key features** fearless, driven, burdened ★ **naturally good at** putting yourself in impossible situations

september 27

character ★ You are a strange combination. Your birth date ruler is Mars, fiery planet of zeal, and this, coupled with your ruling planet, Venus, makes you passionate about life. You have very high expectations of your physical body and energy. You want to become the Duracell Bunny and go on and on and on, but you must realize that this is not humanly possible, advisable, or desirable!

life path ★ You can push yourself too hard, creating an unhappy relationship with yourself. Pay attention to your inner voice: are you friends or enemies with yourself? Harsh or gentle? Work on this and life will be much more relaxed and pleasant. You have the rare ability to be completely present in the moment, which enables you to discover the essence and magic of life.

love ★ You can be a loner and disappear for hours or days contemplating your next grand plan. Lovers try to understand you but must learn to give you space and realize that it is not a reflection on them. An independent Aries, whose ruling planet is also Mars, would be your best match.

best present ★ Relaxation tape, massage oil.

birthday share ★ 1722 Samuel Adams, American revolutionary leader; 1896 Sam Ervin, former U.S. senator; 1972 Gwyneth Paltrow, actress; 1984 Avril Lavigne, singer.

on this day ★ In 1989, Jeffrey Petkovich and Peter Debernardi became the first people to survive going over Niagara Falls's 176-ft.-high Horseshoe Falls in a barrel.

color orange ★ **number** 1, 11, 22 ★ **stone** topaz—makes you smile and gives out good vibes ★ **flora** violet ★ **animal** black cat ★ **occupation** guitarist, bar owner, sculptor ★ **key features** creative, polite, funny ★ **naturally good at** engaging people in conversation

september 28

character ★ You are funny and entertaining but may suffer from shyness or low self-esteem. You hide this well, though, and people are drawn by your gentle allure. You need to be liked, and make a great friend. You have the potential to do well in life as long as you don't give in to your inner demons and do things that you may later regret.

life path ★ You are lovable but may have had a difficult start in life, feeling very alone. You are making up for lost time now and like to have others always around you. You attract beautiful lovers and friends who need your help. You can be a little self-destructive when things go well, so watch out for this. It is essential that you settle down in a home that can give you security.

love ★ You find yourself in serious relationships very quickly, perhaps too quickly. However, it is difficult for you to adjust to losing your personal space, and it may help you to keep a room aside that is used as a music room or chill-out zone just for you. You would harmonize well with a Leo, whose ruling planet is your birth date ruler, the Sun.

best present ★ Guitar, cocktail shaker.

birthday share ★ 1573 Michelangelo Caravaggio, artist; 1902 Ed Sullivan, talk show host; 1934 Brigitte Bardot, actress and animal rights campaigner; 1967 Mira Sorvino, actress.

on this day ★ In 1924, two U.S. Army planes landed in Seattle, having completed the first around-the-world flight in 175 days.

color milky white ★ **number** 2, 11, 22 ★ **stone** moonstone—a fertility stone that balances your moods ★ **flora** golden plum tree ★ **animal** carrier pigeon ★ **occupation** runner, dancer, therapist ★ **key features** instinctive, energized, compulsive ★ **naturally good at** getting to the root of a problem

september 29

character ★ You can find yourself rushing around too much, and you should guard against being manipulated by others. You have an open heart and are always willing to give life your best shot. You may find yourself in a subservient role in friendships but will usually have placed yourself there inadvertently by being too accommodating. Adjust the balance to 50/50.

life path ★ You feel more comfortable helping others through emotional troubles than sharing your own vulnerabilities. You are interested in psychology and New Age practices, as you want to discover your inner self. You have a keen interest in self-help subjects and may go on to become a counselor or therapist. You are a profound soul and need to meet equals who can be fellow travelers on your spiritual journey.

love ★ You can love from afar and never say anything, you can be a loyal friend to the object of your desire … but where will that get you? Stop being a martyr in love and go for it! Why not try a Cancer, whose ruling planet is also your birth date ruler, the Moon?

best present ★ Personal stereo, book on love.

birthday share ★ 1904 Greer Garson, actress, 1913 Stanley Kramer, director; 1935 Jerry Lee Lewis, singer and pianist; 1943 Lech Walesa, president of Poland.

on this day ★ In 1988, United Nations peacekeeping forces were awarded the Nobel Peace Prize for monitoring the world's trouble spots for 40 years.

color purple ★ **number** 3, 12, 21 ★ **stone** amethyst—a sobriety stone that brings wisdom and cures addictive behavior ★ **flora** lavender ★ **animal** husky ★ **occupation** philosopher, midwife, hairdresser ★ **key features** fervent, eloquent, fortunate ★ **naturally good at** looking sophisticated and regal

september 30

character ★ You look good, you feel good, and by golly, you are good! You have high personal morals but are not judgmental. This is quite a feat, so be proud of your emotional and intellectual makeup. You're polite, kind, and generous with your time yet have good personal boundaries. You tend to be rewarded for all this good behavior with unexpected gifts from the universe, such as surprising job offers, lottery wins, and meeting gorgeous lovers.

life path ★ You will do your best in any job and are destined for success. You are likely to do reasonably well financially, as you love the finer things in life, though not in a superficial way—you simply appreciate quality. People tend to open up to you even though you are enigmatic and don't register a reaction to their secrets.

love ★ You are adored and meet lovers who put you on a pedestal; the trouble with pedestals is that everyone falls off eventually, because no one is perfect (although you come close). Your problem is the resulting confused sense of your identity and worth. Refuse to get on next time. A Sagittarius would suit you, as their ruling planet is your birth date ruler, Jupiter.

best present ★ Customized scooter, Armani suit.

birthday share ★ 1921 Deborah Kerr, actress; 1924 Truman Capote, author; 1935 Johnny Mathis, singer; 1980 Martina Hingis, tennis player.

on this day ★ In 1955, movie legend James Dean died in a car crash in Hollywood, California.

october 1

character ★ You need reassurance that you are attractive and talented so you stretch yourself to the limit, working hard to win the accolades you deserve. You may not admit to craving attention and do not seek it in an obvious way but rather subtly and quietly. You generally do end up being noticed and also receiving the admiration you need.

life path ★ You are excellent at being a leader or spokesperson, as your quiet charm can bowl people over. You speak very well and have a sensuous voice like velvet. You pride yourself on your commitment to projects, but actually, if something better came along you would be off like a shot. Be aware of your emotional needs.

love ★ You can be rather a control freak when it comes to love, although again not in an obvious way. You like to know where your partner is at all times and why they are

not with you! Try to loosen the bonds a little. Link up with a Leo, whose ruling planet is also your birth date ruler, the Sun.

best present ★ Silk scarf, piano lessons.

birthday share ★ 1920 Walter Matthau, actor; 1924 Jimmy Carter, 39th U.S. president; 1930 Richard Harris, actor; 1935 Julie Andrews, actress.

on this day ★ In 1971, the Walt Disney World amusement park and holiday resort opened in Florida.

color silvery blue ★ **number** 2, 11, 22 ★ **stone** opal—be warned, this stone makes you face the truth ★ **flora** snowdrop ★ **animal** ostrich ★ **occupation** author, philosopher, peacekeeper ★ **key features** endearing, thoughtful, introspective ★ **naturally good at** putting a different slant on life

character ★ You are unique, playful, and unfathomable. You don't reveal the depths of your spirit to others straight away, but when you do they get a delightful surprise. Life has a deeper meaning for you and you want to get to the bottom of it; the trouble is that the bottom is infinite so you can drown in the depths of your own thoughts. You tend to convey your message with humor.

life path ★ Like the Fool in the tarot cards you leap into life unthinkingly but trustingly. You have faith in your journey most of the time. You often meet characters on your path who have a specific message for you or leave a lasting effect. Life could not be less superficial and you love the vividness of it all.

love ★ You have a huge capacity to love but can talk yourself out of it. This nagging dissatisfaction is not to do with your partner but with an angst within you, which needs to be healed. The only person with whom you can merge totally is you. Why not choose a Cancer, whose ruling planet is also your birth date ruler, the Moon?

best present ★ Crystal ball, poster of Mahatma Gandhi.

birthday share ★ 1869 Mahatma Gandhi, Indian leader; 1890 Groucho Marx, actor; 1949 Annie Leibowitz, photographer; 1951 Sting, singer.

on this day ★ In 1950, the comic strip *Peanuts*, created by Charles M. Schulz, was first published in nine newspapers.

color purple ★ **number** 3, 12, 21 ★ **stone** pink jasper—calms and nurtures you ★ **flora** sweet william ★ **animal** pot-bellied pig ★ **occupation** personal shopper, chef, interior designer ★ **key features** immaculate, pristine, sociable ★ **naturally good at** making things look fabulous

october 3

character ★ You get out and about a lot and love to know what's going on. You are a little nosy and tend to try to keep up with the Joneses. You hate to be out of fashion or not look the part, and people always comment on how well turned out you are. You are great at giving fashion tips to your friends but they may resent your natural flair, so be sensitive.

life path ★ Remember that clothes don't really make the man, or the woman. You are more than your designer clothes. This *Sex and the City* lifestyle will give you a good time but it won't lead you to your life path. You would shine in a course on the healing power of color because you resonate with color so well.

love ★ You usually end up with someone who looks stunning and is successful, your home is like a show home, and you may even have the perfect kids. To make things truly perfect you need to work on intimacy and surrender to your own and your partner's desire. So what if it messes up your hair? That's the way it's meant to be! A Sagittarius, whose ruling planet is Jupiter, would be an ideal match.

best present ★ Louis Vuitton luggage, vintage wine.

birthday share ★ 1867 Pierre Bonnard, artist; 1925 Gore Vidal, author; 1938 Eddie Cochran, singer; 1962 Tommy Lee, drummer.

on this day ★ In 1995, the jury in the OJ Simpson murder trial found the former football star innocent of the 1994 slayings of his former wife, Nicole Brown Simpson, and Ronald Goldman.

october 4

character ★ You're unique, sassy, and bright with a passion for life and all it holds. You will not tolerate being controlled and will never go against your morals. You can be unbending and powerful but are an iron fist in a velvet glove. Attractive and confident, you are a rarity in that the older you get, the more desirable you become.

life path ★ You make an impact even if you don't intend to, and this natural ability to transform places and people is a valuable gift. Your mere presence sparks a reaction and you often act as a catalyst. Use your power for good, always be aware of your inner guide, and you should live a happy life filled with meaning.

love ★ Dedicated and trusting, you give your all when you are truly in love; however, you will also play the field and date all manner of exciting individuals before you find the right soul mate. People may find the partner you eventually pick a strange choice because your partners are usually very different from you, but in your case opposites *do* attract. Why not opt for an Aquarius, whose ruling planet is also your birth date ruler, Uranus?

best present ★ Book of Earth mysteries, smoothie maker.

birthday share ★ 1895 Buster Keaton, actor; 1924 Charlton Heston, actor; 1946 Susan Sarandon, actress; 1976 Alicia Silverstone, actress.

on this day ★ In 1957, the Space Age began when the USSR launched the first man-made Earth-orbiting satellite, *Sputnik 1*.

october 5

character ★ Articulate and loving, you are a great righter of wrongs. At some point in your life you will battle the big bad world and fight for the rights of others. You can be utterly selfless at times. This passion for social reform will burn itself out eventually, and a latent strong desire for a settled family life will then take priority.

life path ★ Perhaps you should jot down some of the ideas you have about making the world a better place. Who knows, you may have it within you to write a revolutionary blueprint for change. You have a deep desire to communicate, and writing is an ideal medium, but it will demand great discipline.

love ★ You seek stability and security in a relationship but it may not arrive until you are in your 40s. If you achieve it before then, you will grow and change within the relationship and perhaps relocate in your 40s instead. Why not search for a Gemini as a partner, as their ruling planet, Mercury, is also your birth date ruler?

best present ★ Set of bongos, laptop computer.

birthday share ★ 1902 Ray Kroc, founder of McDonald's; 1919 Donald Pleasence, actor; 1929 Richard Gordon Jr., NASA astronaut; 1975 Kate Winslet, actress.

on this day ★ In 1989, the exiled Dalai Lama, Tibet's spiritual leader, was awarded the Nobel Peace Prize.

color pink ★ **number** 6, 33, 42 ★ **stone** eulite—the stone of truth ★ **flora** pink rose ★ **animal** stag ★ **occupation** author, chocolatier, makeup artist ★ **key features** sensual, passionate, extreme ★ **naturally good at** loving others unconditionally

character ★ Romance and desire can have too tight a grip on you sometimes and you need to maintain balance in this area. You get caught up in being a lover (or avoiding it if you are blocked) to the exclusion of everything else. You are an exceptional lover and will have some wild adventures.

life path ★ Balancing physicality and spirituality is a big part of your learning curve in life. Meditation may prove something that can transform all that base energy into gold! You have the capacity to love those around you unconditionally and share the gift of love in other ways as well.

love ★ Whether in a relationship or celibate, there is no in-between in your nature. You may have an abundance of lovers or be obsessed with just one and pursue this person until you catch them.

When you do merge with a mutual love you are a fantastic partner. Why not find another Libra, whose ruling planet, Venus, is also your birth date ruler, and who will understand and fulfill you?

best present ★ Rose massage oil, Egyptian cotton sheets.

birthday share ★ 1906 Janet Gaynor, actress; 1908 Carole Lombard, actress; 1942 Britt Ekland, actress; 1963 Elisabeth Shue, actress.

on this day ★ In 1927, the first "talkie" (a movie with sound), *The Jazz Singer*, premiered in New York, with Al Jolson in the starring role.

color ocean blue ★ **number** 7, 34, 52 ★ **stone** stinking water plume agate—allows you to express your intellectual abilities easily ★ **flora** daisy ★ **animal** pug ★ **occupation** diver, artist, songwriter ★ **key features** imaginative, delusional, dreamy ★ **naturally good at** fantasizing about what life should be like

october 7

character ★ You have to watch this tendency to be a fantasist! You can sit all day long staring into space, creating all sorts of scenarios in your mind. Life is about living as well as about dreaming. If you put all that creative energy to practical use you can be a force for profound good in the world.

life path ★ You have been blessed with an abundant imagination and a spiritual bent. However, it is important that you keep yourself grounded in reality or you could lose the plot and get carried away. You may have studied spiritual texts and found your spiritual path; if so, it wouldn't hurt you to be a little superficial sometimes to counteract your earnestness.

love ★ Keep your feet on the ground at the start of relationships and try very hard to see your partners for who they are rather than projecting onto them a fantasy of who you think they are. They want you to love them for themselves, warts and all, rather than as a shining angel on a pedestal. Net yourself a Pisces who can relate to the way you love because your birth date ruler, Neptune, is also their ruling planet.

best present ★ Tarot cards, bonsai tree.

birthday share ★ 1917 June Allyson, actress; 1931 Archbishop Desmond Tutu, Nobel Peace Prize winner; 1935 Thomas Keneally, author; 1968 Thom Yorke, singer.

on this day ★ In 1982, the musical *Cats* opened in New York. It became the longest-running show in Broadway history in 1997.

color olive green ★ **number** 35, 44, 71 ★ **stone** eilat stone—known as "the sage," this is a wise stone that turns negatives into positives ★ **flora** lavender ★ **animal** sea lion ★ **occupation** lawyer, psychiatrist, actor ★ **key features** honorable, strict, persuasive ★ **naturally good at** speaking your mind

october 8

character ★ You have a strong personality and a soft heart. You give the impression that you are fully in control even when this is not the case. Others rely on you and trust your unfaltering allegiance. This faithfulness can be withdrawn as quickly as it was given, though, especially if you are lied to or betrayed.

life path ★ You don't let your guard down very easily and are always alert to what others are thinking about you. You like to be seen as strong but actually are quite sensitive. Your spirits can sink very low and you need space to come out of this phase. Lovers and friends may take this personally or you may blame them for your apparent unhappiness, but in fact this tendency is a part of you that you need to come to terms with.

love ★ You give your heart but not all of it; you have a problem with trust and even when you are swept away by love or infatuation, you can still be on the outside looking in. Why not try a Capricorn, who has Saturn, your birth date ruler, as their ruling planet?

best present ★ Weekend in a log cabin, bath salts.

birthday share ★ 1941 the Reverend Jesse Jackson, civil rights leader; 1943 Chevy Chase, comedian; 1949 Sigourney Weaver, actress; 1970 Matt Damon, actor.

on this day ★ In 1871, a cow overturned a lantern in a barn, causing a fire that led to the Great Fire of Chicago.

color scarlet ★ **number** 27, 45, 63 ★ **stone** snakeskin agate—boosts your emotional energy and helps you find yourself ★ **flora** sweet pea ★ **animal** python ★ **occupation** meditation teacher, hermit, escapologist ★ **key features** solitary, reflective, transcendent ★ **naturally good at** contemplation and self-analysis

october 9

character ★ You can be a loner at times and become confused about what your life is for. Sometimes you are happy to interact and join in the party of life, whereas at other times you need to withdraw and get in touch with your inner peace. Use your own inimitable magic to create a life of realization for yourself.

life path ★ Try not to let yourself be swept away by depression or feelings of loneliness. It is no mistake that you are here on Earth—you have a lesson to complete so you might as well enjoy it! Find a way to express yourself and also to join and connect with people who may appreciate or even need your depth.

love ★ You have a passionate spirit but sometimes you can dismiss physical passion as unspiritual. Intimacy can be a sacred thing and can bring divine enlightenment, so go for it. You might like

to find an Aries, whose ruling planet, Mars, is also your birth date ruler, and so will relate to your power.

best present ★ Meditation beads, vegetarian meal.

birthday share ★ 1891 Otto Schnering, candy bar mogul; 1940 John Lennon, singer; 1948 Jackson Browne, singer; 1958 Mike Singletary, football player.

on this day ★ In 1967, Che Guevara, Argentine-born Marxist revolutionary, was murdered, at the age of 39, by order of the Bolivian military.

color orange ★ **number** 1, 11, 22 ★ **stone** carnelian—harnesses your passion and sparks you up ★ **flora** orange blossom ★ **animal** bee ★ **occupation** playwright, jazz musician, healer ★ **key features** thoughtful, warm, serious ★ **naturally good at** being admired by others

character ★ You have a slightly serious outer persona but also an attractiveness that people are drawn to. Others find you something of a dark horse, deep and magnetic. You rarely smile but when you do, it lights up the room. Your career is important and may entail some form of responsibility. You don't like deafening clubs or any places where you cannot conduct a meaningful conversation.

life path ★ Your mind and your charisma are two qualities that need to be combined. People take notice of you and you are aware of this. You want to put your heart and soul into a career that is fulfilling and meaningful. You get caught up in ideas, and it would be helpful if you discussed your plans with someone who could back you up, rather than trying to achieve everything alone.

love ★ You are loved and fussed over by lovers but can also avoid intimacy. You fear being taken over by love yet it is also something that keeps you balanced. Why not track down a Leo, whose ruling planet is your birth date ruler, the Sun?

best present ★ CD of 1960s music, book on numerology.

birthday share ★ 1813 Giuseppe Verdi, composer; 1900 Helen Hayes, actress; 1917 Thelonious Monk, jazz pianist and composer; 1954 David Lee Roth, singer.

on this day ★ In 1935, George Gershwin's opera *Porgy and Bess* ("the first U.S. opera") debuted on Broadway.

october 11

character ★ You're a big softie, always lending a helping hand and never complaining when asked to work late. Be careful that you don't become too much of a pushover. You are fabulous at giving but find it quite challenging to receive. You can get embarrassed when being given a present. The number 11 is a master number, which imbues you with a touch of magic.

life path ★ Engaging and gentle, you are a ray of light for many people. Perhaps it is time you realized it. You go about doing good deeds in a genuine, altruistic way. It is essential that you form a close-knit circle of friends to support you and with whom you can share your fears and insecurities. Don't be too concerned by these; we all feel insecure or depressed from time to time.

love ★ You can be shy when it comes to love and yet you have a big heart and so much to give. You need to be swept off your feet and treated gently and kindly. Love will come but don't let the past stop you from grabbing it. A Cancer, whose ruling planet, the Moon, is also your birth date ruler, could be just what you need.

best present ★ Hematite bracelet, classic novel.

birthday share ★ 1821 Sir George Williams, founder of the YMCA; 1844 Henry John Heinz, food manufacturer; 1884 Eleanor Roosevelt, U.S. first lady; 1962 Joan Cusack, actress.

on this day ★ In 1984, Kathy Sullivan became the first U.S. female astronaut to perform a space walk.

color purple ★ number 12, 21, 30 ★ stone purple sage agate—helps you build self-esteem and self-love ★ flora poppy ★ animal peacock ★ occupation opera singer, builder, juggler ★ key features expansive, erudite, cultured ★ naturally good at broadening your horizons

character ★ Thanks to Jupiter, your birth date ruler, you have an expansive heart and mind and love to explore life. Not content with staying where you started, you may choose to move around or change your environment often. You have a hunger for learning and enjoy nothing better than studying a new topic.

life path ★ You may end up juggling two different careers at the same time. You love the fact that life is packed full of choices but struggle to make a final decision. Nothing in life is final for you, and you just want to keep moving on to the next adventure.

love ★ It may take time but it is most likely that you will settle with someone who comes from a different culture or life experience from your own. You love diversity, and this stretches to color your love life. If you have children you will be an unconventional and free-spirited parent.

Why not seek out a Sagittarius, whose ruling planet is Jupiter, your birth date ruler?

best present ★ Atlas, airplane ticket to a remote location.

birthday share ★ 1875 Aleister Crowley, author and occultist; 1923 Jean Nidetch, founder of Weight Watchers; 1935 Luciano Pavarotti, opera singer; 1947 Chris Wallace, newscaster.

on this day ★ In 1492, Christopher Columbus had his first sighting of the New World, which he later named San Salvador.

october 13

character ★ You can be likened to polished steel, shiny, hard, and never rusty! You have a strength and power that are awesome and a little dangerous, but if you are one of the very few who are not in touch with their power you may feel totally victimized. You don't mess around, and with sheer gall and grit always rise to the top of the heap.

life path ★ You can be too single-minded and focused. When you are set on some goal or battle you forget about not only your own emotional well-being, but also the emotional well-being of those around you. You can transcend this and discover the way of the peaceful warrior if you try. Open your heart to gentleness.

love ★ You crave security but once you have it, you tend to take your partner for granted or see them merely as an extension of yourself. When you are in a casual relationship or chasing someone, you are much more loving and giving. Think about this. An Aquarius, whose ruling planet, Uranus, is also your birth date ruler, would be very good for you.

best present ★ Bubble-making machine, rose-quartz heart pendant.

birthday share ★ 1925 Lenny Bruce, comedian, and Margaret Thatcher, former prime minister of Britain; 1941 Paul Simon, singer; 1959 Marie Osmond, singer.

on this day ★ In 1992, the pyramids, the Sphinx, and other monuments survived an earthquake in Cairo that killed at least 400 people and injured more than 4,000.

color yellow ★ **number** 5, 23, 41 ★ **stone** yellow jasper—clears your mind ★ **flora** buttercup ★ **animal** dalmatian ★ **occupation** researcher, addiction counselor, office worker ★ **key features** articulate, shy, passive ★ **naturally good at** being able to balance life

character ★ Even though you are quite shy, you love people. You would like to be more open when you socialize but tend to take a step back and wait for others to draw you into a conversation. You have a brilliant mind and need to be more confident about the way you express it. If you let go a little you could be the life and soul of the party.

life path ★ You tend to worry that you are being judged or are not good enough in some way. You carry on a rich inner dialogue with yourself and may love to keep a diary in which you write down your observations. Open up and let them out more! No one but you is judging you. You have a talent for communicating if you could just take the courage to leap in.

love ★ You are a good and considerate lover. In fact giving your partner pleasure can be your main focus within a relationship, but it is important to get your needs met, too. You are fabulous at giving but you need to practice receiving. Why not find a Gemini, who shares your birth date ruler, Mercury?

best present ★ Day at a health spa, lavender bath oil.

birthday share ★ 1894 e. e. cummings, poet; 1927 Roger Moore, actor; 1939 Ralph Lauren, fashion designer; 1940 Cliff Richard, singer.

on this day ★ In 1947, a U.S. Air Force pilot, Charles "Chuck" Yeager, flying a Bell X-1 airplane, became the first person to travel faster than the speed of sound.

october 15

character ★ Your birth date ruler is Venus, as is your Sun sign ruler, so love makes your world go around. You daydream about love and can write beautifuly about it. You tend to love the idea of being in love, and sometimes the object of your desire is secondary to the whole drama. Everyday life seems too boring for you, but love is the dynamite that blows your mind.

life path ★ Unconditional love, universal love, and spiritual love are all essential topics for you to study and understand. It is no good getting cynical about life or disillusioned about love. If this happens it is probably you who are out of balance, not the rest of the world. Romantic love is fab, but it will not provide you with the answer.

love ★ This is your favorite merry-go-round, and even though it never stops, you never get motion sickness. On the other hand, maybe you have been too afraid to get on in the first place—many of you are apt to stay chaste because you dare not release the force of your strong desire. Take heart and leap into the saddle with another Libra, who also loves this ride.

best present ★ Laptop computer, empowerment workshop.

birthday share ★ 1844 Friedrich Nietzsche, philosopher; 1924 Lee Iacocca, businessman; 1946 Richard Carpenter, musician; 1959 Sarah Ferguson, Duchess of York, author, and charity fund-raiser.

on this day ★ In 1993, Nelson Mandela and F. W. de Klerk were awarded the Nobel Peace Prize for their work to end apartheid in South Africa.

color sea green ★ **number** 7, 25, 34 ★ **stone** aragonite—keeps you emotionally balanced ★
flora lilac ★ **animal** jaguar ★ **occupation** mystic, lecturer, conductor ★ **key features**
spiritual, dreamy, intellectual ★ **naturally good at** spiritual practices

october 16

character ★ Whimsical and sensitive, you are probably spiritual or religious and may also be interested in philosophy. You have experienced many trials and tribulations and know what it is to travel right to the edge but somehow manage not to fall off. You can be emotionally fragile. Remember that in the cycle of life, what goes up must come down and vice versa.

life path ★ You have no time for brash or aggressive people and generally limit yourself to a few trusted friends who share your spiritual path. You can get defensive if confronted over your views; you feel them instinctively and don't like to reduce them to words. Spiritual growth does not have to come out of trauma but can also emerge from living in the moment and from pure happiness.

love ★ Love for you is a delicate endeavor. You have to feel it in your spirit and your soul. However, you will tread carefully if you have been hurt before. Your partners will be people you have a deep connection with, so be confident and honest about what you have to offer. A Pisces, whose ruling planet is your birth date ruler, Neptune, could fall for you hook, line, and sinker.

best present ★ Venetian glass, pair of binoculars.

birthday share ★ 1854 Oscar Wilde, author and playwright; 1925 Angela Lansbury, actress; 1938 Nico, singer; 1958 Tim Robbins, actor and director.

on this day ★ In 1978, Polish Cardinal Karol Wojtyla was elected Pope John Paul II, the first non-Italian pope since 1542.

october 17

character ★ You have a determined character and, if you put your mind to it, can achieve seemingly impossible tasks. You find skill attractive, and even when you were a child you practiced things like skipping until you had them down to a fine art. You never give in and are as tenacious as a sheepdog. You need stability but, paradoxically, can be reckless with your security.

life path ★ Your challenge is to learn about opening up and living your inspiration while maintaining balance in other areas. You tend to create your own routines and are rather inflexible if other people need you to change them. We are all free spirits and should be able to do as we please, but consideration and compromise are also essential paths for our spiritual growth.

love ★ You love passionately but can also detach yourself and spend time on your own. You like to be in charge of relationships in a subtle way and may withhold affection if you feel you are not getting the right sort of attention. You might like to try a Capricorn, whose ruling planet is your birth date ruler, Saturn.

best present ★ Silver picture frame, Pogo stick.

birthday share ★ 1918 Rita Hayworth, actress; 1920 Montgomery Clift, actor; 1938 Evel Knievel, stunt man; 1972 Eminem, rap artist and actor.

on this day ★ In 1902, the first Cadillac was produced in Detroit, Michigan.

color red ★ number 9, 27, 45 ★ stone malachite—will help you face your fears and bring change ★ flora fern ★ animal ram ★ occupation tennis player, playwright, archaeologist ★ key features resolute, authoritative, passionate ★ naturally good at bringing a sense of justice to life

character ★ You are fair minded and have an air of authority about you that commands respect. You are naturally good at whatever you feel passionately about and you know where you are going. You will get there. When you love, you love completely.

life path ★ You were born to influence others in some way, and you have an inner core strength that serves you well. You may end up being a guide or an inspiration to those around you. This is helped by your being strong enough to be scrutinized. Not many people could handle the responsibility you will have in your life, but you love it.

love ★ You will find a muse, someone you can adore whom you will chase with all your might. Even if they come to you, you love to be the one who showers them with affection and makes them feel good about themselves. Why not find an Aries, whose ruling planet, Mars, is also your birth date ruler?

best present ★ Leather gloves, silk pajamas.

birthday share ★ 1926 Chuck Berry, singer; 1939 Lee Harvey Oswald, alleged assassin of President John F. Kennedy; 1956 Martina Navratilova, tennis player; 1960 Jean-Claude Van Damme, actor.

on this day ★ In 1873, the first American football rules were formulated at a meeting in New York attended by delegates from Columbia, Princeton, Rutgers, and Yale.

october 19

character ★ You are eager and enthusiastic about life but are easily knocked off your perch. If someone is negative you soak up the criticism like a sponge and take a few days to get over it. You need to protect yourself a little more and not be so easily influenced because it slows you down. However, you are good at cheering and motivating other people.

life path ★ You're gorgeous in your own way and give off little sparks of sensuality. You're not a flirt in the traditional sense but send out a come-hither message quite unawares. People enjoy being in your company and appreciate your take on life. You like to be showered with attention but will often run off for a weekend hike alone, or to a retreat, to regain your equilibrium.

love ★ You come into yourself when in a relationship and have a lot of fun sharing your radiant personality. You can like to have things your way but learn as you get older the validity of other people's point of view. You may like to try a relationship with a Leo, whose ruling planet, the Sun, is also your birth date ruler.

best present ★ Golf lessons, trip to New York.

birthday share ★ 1895 Lewis Mumford, author; 1931 John Le Carré, author; 1945 John Lithgow, actor; 1962 Evander Holyfield, boxer.

on this day ★ In 1987, "Black Monday" occurred when Wall Street stocks plunged a record 508 points, or 22.6 percent. The loss topped the one-day declines of October 28 and 29 in 1929, which heralded the Great Depression.

color milky white ★ number 2, 11, 20 ★ stone gypsum—draws good fortune to you ★ flora petunia ★ animal barn owl ★ occupation drama teacher, songwriter, middle school teacher ★ key features maternal, gentle, emotional ★ naturally good at communicating with children

character ★ You have a kind heart and are very aware of your inner child. You may think a lot about your childhood and perhaps work with children. You like to draw and paint, and love to listen to classical or gentle music. You have a dreamy quality about you and a warm and caring spirit.

life path ★ You are a spiritual soul and need to develop your meditation or relaxation skills. It is also important to clear your energy. A sea salts bath or a space-clearing technique such as smudging, when sage is burned to purify energy, may help you when it is difficult to shift your moods, particularly when you are down. Don't become disillusioned with the world but change it with your big heart.

love ★ You may have experienced pain in this area in the past but lasting love is destined to come to you. Loving yourself is imperative. Build up a solid and secure relationship with yourself and it will be mirrored by a partner. Why not look for a Cancer, whose ruling planet, the Moon, is also your birth date ruler?

best present ★ Moonstone ring, book of poetry.

birthday share ★ 1632 Sir Christopher Wren, architect; 1854 Arthur Rimbaud, poet; 1931 Mickey Mantle, baseball player; 1972 Snoop Doggy Dogg, rap artist.

on this day ★ In 1818, an agreement between Britain and the United States set the 49th parallel as the Canada-U.S. border.

color purple ★ number 3, 12, 21 ★ stone royal plume jasper—balances your spirit, heart, and mind ★ flora dandelion ★ animal labrador retriever ★ occupation chemist, dancer, student ★ key features clever, fortunate, different ★ naturally good at giving sound advice

october 21

character ★ You're a little faster on your feet than most Libras; you have a spring in your step and an eagerness to get things done. Ironically, it can take you ages to complete tasks but this is because you are a bit of a perfectionist. You love to travel and have adventures. You gain peace in your soul when you are in the mountains or remote countryside.

life path ★ It is important for you to see the world and taste and experience different cultures. You are probably excellent at learning languages and have a taste for unusual cuisine. You are not afraid of change if you feel strongly enough about it.

love ★ You need a partner who is adventurous like you or one day, out of the blue, you could up and leave and go on a journey alone. Love is a mixed bag for you, but at some point there will definitely be a love relationship that will blow you away and exceed your expectations, so hang in there because it will be worth it! Perhaps hold out for a Sagittarius, whose ruling planet, Jupiter, is also your birth date ruler.

best present ★ Camping trip, rucksack.

birthday share ★ 1772 Samuel Taylor Coleridge, poet; 1833 Alfred Nobel, inventor; 1917 Dizzy Gillespie, trumpet player; 1956 Carrie Fisher, actress.

on this day ★ 1959, the Solomon R. Guggenheim Museum opened in New York City.

color silver ★ **number** 4, 13, 22 ★ **stone** fluorite—connects you to your higher self ★
flora protea ★ **animal** ferret ★ **occupation** actor, engineer, astronomer ★ **key features**
mercurial, impulsive, inventive ★ **naturally good at** insightful thought

character ★ You are ahead of your time and many people might not understand you. You have ideas, inspiration, and vision that are unique and special. Follow your instincts about your ideas and do not worry if the world lags behind. You're unique and that is the joy of you.

life path ★ You are incapable of conforming and thank goodness for that! If it weren't for forward-thinking people like you, we would still be sitting in caves. However, feeling different or having ideas that people can't follow could feel like a burden sometimes. Celebrate your difference—you're a star in the making!

love ★ You often meet lovers who are either totally elusive or hang on your every word. You are an inspiration to them but also a challenge because you are erratic and changeable. Try an Aquarius, whose ruling planet, Uranus, is also your birth date ruler, and who may be able to handle you!

best present ★ Amber ring, juicer.

birthday share ★ 1920 Timothy Leary, psychologist; 1943 Catherine Deneuve, actress; 1952 Jeff Goldblum, actor; 1968 Shaggy, reggae singer.

on this day ★ In 1960, Cassius Clay (later Muhammad Ali) fought his first professional bout in Louisville, Kentucky.

libra

your ruling planet Venus, of course, is the planet of love. Yes, you are a son or daughter of Aphrodite and your lessons in life are all about love and relationships. Love is your guiding light and you have the grace and charm one would expect of a Venus child. You draw people in with your delicate nature and your steady gaze. Venus rotates backward and this means you can get lost in the past, focusing on mistakes rather than letting go and moving on. You will go out of your way to please your partner and give 100 percent of yourself to a marriage or true-love commitment. Your soft and sweet nature brings out the protective nature of other people. Venus is a very female energy to have, so even if you are male you will emanate a certain gentleness and delicacy.

your natural habitat You love your home and are very aware of the energy it contains. You like to have it perfect but not as perfect as a Virgo home, which is all about neatness. Your perfection lies in making the home a harmonious place to live in. You like color coordination and natural fabrics. You are drawn to gentle colors such as light blues and greens as well as neutral tones like beige, and you like your surroundings to be uncluttered and calm. You may have an altar, shrine, or meditation space, which is a central focus for you. It is a place where you can focus that airy mind and find serenity in this chaotic world. When you cook, it is light and pure, healthful food, full of nutritional value and daintily presented. You like to have a space to exercise or do yoga in, and you are the most body conscious of the air signs.

are you a typical libra?

You are up and down emotionally, and you never know what mood you will wake up in. A cloud of depression can suddenly lower over you for no concrete reason, mostly because you love and need harmony but find it difficult to maintain it in your life. You worship beauty and like to be carefree, light, and airy. You have a strong sense of justice and want everything in life to be fair.

Why you're wonderful! Friendly, charming, and hospitable, you have a great way with people. You love your fellow man and are content just to listen and be supportive. You have a kind heart and a delicate laugh, which seems to captivate others. You like to make friends and enjoy idle chat with them. With your ability to give genuine compliments you are a joy to have on the social scene.

Why you're impossible! You tend to submerge your emotions or not know how to connect with them. You don't talk about your problems but let them build up rather than risk rocking the boat. Unpredictable and prone to mood swings, you can be overwhelmed by a sadness whose cause you cannot place. This makes you retreat deep into yourself, where not even those closest to you can reach. Take courage by the hand and try to express yourself more freely.

Your secret side If you are discontented in a relationship you tend to escape into romantic fantasies and illusions. You daydream about the waitress in the corner coffee shop or the guy who delivers your groceries, but this fantasy can carry you even further away from your partner. You tend to flee from one relationship right into another, leaving your previous partner heartbroken and confused because you never revealed how you felt.

libra love compatibility chart

	aries	taurus	gemini	cancer	leo	virgo
fun	🍾	🍾	🍾	🍾	🍾	🍾
romance	💘	💘	💘	💘	💘	💘
loyalty	🔗		🔗	🔗		
adventure	🎈	🎈	🎈	🎈	🎈	🎈
	💋	💋	💋	💋	💋	💋
	🪑	🪑	🪑	🪑	🪑	🪑
	💡		💡	💡	💡	💡
	🪑		🪑	🪑	🪑	🪑

KEY ▷

 fun romance loyalty adventure

libra	scorpio	sagittarius	capricorn	aquarius	pisces
🍾		🍾	🍾	🍾	🍾
💘	💘	💘	💘	💘	💘
			⭕	⭕	
🎈	🎈	🎈	🎈	🎈	🎈
👄	👄	👄		👄	👄
🪑		🪑	🪑	🪑	🪑
💡	💡	💡		💡	💡
👥			👥		

 passion   **chilling out**   **spontaneity**   **attentiveness**

scorpio

october 23–november 21

color green ★ number 5, 14, 32 ★ stone basalt—this volcanic rock will give you power in challenging times ★ flora desert rose ★ animal rhinoceros ★ occupation talk show host, psychiatrist, private investigator ★ key features intense, probing, suspicious ★ naturally good at unearthing secrets and gathering information

october 23

character ★ You have a probing nature and like to get to the core of people, while revealing little about yourself. You know just what questions to ask and how to gather personal and sometimes top-secret information. Your boredom threshold is low, and you prefer life to be raw and real. You are fascinated by what people conceal, probably because you have such a secret side yourself.

life path ★ Ironically, one of your lessons in life is to learn to trust and let go. Imagine being able to experience life and people without having to analyze and question everything. You are quiet and charming and have a lovely speaking voice that draws listeners to you. Guard well the secrets vouchsafed to you by other people and never use them for manipulative purposes.

love ★ You often get caught up in other areas of life, and even though you are flirtatious and naughty like a typical Scorpio, you tend to talk about love more than experience it deeply. You can have a telepathic connection with lovers once you allow the intimacy to occur. Why not try a Gemini, whose ruling planet is also your birth date ruler, Mercury?

best present ★ Notebook and pen, digital radio.

birthday share ★ 1925 Johnny Carson, talk show host; 1931 Dame Diana Dors, actress; 1935 Chi Chi Rodriguez, golfer; 1940 Pele, soccer player.

on this day ★ In 1915, 25,000 women marched in New York City, demanding the right to vote.

color pink ★ **number** 6, 15, 33 ★ **stone** rose-quartz—opens your heart and fills it with unconditional love ★ **flora** geranium ★ **animal** pony ★ **occupation** athlete, secretary, producer ★ **key features** striking, captivating, untouchable ★ **naturally good at** catching your prey

character ★ You love beautiful things and beautiful people and need to be careful that you don't end up a big-game hunter. You have been accused of sometimes toying with people's emotions as you dip in and out of brief liaisons. You often have the opportunity for secret affairs or unconventional relationships. Others rarely know the extent of your exploits.

life path ★ You have an irresistible quality about you that draws people to you who will defend you to the death. You are ruled by extreme emotions that you battle to control, but you manage to play it cool even when you feel totally out of control inside.

love ★ You have the capacity to love deeply but are scared of being broken in a relationship and usually protect yourself against this, either by always being the one to end things or playing hard to get. Quit the games and surrender—life will be so much easier and more fulfilling. Entrust yourself to a Taurus, whose ruling planet is also your birth date ruler, Venus, planet of love.

best present ★ Designer watch, ylang-ylang bath oil.

birthday share ★ 1923 Denise Levertov, poet; 1936 Bill Wyman, guitarist; 1939 F. Murray Abraham, actor; 1947 Kevin Kline, actor.

on this day ★ In 1861, President Abraham Lincoln received the first telegram via the new coast-to-coast telegram service.

october 25

character ★ You have the mind of a slightly mad genius and tend to live in your head. Always make sure that you socialize or you could become quite reclusive. You are blessed with the imagination of an artist but may spend too much time thinking and not enough time producing. Sometimes you are tempted to tell little white lies … or even great big ones. Try to resist.

life path ★ Although it is tempting, try not to draw other people into a relationship of illusions. You spin a web of intrigue that is beguiling, but if you're not careful you are just as likely as your prey to get stuck in the web. Use that inventive mind for the greater good.

love ★ You have trouble revealing your vulnerabilities in a relationship, or you reveal handpicked ones to put you in a strong position, but either way you hide yourself. This is not good for you or your relationship and you would do much better to open up and trust your partner. Go fishing for a Pisces, whose ruling planet is your birth date ruler, Neptune.

best present ★ Oil paints and canvas, scented candle.

birthday share ★ 1825 Johann Strauss, composer; 1881 Pablo Picasso, painter and sculptor; 1928 Marion Ross, actress; 1941 Helen Reddy, singer.

on this day ★ In 1854, the infamous Charge of the Light Brigade took place at Balaklava, Ukraine, during the Crimean War.

color blood red ★ **number** 8, 44, 62 ★ **stone** jet—helps you deal with the wheel of life: birth, death, and rebirth ★ **flora** cactus ★ **animal** python ★ **occupation** politician, judge, speech writer ★ **key features** powerful, in control, indomitable ★ **naturally good at** overcoming hurdles to succeed

character ★ Powerful and tough, you are not afraid of anything. You have a very clear, reasoned way of communicating, but deep beneath that collected exterior burns a furnace of emotional fire. You also have a strong social conscience and may be interested in global or local politics.

life path ★ You tend to face your inner demons because life has taught you that if you don't they will eventually come and get you. You are resolute and practical, and these assets will take you to the top in your chosen profession. Love can be a minefield because it is where you let your guard down; however, it stretches your spirit and gives you intense pleasure.

love ★ Do not run from your physical longings or repress them—intimacy can release tension and free you. You have a profound depth that you show only to a very close lover once you trust them, and trust is everything to you. Why not seek a Capricorn, whose ruling planet is also your birth date ruler, Saturn?

best present ★ Copy of Leo Tolstoy's *Anna Karenina*, vintage wine.

birthday share ★ 1916 François Mitterand, president of France; 1942 Bob Hoskins, actor; 1947 Hillary Rodham Clinton, U.S. senator and former first lady; 1963 Natalie Merchant, singer.

on this day ★ In 1881, Wyatt Earp, his two brothers, and Doc Holliday were involved in a legendary gunfight at the OK Corral in Tombstone, Arizona.

color scarlet ★ number 9, 45, 54 ★ stone ruby—to light the fire of passion and courage ★ flora red-hot poker ★ animal scorpion ★ occupation soldier, counselor, ambulance driver ★ key features fearless, tempestuous, unsettling ★ naturally good at rallying others to help in a cause or crisis

october 27

character ★ You have a warrior spirit but you really need to watch that temper of yours. You tend to ponder things and then blow up, scaring anyone who experiences your wrath. You ought to calm this anger down because it can eat away at you. Channel that roaring energy into something constructive.

life path ★ You have dark thoughts when you are alone, but this can be resolved by taking up meditation and positive visualization. This will help to control what is in your head—if you don't like it, change it. You have thought a lot about life and death and would make an excellent grief counselor. Focusing your boundless compassion on people who need you will transform your base energy into gold.

love ★ Physical intimacy can take you to such heights that, coupled with love, it can be a little scary for you. See this ability to fly as a gift and throw yourself into it with a pure heart. An Aries would make for a cloud-nine coupling, as your birth date ruler, Mars, is also their ruling planet.

best present ★ Day of stock-car racing, trip to the seaside.

birthday share ★ 1728 Captain James Cook, naval explorer; 1914 Dylan Thomas, poet; 1932 Sylvia Plath, poet; 1939 John Cleese, comic actor.

on this day ★ In 1938, the DuPont company introduced its new synthetic yarn, nylon.

color orange ★ **number** 1, 11, 22 ★ **stone** fire opal—this rare opal inspires your creativity and enhances your appeal ★ **flora** starflower ★ **animal** gibbon ★ **occupation** chess champion, web site designer, researcher ★ **key features** thorough, studious, magical ★ **naturally good at** being the best in your field

character ★ You are committed to your career and nearly always reach the top of your field. You put the effort in and have an eye for detail that others lack. You love being around people but are quite quiet and reserved. As an alchemist you can turn the mundane into something precious.

life path ★ You are lucky with money and good at investments. You like to be secure and can appear a little too frugal, but you have generosity of spirit, so spread the cash a bit more. The universe is full of abundance and you know how to unearth it, so relax and enjoy your rewards.

love ★ You are likely to start your love life quite late and gain confidence as a lover as time passes. You can be rather reserved to begin with in a relationship, but you may surprise your lover with your ardor once you feel confident. Choose Leo, whose ruling planet is also your birth date ruler, the Sun.

best present ★ Sheepskin rug, lava lamp.

birthday share ★ 1903 Evelyn Waugh, author; 1909 Francis Bacon, artist; 1941 Hank Marvin, guitarist; 1967 Julia Roberts, actress.

on this day ★ In 1492, Christopher Columbus discovered Cuba and claimed it in the name of Spain.

color pure white ★ **number** 2, 11, 20 ★ **stone** clear quartz—the magic wand of crystals, this will magnify whatever you put into life ★ **flora** lotus ★ **animal** giraffe ★ **occupation** children's author, nursery school teacher, stand-up comic ★ **key features** lively, funny, naive ★ **naturally good at** making others laugh

october 29

character ★ You have a delightful childlike quality that you can use creatively. You see the world through childlike eyes and find responsibility or stress impossible to handle. You can often be an escapist when reality seems too harsh. You have difficulty responding when other people make demands on you, but you have a big heart.

life path ★ In a way you will never grow up, but you do need to take more care in the day-to-day running of your life. The universe often saves you from disaster at the last minute, but you can't always throw away bills or hide them in your sock drawer. Some more attention here would not go amiss.

love ★ Your juvenile nature has pros and cons when it comes to love. On the one hand you are very entertaining and spontaneous, but on the other you are self-obsessed and demanding. Perhaps it would be wiser to grow up for some of the time? A Cancer, whose ruling planet is also your birth date ruler, the Moon, could tenderly show you how.

best present ★ Pogo stick, yo-yo.

birthday share ★ 1891 Fanny Brice, actress and singer; 1897 Paul Joseph Goebbels, propagandist; 1947 Richard Dreyfuss, actor; 1971 Winona Ryder, actress.

on this day ★ In 1929, prices collapsed at the New York Stock Exchange on Wall Street. The day became known as "Black Tuesday" and led to the Great Depression of the 1930s.

color amethyst ★ **number** 12, 21 30 ★ **stone** jade—this sacred chinese stone will draw financial assets to you ★ **flora** fern ★ **animal** koala bear ★ **occupation** director, literary agent, publisher ★ **key features** clever, organized, good at making plans ★ **naturally good at** laying foundations

character ★ You like security and success, will avoid risks unless they are carefully calculated, and spend much of your life building a secure home environment and career. You are single-minded and persistent and often have a job in which you supervise others. You like to keep your personal life very private and hate for anyone to pry.

life path ★ You build firm foundations not only for yourself but also for the people you love. However, you tend to have almost a business partnership with lovers and are quite formal and reserved. You are likely at some stage to meet someone in life who shakes those cast-iron foundations and is intent on leading you astray.

love ★ You need someone who can challenge you, excite you, and loosen you up. Beneath that reserved surface you have a sizzling physicality like all Scorpios. Why not try a Sagittarius, whose ruling planet, Jupiter, is also your birth date ruler?

best present ★ Fountain pen, gold chain.

birthday share ★ 1885 Ezra Pound, poet; 1939 Otis Williams, singer; 1945 Henry Winkler, actor and producer; 1967 Gavin Rossdale, singer.

on this day ★ In 1938, Orson Welles broadcast a radio dramatization of *The War of the Worlds* by H. G. Wells, causing panic throughout the United States as listeners believed a Martian invasion was really occurring.

october 31

character ★ You have a slightly disturbing air about you, as you tend to keep your face free of emotion, afraid of revealing your feelings or appearing vulnerable. Learn to trust others more. Combative and fearless, you should be excellent at martial arts. You either enjoy all sports or you go to the opposite extreme and let your body go completely—there is no middle ground.

life path ★ You may have been let down or disappointed by someone when you were small, and this has left a deep emotional scar. You have to take things less personally because you are keeping yourself from receiving much love. You are delicious, and if you weren't so spiky you would have admirers beating a path to your door.

love ★ Love is letting go of fear and allowing your partner the freedom to be who they are in the world. You are lovable and love surrounds you, so don't get obsessive or possessive with potential lovers or you could frighten them away. Look for an Aquarius, whose ruling planet is also your birth date ruler, Uranus.

best present ★ New Age book on forgiveness, Buddha statue.

birthday share ★ 1795 John Keats, poet; 1930 Michael Collins, astronaut; 1950 John Candy, comedian and actor; 1968 Vanilla Ice (Robert Van Winkle), singer.

on this day ★ In 1984, India's prime minister, Indira Gandhi, was shot and killed in her garden in New Delhi by Sikh extremists.

color hunter green ★ **number** 1, 11, 22 ★ **stone** gold tiger's eye—for protection and mental stimulation ★ **flora** clover ★ **animal** ostrich ★ **occupation** engineer, academic, farmer ★ **key features** confident, controlling, critical ★ **naturally good at** making yourself indispensable

character ★ You like to have total control over your environment but don't wield your power in an obvious way. You use the voice of apparent reason to control and place discipline and firm boundaries on those around you. You need to be more up front about your motives; you like attention but can use underhanded tactics and manipulation to get it. If you are highly evolved you will express all your fears honestly.

life path ★ When you grow in spirit you will have a better understanding of other people's fears and vulnerabilities. If you have a relationship with someone who is open about their deepest issues, it would be more honest and fair to share yours in return. Why are you afraid to be as open? Once you have dealt with your issues on disclosure, life will become much easier and lighter.

love ★ You will not let a loved one go if you still love them, hanging on to the bitter end, seeking to rekindle the flame. Even though you love relationships, you can feel alone in the most committed partnership. Have you given your lover a chance to really see you? If not, remember that it is your responsibility, not theirs. A Leo whose ruling planet is also your birth date ruler, the Sun, would press all the right buttons.

best present ★ Parachute jump, cognac.

birthday share ★ 1936 Gary Player, golfer; 1942 Larry Flynt, magazine publisher; 1957 Lyle Lovett, singer and actor; 1972 Jenny McCarthy, actress.

on this day ★ In 1995, South Africans voted in their first all-race local government elections, completing the destruction of the apartheid system.

november 2

character ★ You see life as a deeply meaningful experience; you don't believe in coincidence but think everything is a signpost to your ultimate destiny. You are intuitive and would make a great clairvoyant. However, you can be too subjective sometimes and get lost in the depths of your analytical mind.

life path ★ It is as if you have been given extra-special insight into the workings of the human psyche. You understand why people behave in certain ways by reading between the lines when people speak to you and by observing body language. You reveal little about yourself but play the therapist with your friends, who admire you for your understanding. You crave the profound and get very low if life is too mundane.

love ★ You plunge into your lover's soul and dance in their eyes. No superficial relationships for you, although you may be tempted by one-night stands occasionally to satisfy your fun-loving side. You are an emotional healer and need to focus that energy back into yourself. Why not find a Cancer, whose ruling planet, the Moon, is also your birth date ruler?

best present ★ Tarot cards, incense.

birthday share ★ 1913 Burt Lancaster, actor; 1934 Ken Rosewall, tennis player; 1942 Stefanie Powers, actress; 1961 k.d. lang, singer.

on this day ★ In 1947, the *Hughes H-4 Hercules*, an eight-engine flying boat built by Howard Hughes, made its one and only flight of just over a mile in Los Angeles harbor.

color green ★ **number** 3, 12, 21 ★ **stone** green aventurine—for protection in travel and to draw abundance to you ★ **flora** mistletoe ★ **animal** panda ★ **occupation** business person, store owner, construction worker ★ **key features** enigmatic, powerful, unusual ★ **naturally good at** escaping from danger

november 3

character ★ You have been in some risky situations and danger has often loomed in some form, but you always manage to avoid damage and survive unscathed. Clearly you have a guardian angel and end up landing on your feet no matter how bad things become. You emanate a silent charm that draws people to you.

life path ★ Like the myth of the goddess Innana and the dance of the seven veils, your life has very clear cycles. At some point you may find that you feel stripped naked, but you will reemerge stronger than before. You are something of a phoenix, and because of this you have nothing to fear—you will always return after setbacks.

love ★ You are all or nothing. You will share your heart only with someone you connect with as if they were your missing piece, giving your all to this one great love and soul mate. Anybody else will only ever get 60 percent. Perhaps there is more than one soul mate out there for you, but you feel you will experience true love only once. It could be with a Sagittarius, whose ruling planet is also your birth date ruler, Jupiter.

best present ★ Watch, eternity ring.

birthday share ★ 1921 Charles Bronson, actor; 1952 Roseanne Barr, actress, comedienne, and talk show host; 1954 Adam Ant, singer; 1959 Dolph Lundgren, actor.

on this day ★ In 1992, Bill Clinton was elected President of the United States, defeating George Bush.

color silver ★ **number** 4, 13, 22 ★ **stone** lapis lazuli—sacred to the ancient egyptians, this stone protects and enlightens you ★ **flora** hydrangea ★ **animal** flamingo ★ **occupation** entrepreneur, cowboy/girl, clown ★ **key features** eccentric, deep, vibrant ★ **naturally good at** staying in touch with childhood dreams

november 4

character ★ Bouncy and intense, you have irrepressible energy and a love of adventure. Your childlike spontaneity may stem from too many restrictions when you were young. Responsibility at an early age has made you fearful of being pinned down now.

life path ★ You have wild ideas and are slightly crazy, but in a good way! You stun people with your wacky take on life, but within the wackiness is divine truth. Like the Fool in the tarot cards you are foolish on the surface but have wisdom inside. It would be a fool who took you at face value and dismissed you.

love ★ You may feel disappointed in this area or rather insecure. This disappointment comes from the past, not the present. Love yourself for who you are and you will delight and inspire lovers with your kooky charm. You are an inventive lover and need to relax

and enjoy this part of you. Why not try an Aquarius, whose ruling planet is also your birth date ruler, Uranus?

best present ★ Whiskey, cartoon DVD.

birthday share ★ 1923 Alfred Heineken, brewer; 1937 Loretta Swit, actress; 1969 Sean John Combs (Puff Daddy), rapper and producer, and Matthew McConaughey, actor.

on this day ★ In 1946, the United Nations Educational, Scientific, and Cultural Organization (UNESCO) was established.

color green ★ **number** 14, 23, 50 ★ **stone** smoky quartz—helps you face your fears ★
flora orchid ★ **animal** gray cat ★ **occupation** housing manager, homeopath, shaman ★
key features secretive, analytical, furtive ★ **naturally good at** multitasking

november 5

character ★ You are deeply philosophical and sizzlingly attractive. Lovable and outgoing, you remain secretly insecure, but with your great wisdom and insight you could rise to your full potential with confidence. You have many close friends but tend to share different parts of yourself with different people. You often have a problem telling the whole truth and like to hedge your bets in typical Scorpio fashion.

life path ★ Your lesson in life is to overcome your natural shyness and insecurity because you actually have a strong spirit and ooze magnetic charm. You can be too easily swayed by words and equally can sway others with your seemingly rational thought. Always trust your intuition more than words.

love ★ You will have many great loves in your life but may never give the whole of yourself to any one relationship. Part of you is scared you will disappear if you do. Perhaps it's time to stop avoiding intimacy and practice giving love and sharing space? Choose a Gemini, whose ruling planet is also your birth date ruler, Mercury.

best present ★ Trip to Amsterdam, tandem bicycle.

birthday share ★ 1913 Vivien Leigh, actress; 1943 Sam Shepard, actor; 1959 Bryan Adams, singer; 1963 Tatum O'Neal, actress.

on this day ★ In 1940, President Franklin D. Roosevelt was elected for an unprecedented third term in office.

color pink ★ number 6, 15, 33 ★ stone garnet—a healing stone and aphrodisiac ★ flora hollyhock ★ animal pair of lovebirds ★ occupation dancer, party planner, lingerie designer ★ key features magnetic, sizzling, funny ★ naturally good at winning friends and influencing people

november 6

character ★ Voluptuous and vibrant, you simply cannot cover up your scorching appeal. Even when you are being quite innocuous, people may feel you are flirting with them or have some ulterior motive. Although on the one level you quite enjoy this, it can be very tiring when people get the wrong impression. Make sure you have good boundaries with your friends or they could become obsessive.

life path ★ Putting that hot nature of yours to good use is going to be a challenge. You can get caught up in wild relationships that distract you from your path. You may avoid intimacy altogether for fear of losing yourself. However, it would be better to explore the spiritual quality of love and just enjoy your gift.

love ★ You can play with love and are often attracted to unobtainable or aloof partners. This is a way of protecting yourself, but

whatever you do, don't become a martyr to love—it doesn't suit you. A Libra, whose ruling planet is also your birth date ruler, Venus, would be an ideal match.

best present ★ Book on spirituality, beaded candleholder.

birthday share ★ 1814 Adolphe Sax, inventor of the saxophone; 1946 Sally Field, actress; 1970 Ethan Hawke, actor and author; 1972 Thandie Newton, actress.

on this day ★ In 1923, Colonel Jacob Schick was granted a patent for the first electric shaver.

color sapphire blue ★ **number** 16, 34, 52 ★ **stone** sodalite—helps you reveal your personal truth ★ **flora** dockleaf ★ **animal** monkey ★ **occupation** medium, navy captain, psychiatrist ★ **key features** wistful, deep, overwhelming ★ **naturally good at** plunging into the unconscious

november 7

character ★ You are psychic and have a vivid imagination, which is quite a challenging combination—it may be difficult for you to distinguish between your imagination and reality. It would be wise to double-check any assumptions you make intuitively, just in case. You may also have revelations and flashes of insight that are awesome. It is easy for you to get lost in a world of your own.

life path ★ You are supersensitive, and this has made you feel very vulnerable. You may periodically hide away and retreat from this harsh old world. Make sure that you remember to come back out and play, because as sad as life is, it is also joyous, as dangerous as it is, it is also miraculous, and you are genuinely much safer than you sometimes feel.

love ★ You can dive to depths of intensity of which mere mortals can only dream. The problem is that you have to come up for air occasionally! Don't go too deep too soon. You are a superb lover and should have no problem delighting your partner. The lucky one could be a Pisces, whose ruling planet is also your birth date ruler, Neptune.

best present ★ CD of rock music, New Age self-help book.

birthday share ★ 1867 Marie Curie, physicist; 1879 Leon Trotsky, Communist leader; 1913 Albert Camus, author; 1943 Joni Mitchell, singer.

on this day ★ In 1783, the last public hanging in Britain took place at Tyburn, near Marble Arch in London.

november 8

character ★ You are too charming to be shifty, but you are secretive and love to keep a foot in two different worlds. One is straightforward and transparent, the other is a shadow world, where all sorts of possibilities tempt you. This tightrope act is an accomplished game that is part of your nature. Whether you ever become fully submerged in the shadow land or just think about it remains to be seen.

life path ★ Duplicity and intrigue are always following you. You may ignore them and be the most respectable Joe on the block but you cannot deny that they are there. How you deal with them is your big challenge in life. Whatever decision you take is not necessarily wrong—you must be your own moral judge.

love ★ Passionate but reserved, you have strong desires. You are tempted to date lovers who are mad, bad, and dangerous to know, but you rarely follow through with it. You may appear to be detached from your partner but this could not be further from the truth. A Capricorn, whose ruling planet is also your birth date ruler, Saturn, would best suit your needs.

best present ★ Book on philosophy, pair of sunglasses.

birthday share ★ 1656 Edmond Halley, astronomer; 1847 Bram Stoker, author; 1900 Margaret Mitchell, author; 1949 Bonnie Raitt, singer.

on this day ★ In 1837, the Mount Holyoke Female Seminary in Massachusetts became the first U.S. college founded for women.

color red ★ number 36, 45, 90 ★ stone bloodstone—grounds you and gives you energy ★ flora rock rose ★ animal cougar ★ occupation soldier, firefighter, mountaineer ★ key features vital, strong, energetic ★ naturally good at having unexpected adventures

character ★ Fiery and fearless, courageous and bold, you have amazing energy, striking physical presence, and a confident air. You can spot weaknesses in others but rarely use them against them. You have a nose for danger and so manage to avoid it. You would do very well in the army.

life path ★ Many adventures will come your way and you have the stamina to overcome all obstacles or blockages. You have a passionate nature and enjoy the cut and thrust of sport with members of the opposite sex, such as tennis mixed doubles or beach volleyball. Females born on the 9th are confident and assertive, giving any lovers a run for their money.

love ★ You love intensely and may be caught up in a romantic obsession. Mars, your birth date ruler, is the planet of energy and passion. This, linked to your extremely potent ruling planet, Pluto, gives you strong yearnings. As with all Scorpios it is possible you will decide to be celibate and totally renounce this tireless force. If not, an Aries, whose ruling planet is Mars, could be the perfect answer.

best present ★ Football, silk shirt.

birthday share ★ 1928 Anne Sexton, poet and author; 1934 Carl Sagan, astrophysicist and author; 1935 Bob Gibson, baseball player; 1951 Lou Ferrigno, actor and bodybuilder.

on this day ★ In 1938, anti-Jewish riots took place in much of Germany after the murder of a German official in Paris. The streets of the main cities were littered with broken glass, and the night became known as "Kristallnacht," or Crystal Night.

november 10

character ★ You have traveled to the depths of despair and to the heights of pleasure and happiness. You have seen it all psychologically and should be emotionally intelligent because of this. Your natural ability to look beyond a crisis, toward the light at the end of the tunnel, helps you stimulate and push other people to go beyond their limits.

life path ★ You were born with an acute awareness of life—the good, the bad, and the ugly—and your mission is to learn to accept everything as part of life's rich tapestry. You may well have achieved this already and become a laid-back and kind individual, accepting of human frailty and always willing to lend a hand.

love ★ You have the ability to heal your partner's psychological problems and may attract lovers with deep-rooted emotional damage. You're a cathartic and passionate romancer. Always be aware of the huge effect you have on loved ones. Why not try a Leo, as their ruling planet, the Sun, is also your birth date ruler?

best present ★ Ride on a Harley-Davidson, hip flask.

birthday share ★ 1483 Martin Luther, religious reformer; 1925 Richard Burton, actor; 1932 Roy Scheider, actor; 1949 Donna Fargo, singer.

on this day ★ In 1970, the Great Wall of China opened to the world for tourism.

color white ★ **number** 2, 11, 110 ★ **stone** pearl—to put you in touch with your emotions ★ **flora** cowslip ★ **animal** rabbit ★ **occupation** lawyer, counselor, judge ★ **key features** political, motivated, aware ★ **naturally good at** taking control of organization

november 11

character ★ You are emotionally complex and have a tendency to overreact to slights and imagined conflict. You like to be respected and to know where you stand with people. In your view the world is either for you or against you. However, you are a softie underneath this hard exterior, and once you give your heart you are generous and loving.

life path ★ You can be ruthless if you think something is important enough. You have the potential to evolve quickly and become very emotionally aware. Your tendency to go to extremes needs to be tempered, and you must make sure that you don't succumb to paranoia. Being loving and forgiving should be your goal in life, and learning not to judge a book by its cover.

love ★ What's yours is yours lovewise and heaven help anyone who tries to tamper with your relationship. You may find yourself attracted to a parental figure because you like to be looked after and cooked for by a loved one. A Cancer, whose ruling planet is also your birth date ruler, the Moon, could be just your cup of tea.

best present ★ Water pistol, chess set.

birthday share ★ 1934 Charles Manson, cult leader; 1962 Demi Moore, actress; 1964 Calista Flockhart, actress; 1974 Leonardo DiCaprio, actor.

on this day ★ In 1918, World War I ended with the signing of the armistice agreement between the Allies and Germany. This day is now commemorated as Veterans Day.

november 12

character ★ You have a mesmerizing air and piercing eyes—others feel you look not just into their eyes but into their very soul. You attract people who either love you or hate you but are drawn like moths to a flame because of this magical aura; some will find you wonderful, others sinister.

life path ★ Because it is easy for you to have power over others, it is essential that you monitor yourself and check your motives regularly. Some people born on this day become very insecure and are not aware of their incredible hypnotic power. Open yourself up to a path of enlightenment and unconditional love, but keep yourself firmly on the ground.

love ★ You are lucky in love and attract a number of special and lovely partners. Learn to receive their love and don't question them as to why they love you—you can overcomplicate relationships with your probing and interrogating. Chill out and enjoy. Why not find a Sagittarius, whose ruling planet is also your birth date ruler, Jupiter?

best present ★ Rose massage oil, book on spirituality.

birthday share ★ 1840 Auguste Rodin, sculptor; 1929 Grace Kelly, Princess Grace of Monaco; 1945 Neil Young, singer; 1966 David Schwimmer, actor.

on this day ★ In 1859, in Paris, the first flying trapeze act was performed by Jules Leotard at the Cirque Napoleon without a safety net. The body-hugging costume he used was later named after him.

color silver ★ **number** 13, 22, 40 ★ **stone** hematite—to increase your self-confidence ★ **flora** peace lily ★ **animal** iguana ★ **occupation** acrobat, rap artist, comic ★ **key features** changeable, spontaneous, eccentric ★ **naturally good at** overcoming adversity

character ★ You are a live wire. You are all over the place and can never sit still. You have so many ideas streaming through your mind that when you have a conversation, other people find it difficult to keep up with you. Talkative and funny, you know how to capture an audience, but you seem to be completely without ego.

life path ★ You can do whatever you wish, as long as you know this is so. No one can hold you back or tie you down except you. You are your own worst enemy or own best friend, so focus on building a positive relationship. You may have an interest in unexplored mysteries, UFOs, or coincidences.

love ★ You may experience many unconventional relationships or have a very broadminded view of what love is all about. As long as you are up front and honest, that's cool. Why not try an Aquarius for a lover, as your birth date ruler is Uranus, the ruling planet of Aquarius?

best present ★ Book on dream interpretation, oil paints.

birthday share ★ 1850 Robert Louis Stevenson, author; 1938 Jean Seberg, actress; 1954 Chris Noth, actor; 1955 Whoopi Goldberg, actress.

on this day ★ In 1956, the U.S. Supreme Court ruled that segregation of people of different races on public buses was unconstitutional.

november 14

character ★ When you want information you are like a dog with a bone. You won't even allow lovers or family members to get away with anything. Truth is very black and white for you even though you yourself are quite secretive. Hypocritical? No! You just feel that you keep secrets so that you don't hurt other people. But maybe that's why other people do, too! Relax—if we all knew everything in everyone's heads it would be unbearable.

life path ★ You take life and work very seriously and should be in a job that involves information or communication. You have a clear and precise way of expressing yourself and also listen very attentively. You are a close observer of life and of people. Fiercely protective of those you love, you will fight to the death to defend them if need be.

love ★ Relationships are very important to you and you give your all. Trust is imperative, and although you may test someone for a while before you hand over your heart, once you trust it is usually forever, even when that trust is betrayed. Why not choose a Gemini, who shares your birth date ruler, Mercury?

best present ★ Magnifying glass, kite.

birthday share ★ 1840 Claude Monet, impressionist artist; 1922 Boutros Boutros-Ghali, secretary general of the United Nations; 1935 King Hussein of Jordan; 1948 Prince Charles, Prince of Wales.

on this day ★ In 1963, a new island was created off the Icelandic coast by an undersea volcanic eruption.

color pink ★ **number** 15, 33, 60 ★ **stone** blue lace agate—to cool some of your passion and bring balance ★ **flora** cornflower ★ **animal** poodle ★ **occupation** bodyguard, commando, secret agent ★ **key features** daring, loving, aggressive ★ **naturally good at** getting into trouble

character ★ Often stalked by danger or mystery, you seem never to have a straightforward existence. You can get addictive about people or things so need always to keep an eye on the balance in your life or lack of it. You have a heart of gold but find it hard to trust. You are very self-reliant and may be attracted to dangerous sports or pursuits.

life path ★ You tend to bump into interesting and unusual people but are often on the outside looking in. You can make some rash career choices that are adventurous and involve some element of risk. You tend to feel that life is a battle, but perhaps the battle has stopped and you have forgotten to put down your sword.

love ★ This is one of the most important learning areas of your life, and you need to work hard on yourself here. Relationships bring out the primal in you, making you feel emotions like jealousy, which in turn makes you uncomfortable. You need to learn about being free and allowing others to be free in your love. A Libra, whose ruling planet is also your birth date ruler, Venus, could be an inspiring teacher.

best present ★ Rose-quartz heart pendant, gift certificate from a bookstore.

birthday share ★ 1887 Georgia O'Keeffe, artist; 1930 J. G. Ballard, author; 1932 Petula Clark, actress; 1954 Beverly D'Angelo, actress.

on this day ★ In 1969, about 250,000 people marched in Washington D.C. to protest against the Vietnam War.

november 16

character ★ You are wild at heart and happily get yourself in trouble. You like a bit of mischief and others love you for it. You're a high roller who plays for big stakes, and your reckless attitude may bring you major disasters financially … but who knows? It might make you a fortune as well!

life path ★ You have a rich imagination and your finger is on the pulse of current trends; sift your ideas through the sieve of practicality. Alcohol can be irresistible to you so you have to be careful; it makes you feel good but it can lead to problems. If you have an addiction problem, deal with it sooner rather than later. You have much to offer—don't throw it away.

love ★ Your idea of what you want as a lover is something of a fantasy. Wake up and smell the coffee! Your partner probably has hidden depths and the real person beside you may be better than any fantasy!

You can have erratic emotions, but if you are patient and wait for them to stabilize, you will make love less of a lottery. Net yourself a Pisces, whose ruling planet is also your birth date ruler, Neptune.

best present ★ Set of golf clubs, magnolia tree.

birthday share ★ 1908 Burgess Meredith, actor; 1935 Elizabeth Drew, author; 1967 Lisa Bonet, actress; 1970 Martha Plimpton, actress.

on this day ★ In 1933, the United States and the USSR established diplomatic relations.

color burgundy ★ number 35, 44, 62 ★ stone chrysocolla—increases your inner strength ★ flora chrysanthemum ★ animal eagle ★ occupation personal coach, soldier, social activist ★ key features steadfast, stubborn, hardy ★ naturally good at taking command

november 17

character ★ You are tough, strong, and powerful and usually gravitate to positions of power in society. You have firm opinions, and once you have taken a view, you will not be persuaded to change by anyone or anything. Although this is admirable in some ways it can lead to trouble in personal relationships, because a partner can find your unbending attitude disempowering.

life path ★ You would make a great general but life is not a war to be battled through. Half the joy of life is that it throws up the unexpected, yet you tend to want to regiment your life to the point where this does not happen. Impossible! Embrace the unexpected, because sometimes it can lead to wonderful surprises and great happiness.

love ★ You tend to have committed long-term partnerships with faithful and loyal companions. However, it is important that you allow them to stand on their own two feet or resentment can build up eventually. A Capricorn whose ruling planet is also your birth date ruler, Saturn, would harmonize well.

best present ★ Pair of boxing gloves, fragrance.

birthday share ★ 1925 Rock Hudson, actor; 1942 Martin Scorsese, director; 1944 Danny DeVito, actor; 1960 RuPaul, actor and entertainer.

on this day ★ In 1973, President Richard Nixon told an Associated Press managing editors meeting in Orlando, "People have got to know whether or not their president is a crook. Well, I'm not a crook."

november 18

character ★ You are sturdy, with a strapping body and the personality to match. You love to rush around performing seemingly impossible feats or heroic acts. If you're female you are incredibly strong-willed and see yourself as equal to any man.

life path ★ You can be excitable and explosive. You love a good argument or battle and don't take any prisoners. If you are really pushed to the limit you can play dirty to win, and you justify this if you think you have the moral high ground. Passion quells your anger so celibacy would not suit you— it would make you moody and irritable.

love ★ You have endless energy and an insatiable appetite for love. Being in a relationship is particularly good for you, and communication is the key that will make your relationships work. If you feel misunderstood you can become unreasonable and sulky. Avoid this by choosing an Aries, whose ruling planet is also your birth date ruler, Mars.

best present ★ Thai meal, full-body massage.

birthday share ★ 1906 Sir Alec Issigonis, designer of the Morris Minor and Mini automobiles; 1923 Alan Shepard Jr., astronaut; 1939 Margaret Atwood, author; 1942 Linda Evans, actress.

on this day ★ In 1995, the Vatican announced the Roman Catholic ban on the ordination of women as priests was a definitive, infallible and unquestionable part of the church's doctrine.

november 19

character ★ You may or may not be famous but you have an air of success about you. When you are out and about, people often stop and stare. Part of your attraction is that you are enigmatic and live enveloped in mystery; other people become fascinated by you but they usually respect your boundaries and do not probe too much.

life path ★ It should be easy for you to become well known because the magnetic energy you exude draws opportunity to you. You have something important to say, so take time to explore within and connect with your higher purpose. You have a great sense of humor, which you use to cover deep emotions.

love ★ You are secretive about your lovers, which may hurt them, as they may feel you are embarrassed by or ashamed of them. This could not be further from the truth.

Really you want to keep them all to yourself and not share them with all and sundry. Why not try a Leo, whose ruling planet is also your birth date ruler, the Sun?

best present ★ Video camera, laptop computer.

birthday share ★ 1917 Indira Gandhi, former prime minister of India; 1942 Calvin Klein, fashion designer; 1961 Meg Ryan, actress; 1962 Jodie Foster, actress.

on this day ★ In 1863, President Abraham Lincoln delivered his Gettysburg Address at the dedication of the national cemetery on the Civil War battlefield of Gettysburg, Pennsylvania.

color silvery white ★ **number** 2, 11, 20 ★ **stone** amazonite—gives you courage and strength ★ **flora** lupine ★ **animal** dolphin ★ **occupation** dj, hockey player, pr executive ★ **key features** changeable, reckless, adventurous ★ **naturally good at** getting yourself into mischief

november 20

character ★ You are ruled far too much by your ever-changing emotions. One minute you are on top of the world, the next in the depths of despair. Try to regulate your moods and, as your birth date ruler is the Moon, become aware of how the cycles of the Moon affect you. Meditate to balance your erratic feelings.

life path ★ You can be rash and impulsive and don't see danger when it is staring you in the face. This is very untypical Scorpio behavior! You like to show off your fearlessness and must be careful of going too far in dangerous sports. You love the thrill of adrenaline surging through your body and will pursue whatever brings on this feeling. You are tempted by jobs that can bring you an element of drama.

love ★ You can declare undying love one minute, then for no good reason decide it is all over. You have chased impossible lovers

who were bound to turn you down simply because you adore the thrill of the hunt. Instead, go after a Cancer, whose ruling planet is your birth date ruler, the Moon.

best present ★ Model powerboat, day at the races.

birthday share ★ 1889 Edwin Powell Hubble, astronomer; 1914 Emilio Pucci, fashion designer; 1925 Robert F. Kennedy, U.S. senator; 1956 Bo Derek, actress.

on this day ★ In 1945, 24 Nazi leaders went before an international war crimes tribunal in Nuremberg, Germany.

color purple ★ **number** 3, 12, 21 ★ **stone** pecos diamond—soothes your emotions ★ **flora** dahlia ★ **animal** stray cat ★ **occupation** musician, philosopher, summer camp leader ★ **key features** unusual, intelligent, lucky ★ **naturally good at** coming up with original ideas

november 21

character ★ You have a sharp and intellectual mind. Even if you have had little formal education you are smarter than most people. You can spin any idea to come up with a different angle. It would benefit you to travel and see the world because you can get stuck in a rut, and with your chameleon nature, you may become what people expect of you. Yet there is so much more inside you.

life path ★ You have limitless talent and must be sure to keep your life moving on to avoid stagnation. Get those ideas out of your head and onto paper. Perhaps you will write a Hollywood script or design the next must-have shoes. Who knows? It is all up to you and you are the only one who can do it. Otherwise your catchphrase will be "what if?"

love ★ You are likely to have some fantastic, inspiring lovers who appear out of the blue, sweep you off your feet, and have a divine message for you! Wow, fab, look out for them! They are likely to be a Sagittarius whose ruling planet is also your birth date ruler, Jupiter.

best present ★ CD of French love songs, around-the-world air ticket.

birthday share ★ 1898 Rene Magritte, artist; 1945 Goldie Hawn, actress; 1965 Bjork, singer; 1969 Ken Griffey Jr., baseball player.

on this day ★ In 1934 the Cole Porter musical *Anything Goes* opened on Broadway.

scorpio

your ruling planet **Pluto** was lord of the underworld and this certainly poses a challenge for you. The planet Pluto is the darkest in the known universe because it is farthest from the Sun. Perpetual darkness can be dispiriting and forces you constantly to question yourself. This shadow land encourages you to look at any hidden motivation and to know your own dark side; we all have a shadow side but you need to embrace and accept yours. Pluto is the only planet that has never been visited by a spacecraft; like you it is shrouded in mystery and its enigmatic spirit has never been sounded. Pluto's orbit is not straightforward—it rotates in the opposite direction from all the other planets—and you, too, have a tendency to go around the reverse way to reach your destination. You may spend an awful lot of time being indirect and lurch from inner crisis to inner crisis because of this. Pluto is all about facing your fears and surrendering—not giving up but throwing yourself into the flow of life and trusting that it will embrace and carry you to the right places.

your natural habitat You're quite obsessive about most things, including your home. You like to convey a welcoming atmosphere to guests, but your bedroom is a different matter and totally private. This is your inner sanctum, your boudoir, and is to be entered only by the privileged few. You spend a lot of time thinking in your bedroom and may wake up in the morning and take 15 minutes or so to reflect on your dreams. If you have a new sweetheart you will rarely invite them to spend the night because you like to wake up alone. The exception would be someone with whom you have a very intimate bond. You are sensitive to smell and may have a signature scent or perfume that you like to spray around your home when you have company; you like to surround your guests with your fragrant welcome. You would suit red satin sheets and heavy drapes but may go for a light and airy look instead to disguise your intensity. Dark colors on the wall will soothe you and make you feel secure. You may keep a trunk or drawer full of hidden treasures from the past, love letters, photographs, and so on, which you open occasionally, but even the best burglar could not pry it open once you have locked it. You can be too attached to your home and need to make sure you get out enough.

are you a typical scorpio?

You are sultry, confident, and disarmingly charming. You are not obvious about anything but slink around being noticed despite not saying a word. The air of mystery and intrigue that surrounds you is compelling. You have a lot of secrets and never share the real you, not even with your nearest and dearest. You don't trust easily, if at all, and always expect the worst, but you still believe you can control life by being something of a magician.

Why you're wonderful! You are deliciously attractive in an unconventional way, with huge personal power even though you probably come across as very gentle. Your experience of life is very raw and alive; there's nothing superficial about you. Your lessons in life are to do with sexuality and endings; you will need to master your tendency to tempestuous entanglements and learn that true freedom and fulfillment are the rewards of fidelity in love. Your magnetic allure drives your lovers wild.

Why you're impossible! Dark and secretive, you can be moody and dissemble rather than reveal your true vulnerability. You feel that everyone is out to get you or not being up front with you, but this may be a result of how you project yourself. If you were more open about yourself you would be protected and nurtured by those close to you, not thrown to the dogs as you fear.

Your secret side You can be flirtatious, wild, and generally a very outrageous Scorpio indeed. You can be ruled by fear and self-reproach and torn by internal conflict over who you should be in the world. You need to find balance in this area. You like to have a secret life that no one knows about except you. However, all this cloak-and-dagger stuff may not serve you well in the end. Try just creating space and being more open about your need for independence.

scorpio love compatibility chart

	aries	taurus	gemini	cancer	leo	virgo
fun		🍾		🍾		🍾
romance	❤	❤		❤	❤	❤
loyalty		🔗		🔗	🔗	🔗
adventure	🎈	🎈		🎈		🎈
kiss	👄	👄		👄	👄	👄
relax		🪑		🪑		🪑
ideas				💡		💡
friends		👥		👥		👥

	libra	scorpio	sagittarius	capricorn	aquarius	pisces
		🍾		🍾	🍾	🍾
	❤	❤	❤	❤	❤	❤
		⭕		⭕	⭕	⭕
	🎈	🎈	🎈	🎈	🎈	🎈
	👄	👄	👄	👄	👄	👄
		🪑		🪑	🪑	🪑
	💡				💡	💡
		👥		👥	👥	👥

 passion   **chilling out**   **spontaneity**   **attentiveness**

sagittarius

november 22–december 21

color silver ★ number 4, 13, 22 ★ stone amber—soaks up negativity and helps you deal with the past ★ flora salvia ★ animal parrot ★ occupation athlete, scientist, social reformer ★ key features eccentric, liberated, eager ★ naturally good at transcending boundaries

november 22

character ★ Even as a child you felt that you thought differently from other people. You were always one step ahead and perhaps rather grown up for your age. You may have an unusual talent for inventing things. You are bold and thoughtful and need lively and bright people to swap ideas with or you will get bogged down by life.

life path ★ You were born under a master number, 22, which gives you a bonus in the journey of life. If you put the effort in, you will be rewarded—life will shower you with gifts for your audacity. It is essential that you visualize how you want life to be and get excited about it. Those born under the number 22 are considered master builders, and you have the good fortune to be able to construct your own life. To what amount is entirely up to you.

love ★ It is important not to give into fear in this area. You can be swept away by love and because of this may become paranoid about giving your heart or yourself. Don't be suspicious when love greets you but instead welcome it with open arms and trust. Why not try an Aquarius, whose ruling planet is also your birth date ruler, Uranus?

best present ★ Book on Nostradamus, Internet account.

birthday share ★ 1932 Robert Vaughn, actor; 1943 Billie Jean King, tennis player; 1958 Jamie Lee Curtis, actress; 1967 Boris Becker, tennis player.

on this day ★ In 1963, President John F. Kennedy was shot and killed by an assassin in Dallas, Texas.

color flint gray ★ **number** 5, 14, 32 ★ **stone** peacock ore—to raise your optimism and increase your creativity ★ **flora** orchid ★ **animal** carrier pigeon ★ **occupation** writer, statesman/woman, artist ★ **key features** blunt, communicative, mercurial ★ **naturally good at** talking a blue streak

character ★ You are engaging, frisky, and fun to be around. You always have something to say on every subject, but remember that sometimes it is important to engage the brain before opening the mouth! You are not the most sensitive of creatures and can be incredibly blunt. Although this is refreshing and exciting most of the time, it can be offensive and hurtful to loved ones who get an ear bashing if they fall short of your expectations.

life path ★ Use that passionate desire to communicate constructively. You are a savage hunter of truth and could perhaps think about becoming a journalist or writing the odd article with your stimulating views. Life should be exciting and optimistic as long as you are being true to yourself.

love ★ You are very good at seduction but can be inclined to talk about it too much. An eager lover, you need a smart partner to spar with mentally before you get physical. Find a Gemini, whose ruling planet is also your birth date ruler, Mercury.

best present ★ Complete works of William Shakespeare, writing course.

birthday share ★ 1804 Franklin Pierce, 14th U.S. president; 1859 Billy the Kid, outlaw; 1887 Boris Karloff, actor; 1888 Harpo Marx, comedy actor.

on this day ★ In 1835, Henry Burden patented a machine for the production of horseshoes.

color pink ★ number 6, 33, 42 ★ stone red coral—for passion and motivation, this mineral heats you up and lights your fire ★ flora viola ★ animal cougar ★ occupation dating agency consultant, party organizer, toy designer ★ key features warm, spontaneous, loving ★ naturally good at playing cupid and arranging blind dates

november 24

character ★ Funny, bouncy, and loving, you have a lovely energy. People are drawn to you even though you are a social butterfly. You like to be part of the "in" crowd but are not in the least superficial. You love life and you love to love.

life path ★ Venus is your birth date ruler and this planet of love influences your life significantly. You may get involved in your friends' relationships as a counselor of sorts. You have a little intrigue in your own love life and affairs of the heart are constantly on your mind. You will have the opportunity to travel abroad to a country that feels like home. This may give you a choice of where to live out your grand passions.

love ★ You may find yourself drawn into love triangles or mysterious encounters. Keep your balance in this area. There is never a dull moment in your love life, unless you are one of the few who spend their time living love in your head. Love is out there for you and indeed has probably arrived. You have wonderful romantic adventures. Perhaps try a Libra or a Taurus, whose ruling planet is Venus, your birth date ruler.

best present ★ Country picnic, book of Lord Byron's poems.

birthday share ★ 1864 Henri de Toulouse-Lautrec, artist; 1937 Marlo Thomas, actress; 1940 Johnny Carver, country singer; 1942 Billy Connolly, comedian and actor.

on this day ★ In 1963, Lee Harvey Oswald, alleged assassin of President Kennedy, was shot dead by Jack Ruby in the parking garage of Dallas Police headquarters.

color sea green ★ number 7, 16, 43 ★ stone aquamarine—the stone that helps you speak your truth ★ flora waterlily ★ animal polar bear ★ occupation sailor, expedition leader, travel writer ★ key features deep, intense, adventurous ★ naturally good at taking a trip on the spur of the moment

character ★ You are more sensitive than most Sagittarians, loyal but changeable, and you try to be kind with your words. You think about emotions a lot, your own and other people's, and can get lost in fantasy if you are not careful. Although it may enable you to be the life and soul of the party, you should be careful of your liking for alcohol.

life path ★ You have a vivid imagination and unique dress sense. Other cultures fascinate you and you love to travel and explore the world as well as your own country. You prefer remote locations to tourist traps. Try not to get too caught up in overanalyzing your emotions, because you can be swept away and caught between reality and illusion.

love ★ You need a partner who is not frightened of traveling on the sea of love; you like it calm, you like it stormy, and most of all you like it deep. You merge with your loved one, at least for a while, and dive into their spirit. Things would go swimmingly with a Pisces, whose ruling planet is your birth date ruler, Neptune.

best present ★ Leather bound journal, trip to the seaside.

birthday share ★ 1914 Joe DiMaggio, baseball player; 1920 Ricardo Montalban, actor; 1960 Amy Grant, singer; 1971 Christina Applegate, actress.

on this day ★ In 1783, the last British troops left New York City at the end of the Revolutionary War.

november 26

character ★ Spirited but somewhat stern, you manage to find freedom in the conservative. You generally play by society's rules but sometimes bend them just a fraction. You appear to be a pillar of the community, but under that straight exterior lies a maverick streak that you keep hidden most of the time. You show flashes of genius in your life and have a knack for making business work with your innovative ideas.

life path ★ You are cautious but once in a while might feel compelled to take a risk— usually a huge risk. However crazy these risks may look to an outsider, you will have done your homework and they are carefully calculated. You may suddenly change your career or your home but it usually pays off big time. You love to listen to others and are fascinated by their lives and choices.

love ★ You need someone who can accept you as you are. You want a gorgeous, possibly younger, lover who looks up to you, and luckily this is what you tend to attract. You play the role of teacher or guru to your partners. Seek a Capricorn, whose ruling planet, Saturn, is your birth date ruler.

best present ★ Plaid bathrobe, walking boots.

birthday share ★ 1607 John Harvard, college founder; 1910 Cyril Cusack, actor; 1922 Charles M. Schulz, cartoonist; 1939 Tina Turner, singer.

on this day ★ In 1922, archaeologists Howard Carter and Lord Carnarvon became the first people to enter King Tutankhamen's tomb in Egypt since it was sealed more than 3,000 years before.

november 27

character ★ You are very tough, with a formidable physical presence. You are quick to anger, but also quick to forgive. You can get into trouble because of your temper, so calm down. You will defend those you love to the death and are fiercely protective of everyone you know. Loyalty is a big issue for you; when you give it, you will demand it in return.

life path ★ It is good for you to get fit and to burn off some of that overwhelming energy. You are a force to be reckoned with and exude physicality and vitality. You like male company best, whether you are male or female. Bold and captivating, with a host of admirers who worship you from afar, you love team games (as long as you're the captain), and they provide the perfect opportunity for your fans to cheer you on.

love ★ You seem to need physical contact as much as the air you breathe. Combined with love it is awesome. Brief flings tempt you but leave you feeling empty. Even so, you find temptation almost impossible to resist because you are so impulsive and ardent. An Aries, whose ruling planet, Mars, is your birth date ruler, would best satisfy your cravings.

best present ★ Football, mountain bike.

birthday share ★ 1701 Anders Celsius, astronomer and inventor; 1940 Bruce Lee, martial arts expert and actor; 1942 Jimi Hendrix, singer and guitarist; 1964 Robin Givens, model and actress.

on this day ★ In 1895, Alfred Nobel established the Nobel Prize.

color orange ★ number 1, 11, 22 ★ stone carnelian—used by the romans to bring good fortune ★ flora magic carpet ★ animal lion ★ occupation actor, nightclub owner, broadcaster ★ key features charismatic, daring, charming ★ naturally good at promoting yourself

november 28

character ★ You are unusual and attractive. You have a slightly different take on the world from most people and a humorous way of expressing your sometimes outrageous views. You never annoy people even if you totally contradict their views because you have such a charming and persuasive manner. People like to hang out with you.

life path ★ You're cool and fashionable even if you don't dress in the latest style. You have natural flair and allure and are invited to all the best parties and social engagements. You like to make others feel special, and even though you are gorgeous and sought after, you take care to pay attention to people who are usually ignored or derided, making them feel attractive.

love ★ You have plenty of opportunities for love but prefer to have relationships that leave you space. Lovers worship you and feel honored that you have chosen them. Never date anyone who thinks they are better than you—it will dent your self-esteem and disempower you. Look out for a Leo, whose ruling planet, the Sun, is also your birth date ruler.

best present ★ Gold ring, orange candle.

birthday share ★ 1757 William Blake, poet and artist; 1908 Claude Levi-Strauss, anthropologist; 1950 Ed Harris, actor; 1967 Anna Nicole Smith, model and actress.

on this day ★ In 1934, the U.S. bank robber George "Baby Face" Nelson was killed near Barrington, Illinois, by FBI agents.

color white ★ number 2, 11, 22 ★ stone moonstone—connects you to your natural rhythms ★ flora white poppy ★ animal white german shepherd ★ occupation nurse, midwife, psychic ★ key features intuitive, passionate, profound ★ naturally good at following your gut instinct

november 29

character ★ You have a need to reach out to other people emotionally, seeming to gain strength and self-esteem when you support others. This leads you into some interesting and treasured friendships. You connect naturally with people and share yourself openly.

life path ★ Adventurous and compassionate, you are skilled at balancing your own needs against the needs of those close to you. You live a life in which you enjoy personal freedom as well as responsibility. You don't like to be tied down to a routine and often change your schedule on an emotional whim. You may have an interest in developing your spirituality or studying philosophy.

love ★ Your heart is as wide as the ocean, and when you love, you love completely. You are very sensitive in relationships and can be easily offended and hurt if you feel you are not being taken into consideration. A Cancer, whose ruling planet, the Moon, is also your birth date ruler, would certainly float your boat!

best present ★ Crystal glasses, heart-shaped locket.

birthday share ★ 1832 Louisa May Alcott, author; 1898 C. S. Lewis, author; 1932 Diane Ladd, actress; 1954 Joel Coen, writer and director.

on this day ★ In 1907, Florence Nightingale, aged 87, was awarded the Order of Merit by King Edward VII of Britain.

color purple ★ number 3, 12, 21 ★ stone amethyst—the sobriety stone that bestows wisdom and increases intuition ★ flora nasturtium ★ animal monkey ★ occupation politician, statesman/woman, mountaineer ★ key features generous, outgoing, spontaneous ★ naturally good at daring acts of courage

november 30

character ★ No one could miss you in a crowd; you are bold, forthright, extravagant, and unrestrained. You may have a tendency to put on weight because of your love of overindulgence and luxurious living. This doesn't make you any less attractive, though. You are eccentric but can still communicate well with all those you meet.

life path ★ You have a calling to be different and to be accepted for your difference. You follow your own path and dance to your own tune on it, managing to make a statement without saying a word. People find you a catalyst for change or you give them the confidence just to be themselves. You love to explore people, places, and food. Make sure you rest sometimes.

love ★ You are attracted to lovers who are unusual or gifted. Partners from a different culture thrill you, and you can sit happily for hours trying to gather information about them and their personal history. You are a tactile lover who is eager and inventive. Perhaps try another Sagittarius, as your birth date ruler is the same as your ruling planet, expansive Jupiter.

best present ★ Antique map, backpack.

birthday share ★ 1667 Jonathan Swift, author and satirist; 1835 Mark Twain, author; 1874 Sir Winston Churchill, British prime minister; 1965 Ben Stiller, actor.

on this day ★ In 1995, Bill Clinton became the first U.S. president to visit Northern Ireland. He was greeted like a hero by Protestants and Roman Catholics alike and said: "The time has come for the peacemakers to triumph in Northern Ireland."

color orange ★ **number** 1, 11, 100 ★ **stone** gold—provides protection and inspiration ★ **flora** crocus ★ **animal** goat ★ **occupation** stand-up comic, talk show host, chef ★ **key features** hilarious, witty, outrageous ★ **naturally good at** making shocking statements

december 1

character ★ You spell trouble! You love attention and know how to captivate an audience. If you're not on the stage you should be. You have a wicked sense of humor, backed up with a loud and raucous laugh. You rarely show your vulnerability unless it is attached to a self-effacing joke.

life path ★ Born with an uncanny ability to lighten any situation, you bounce into people's lives and warm them with your blazing love. You have real generosity of spirit, and although you can be a demanding friend (you have some intense friendships), you give more than you take. You're a great cook and love foreign food.

love ★ Fun loving and uninhibited, you will come into your physical prime when you are older. When you are young you may feel a bit shy. However, you can still attract a mate later in life. Don't put yourself down—you are it! Why not run after a Leo, whose ruling planet, the Sun, is also your birth date ruler?

best present ★ DVD of a Woody Allen movie, microphone.

birthday share ★ 1935 Woody Allen, comedian, actor, and director; 1940 Richard Pryor, actor; 1945 Bette Midler, actress and singer; 1946 Gilbert O'Sullivan, singer.

on this day ★ In 1989, Mikhail Gorbachev became the first Soviet leader to visit the Vatican and meet the Pope. This meeting ended 72 years of Kremlin atheist ideology.

december 2

character ★ You find it hard to believe you're irreplaceable and talented but you are! You demand attention and can become very insecure when with those you love. This can lead to spontaneous, fiery arguments during which you say things you don't mean. However, once you have worked on your insecurity, life will seem a dream. You lavish gifts on those you love and will never leave a partner once you give your heart.

life path ★ Heart and mind are perpetually connected for you, and in fact your heart rules your head. You are magnificent at grand gestures and will travel to your lover wherever they are. You dress to impress and have expensive and sentimental tastes. Wild and free, you can be a bit of a handful, but this is all part of your charm. You love children but may want to have your own only later in life when you are ready to settle down and commit yourself fully to parenthood.

love ★ You have an innocent look about you but are actually full of mischief in love. You don't mean to be but you're an incorrigible flirt, leading people up the garden path while all the time remaining totally committed and loyal to your partner. Search for a Cancer, whose ruling planet is also your birth date ruler, the Moon.

best present ★ Diamond jewelry, tickets to an opera.

birthday share ★ 1923 Maria Callas, opera singer; 1946 Gianni Versace, fashion designer; 1973 Monica Seles, tennis player; 1981 Britney Spears, singer.

on this day ★ In 1901, King Camp Gillette introduced a safety razor with a double-edged disposable blade.

color purple ★ **number** 12, 21, 30 ★ **stone** topaz—lights your spirit ★ **flora** fig tree ★ **animal** pony ★ **occupation** pilot, dog handler, pr executive ★ **key features** energetic, lucky, magnanimous ★ **naturally good at** traveling to far-off lands

character ★ Philosophically minded, you ponder life's trivialities to find hidden nuggets of wisdom. You plan your future with optimism and often go from one wacky arrangement to another. You are good at sketching your ideas out to others and often get even the most cautious people to back you in your adventures.

life path ★ You are hardworking but have to do things your way. There is method in your madness and you get excellent results, much to the astonishment of your colleagues. You are hyperactive and may have disturbed sleep at night. Be careful you don't get run down with all that bounding about. Try not to eat on the go, and pay attention to your diet.

love ★ Expressive and zany, you make a lighthearted and ardent lover. Why not try another Sagittarius, as your birth date ruler is also your ruling planet—Jupiter?

best present ★ Apple tree, white wine.

birthday share ★ 1927 Andy Williams, singer; 1948 Ozzy Osbourne, singer; 1960 Daryl Hannah, actress; 1968 Brendan Fraser, actor.

on this day ★ In 1947, the Tennessee Williams play *A Streetcar Named Desire* made its Broadway debut.

december 4

character ★ Strong and argumentative, you need to explore your soft side more. You have a cast-iron will and will not be budged for any reason. Your home is your castle and you may have an obsession with keeping it safe and secure, installing elaborate locks or burglar alarms.

life path ★ Some people perceive you as dogmatic and authoritarian but you quite like this. You keep your guard up with those you don't know and are loath to part with your protective shield. You can be rather reclusive and spend hours alone in your private hideaway reading and plotting your path to future goals.

love ★ You enter into relationships with gusto but will ask someone for a date only if you are sure they like you. Once you find someone you really like, you pursue them, until you possess them completely. However, you still like to have your personal space and may choose to live on your own. An Aquarius, whose ruling planet, Uranus, is your birth date ruler, could complement you well.

best present ★ Silver pen, designer key ring.

birthday share ★ 1892 General Francisco Franco, dictator; 1949 Jeff Bridges, actor; 1964 Marisa Tomei, actress; 1973 Tyra Banks, model and actress.

on this day ★ In 1918, President Woodrow Wilson sailed for Versailles, France, for the World War I peace talks. He was the first U.S. president to travel abroad while in office.

color turquoise ★ **number** 14, 23, 32 ★ **stone** peacock ore—to awaken your creativity and optimism ★ **flora** marjoram ★ **animal** alligator ★ **occupation** journalist, radio dj, dancer ★ **key features** intellectual, rash, assertive ★ **naturally good at** telling the bare truth

december 5

character ★ You have an agile mind and express your views clearly and eagerly. You can be frank, even a little too direct, sometimes. You love to banter and argue, and words are food and drink to you. You believe in brutal honesty at all times and will haul someone over the coals if they have the nerve to tell you even the minutest white lie.

life path ★ You venture forth, treading on many toes as you scour the horizon for new battles to be won. You are never content with your position in life and strive to get on. One of the reasons why you may not have achieved all you desire is your unwillingness to be controlled or to obey superiors. You are wild and free and will make it under your own terms.

love ★ You like security but love to argue and bicker with your partner, seeing this as just a bit of fun that whets your appetite for the making up. Your partners may see this differently and feel stressed out by your confrontational manner, however gentle. Why not try a Gemini, whose ruling planet is Mercury, your birth date ruler?

best present ★ Board game, complete works of Charles Dickens.

birthday share ★ 1839 George Armstrong Custer, cavalry commander; 1901 Walt Disney, cartoonist; 1906 Otto Preminger, director; 1932 Little Richard (Richard Wayne Penniman), singer.

on this day ★ In 1933, Prohibition in the United States was repealed after 14 years.

color pink ★ **number** 24, 33, 60 ★ **stone** rose-quartz—the stone of unconditional love to soothe your heart ★ **flora** geranium ★ **animal** mouse ★ **occupation** promoter, nurse, pr consultant ★ **key features** sexy, eccentric, amusing ★ **naturally good at** having unusual partners

december 6

character ★ You have a warm glow about you and an irrepressible wit, seeing the funny side of even the most serious subjects. You are quick to point out your own failings; this self-deprecation wins you many good friends and an abundance of acquaintances who are all highly amused by you. You always seem to get the girl or boy you go for, even if it is an unlikely match.

life path ★ You want to lead a worthy life in which you help others, learn, and generally grow in spirit; however, you are all too prone to get lost in the moment and never seem to find time for your loftier ideals. Once you discipline yourself to do at least one of these things each week you will feel better about yourself.

love ★ You tend to leap in and out of love with extreme fervor. Passion grips you and in you plunge at the deep end—without any oxygen. You usually come out unscathed but find it difficult to give your commitment for longer than four years. Search for a Libra or a Taurus, whose ruling planet is Venus, planet of love and your birth date ruler.

best present ★ Tape of positive affirmations, ice-skating lesson.

birthday share ★ 1896 Ira Gershwin, musician and lyricist; 1920 Dave Brubeck, musician; 1932 Don King, boxing entrepreneur; 1948 JoBeth Williams, actress.

on this day ★ In 1921, Ireland's 26 southern states were granted independence from Britain, becoming the Irish Free State.

color azure ★ number 16, 34, 70 ★ stone lapis lazuli—sacred to the ancient egyptians, this stone represents the heavens and bestows clarity and wisdom ★ flora curry plant ★ animal meerkat ★ occupation singer, jockey, cowboy/girl ★ key features spiritual, scatterbrained, unstable ★ naturally good at daydreaming for hours

december 7

character ★ You are determined to find meaning in your life. You sense that there is a special purpose for you but seem unable to pin it down. You're a dreamer and talk more than you act. People may dismiss you because your plans never seem to come to fruition, but you are likely to surprise them one day when, out of the blue, everything falls into place.

life path ★ You are fascinated by philosophy and spirituality and swing from feeling that you are on your path and connected to your higher power to feeling lost and abandoned. This is partly because you are so deep that you get lost in your own ideas; meditation will help you. You are also very magical and need to find like-minded magicians with whom to explore the supernatural.

love ★ You dream of finding your soul mate. You may have touched true love but it still feels like an elusive concept. You have had intimacy, physical bliss, and healthy relationships but you are seeking romantic nirvana. Float your way there with a Pisces, as their ruling planet, Neptune, is also your birth date ruler.

best present ★ Shell necklace, tarot cards.

birthday share ★ 1926 Victor Kiam, businessman and former chairman of Remington; 1928 Noam Chomsky, linguist; 1932 Ellen Burstyn, actress; 1949 Tom Waits, singer and actor.

on this day ★ In 1941, the Japanese launched a surprise attack on Pearl Harbor, Hawaii, dealing fatal blows to two battleships hundreds of U.S. sailors.

color maroon ★ **number** 8, 26, 44 ★ **stone** calcite—to teach you compassion ★
flora lupine ★ **animal** giraffe ★ **occupation** police sergeant, revolutionary, songwriter ★
key features strong-minded, extreme, commanding ★ **naturally good at** backing
controversial views

december 8

character ★ You're a warrior of sorts. Belligerent, outspoken, and charismatic, you are prepared to speak the unspeakable and are not afraid of controversy. What you believe in, you will fight for with your life. You have such strong convictions that you often sail close to the wind and could end up in trouble.

life path ★ You are here to shake people up and make them confront reality. You cannot stand people who bury their head in the sand. Tread a little more gently and you may get your message across to more people. You like to cause mayhem and can go over the top when you let your hair down.

love ★ You have tempestuous relationships with people who hold opposing views. Watch out that you are not feeding off arguments and disharmony. You love to be caught up in an all-consuming passion and rarely resist, as your view is that everything should be tried once. Why not find yourself a Capricorn, whose ruling planet is Saturn, your birth date ruler?

best present ★ Meditation tape, camping trip.

birthday share ★ 1943 Jim Morrison, singer; 1953 Kim Basinger, actress; 1964 Teri Hatcher, actress; 1966 Sinead O'Connor, singer.

on this day ★ In 1980, musical icon John Lennon was shot and killed in New York City. He was 40 years old.

color red ★ **number** 36, 45, 90 ★ **stone** ruby—held sacred by the ancient hindus, this gem will stoke your excitement ★ **flora** poppy ★ **animal** leopard ★ **occupation** actor, dj, soldier ★ **key features** powerful, fervent, intense ★ **naturally good at** exploring your psyche

character ★ You are impulsive and broad-minded. Life is for living and you want to pack in as many good times as you can. You have an air of mystery about you but actually you are quite straightforward. You have few close friends, but those you have you would die for. Many people hang out with you but you don't let them into your inner circle.

life path ★ You have dramatic allure and may have dreamed of being a movie star. Seriously consider those acting lessons because you have what it takes. You have a close relationship with your mother but probably live in a different city or country, as you have a wanderer's spirit.

love ★ You're an incurable romantic and are brimming with passion. You love to challenge your partner, and push them to the limit, physically, mentally and spiritually. Try a little softness or things could get out

of hand. An Aries whose ruling planet is your birth date ruler, fiery Mars, could have a passion that matches yours.

best present ★ Whiskey, massage oil.

birthday share ★ 1608 John Milton, poet; 1886 Clarence Birdseye, pioneer of frozen food; 1916 Kirk Douglas, actor; 1957 Donny Osmond, singer.

on this day ★ In 1992, Prince Charles, Prince of Wales, and Princess Diana announced plans to separate.

december 10

character ★ You have the drive to succeed where others fail. You are so keen to make it that it is infectious. If a problem or stumbling block occurs you don't hesitate to see it as an opportunity rather than a hazard. You put a positive spin on all situations and this encourages good fortune to find you.

life path ★ It is essential that you don't let others quell this excellent optimistic streak. If you succumb to other people's cynicism you will wither and become a shadow of your true self. Those negative types are drawn to you because they gave up a long time ago. Be the perky, positive person you are and you will be rewarded big time.

love ★ You can end up falling in love with someone who lives miles away, but you're so special that they could eventually move to be with you. Always love freely but never give away your power and do keep space for yourself. In time a magnificent love affair will bring you a true marriage of hearts, minds, and souls. It's likely to be with a Leo, whose ruling planet, the Sun, is also your birth date ruler.

best present ★ Statue of Aphrodite, trip to a natural history museum.

birthday share ★ 1830 Emily Dickinson, poet; 1908 Olivier Messiaen, composer; 1952 Susan Dey, actress; 1960 Kenneth Branagh, actor, director, and producer.

on this day ★ In 1903, Marie Curie became the first woman to receive a Nobel Prize along with Pierre Curie and Henri Becquerel for research on the phenomena of radiation.

color white ★ **number** 2, 11, 20 ★ **stone** clear quartz—the magic wand of crystals, it will attract what you desire ★ **flora** yew tree ★ **animal** owl ★ **occupation** teacher, trainer, defense lawyer ★ **key features** fair, sympathetic, compassionate ★ **naturally good at** weighing evidence

character ★ You are emotional and versatile and generally think of others' good before your own. You have a strong sense of justice and fairness and fight for the rights of other people as well as for yourself. Even as a child you were outspoken and supportive and had an old head on young shoulders.

life path ★ All those born on this day should have a fascinating life. You cannot ignore your own rules and sense of morality, and this seems to have speeded up your karma—what you give out returns to you tenfold. The king and queen of numerology, 11 and 22, are master numbers, and are said to bestow upon you extra magic. They bless you with the gift of awareness, so you should never lie to yourself.

love ★ You love earnestly and deeply. You are nurturing and caring of those you love, and you try to find an equal balance between your needs and theirs. You particularly like to go on vacation with your lover, which brings out the best in you. Why not try a Cancer, whose ruling planet is the Moon, your birth date ruler?

best present ★ Midnight swim in the ocean, vase.

birthday share ★ 1931 Rita Moreno, actress; 1942 Donna Mills, actress; 1944 Brenda Lee, singer; 1954 Jermaine Jackson, singer.

on this day ★ In 1936, King Edward VIII abdicated the throne of Great Britain to marry U.S. divorcee Wallis Simpson.

color lilac ★ **number** 12, 21, 30 ★ **stone** marble—to calm you down and cool you ★ **flora** violet ★ **animal** bald eagle ★ **occupation** judge, pilot, travel agent ★ **key features** energetic, lively, generous ★ **naturally good at** being objective when necessary

december 12

character ★ Enthusiastic and bubbly, you throw yourself into life. You are easily bored so you like to take on new challenges; you thrive on them and are not one to give in. Others may see you as slightly neurotic because you have so much energy, but you love having people around you. You are especially drawn to the study of history and geography.

life path ★ If you don't take up some form of exercise you will find you put on weight easily. Your body fluctuates, depending on your frame of mind. Physical activity will prove a form of meditation to you, so get going! You're a deep thinker and are rarely superficial.

love ★ You have a huge capacity to love and as long as you are not confined will offer all of yourself. You don't like being told what to do in a relationship and will not be controlled. You need to find another freedom-loving individual who will join you in the waltz of life. Why not go for another Sagittarius, as your ruling planet and your birth date ruler are both Jupiter?

best present ★ Sneakers, baseball cap.

birthday share ★ 1821 Gustave Flaubert, author; 1863 Edvard Munch, artist; 1915 Frank Sinatra, singer and actor; 1940 Dionne Warwick, singer.

on this day ★ In 1800, Washington, D.C., was established as the capital of the United States.

december 13

character ★ Slightly strange and unpredictable, you have a zany streak that others may fail to understand. You need the freedom to follow your own path and can become very drained if you have to live a 9-to-5 existence. You are talented musically and may be fascinated by astronomy or astrology.

life path ★ You may often have the sense that in some way you are the odd one out or don't fit in. This sense of alienation needs to be turned on its head. Perhaps it is you who have rejected others, not the other way around. Not everyone is judgmental, and many people would love you for your unique take on life. Let the love in!

love ★ Your love life has been sporadic and unconventional. You need someone to bounce ideas off and someone who challenges you. There have been many sudden endings in your love life but also sudden beginnings, so take heart—you will find what you are looking for. It could well be an Aquarius, whose ruling planet is Uranus, your birth date ruler.

best present ★ Telescope, star named after you.

birthday share ★ 1818 Mary Todd Lincoln, former U.S. first lady; 1925 Dick Van Dyke, actor; 1927 Christopher Plummer, actor; 1957 Steve Buscemi, actor.

on this day ★ In 1918, President Woodrow Wilson arrived in France, becoming the first U.S. president to visit Europe while in office.

december 14

character ★ Lively and sociable, you have a good rapport with people at work. You have a forceful personality and hate to be misunderstood. You express exactly what you are feeling so some people think you are moody. You may be reclusive occasionally when life gets on top of you, but interaction with others is essential for your growth.

life path ★ You have a talent for communication and love to listen to the radio. You're hungry to learn and gobble up books, usually in one sitting. There are so many subjects you're interested in, but maybe if you focused on one or two you would achieve more. Learn to listen as well as talk—your ideas come tumbling out and other people can't get a word in edgewise.

love ★ You need a lover who is intellectual and unusual. You're easily bored and need to be mentally, as well as physically, stimulated. You're affectionate and devoted once you get to know someone and like to send playful e-mails or text messages. Why not choose a Gemini, whose ruling planet, Mercury, is also your birth date ruler?

best present ★ Notebook, fountain pen.

birthday share ★ 1503 Nostradamus, astrologer; 1932 Charlie Rich, singer; 1935 Lee Remick, actress; 1946 Stan Smith, tennis player.

on this day ★ In 1911, the Norwegian explorer Roald Amundsen became the first man to reach the South Pole.

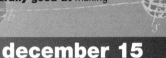

color pink ★ **number** 6, 24, 33 ★ **stone** rose-quartz—emits universal love and soothes your heart ★ **flora** red rose ★ **animal** grizzly bear ★ **occupation** bar manager, beautician, television host ★ **key features** affable, gregarious, likable ★ **naturally good at** making others feel comfortable

december 15

character ★ Seductive and a little extreme, you certainly like the good things in life. You are a born flirt with a tangible charisma that attracts both men and women. You enjoy living life to excess, particularly when it comes to loving and partying. You have great natural rhythm and know how to strut your stuff.

life path ★ One of your lessons in life is learning how to balance that hedonistic personality. Life is for living, but you will burn out if you burn the candle at both ends over a long period. There is something of the Peter Pan about you. You have no intention of ever growing up and tend to dress in the latest styles with a splash of unique jewelry for good measure.

love ★ So many choices, so little time. Lovers are plentiful and you can cast them aside like last year's fashion accessory. You sometimes play the needy, vulnerable child in a relationship but this past pattern does not serve you anymore. Create a new pattern with a Libra or a Taurus, as their ruling planet, Venus, is also your birth date ruler.

best present ★ Antique 1920s jewelry, ornate glass bowl.

birthday share ★ A.D. 37 Nero, Roman emperor; 1832 Alexandre Gustave Eiffel, engineer; 1892 J. Paul Getty, petroleum magnate; 1949 Don Johnson, actor.

on this day ★ In 1961, Adolf Eichmann, a fanatical Nazi and SS colonel in World War II, was sentenced to death in Jerusalem for organizing the deportation of Jews to concentration camps.

color blue ★ **number** 7, 25, 34 ★ **stone** sapphire—the ancient persians believed the earth lay on a giant sapphire and its reflection colored the sky, bringing clarity and truth ★ **flora** jasmine ★ **animal** conger eel ★ **occupation** set designer, writer, composer ★ **key features** dreamy, intriguing, idealistic ★ **naturally good at** mixing cocktails

december 16

character ★ You live in a world of your own and need to take a reality check sometimes. You are so imaginative that you may become confused by your own creative thinking. You want the world to be a certain way so you choose to see it that way.

life path ★ You tend to get yourself into tight spots. You are drawn to danger and can abandon common sense—if you want to do something you do it and that's that. You are brave and spiritual but can lack practical skills. You need a career in which you are able to use that ethereal and sensitive mind.

love ★ You have a poetic spirit and long for a passionate affair with someone you can adore, but you sometimes dive into love without thinking. You assume you are a good judge of character because you are intuitive, yet in fact you look so deep within

that you see the other person's soul and miss the outer complexities; however pure someone's soul, the layers on top could still cause you problems. Don't seek out a partner to save, as a relationship built on that foundation will be doomed. A Pisces, whose ruling planet, Neptune, is your birth date ruler, would be a wise choice.

best present ★ Fishing net, piano.

birthday share ★ 1485 Catherine of Aragon, first wife of King Henry VIII of England; 1775 Jane Austen, author; 1899 Sir Noel Coward, playwright, actor, producer, and director; 1946 Benny Andersson, singer.

on this day ★ In 1773, the Boston Tea Party took place when the *Sons of Liberty* dumped its cargo of tea into the sea.

color maroon ★ **number** 8, 35, 44 ★ **stone** obsidian—helps you integrate your shadow side ★ **flora** nicotiana ★ **animal** pheasant ★ **occupation** banker, historian, cartoonist ★ **key features** creative, conservative, strong-willed ★ **naturally good at** following an ordnance survey map

character ★ Powerful and creative, you have the presence and ability to take charge. You have a magnanimous nature and are very generous to those you love. You tend to test people before you give them your trust and are usually right in your first opinion of people. You have the heart of a lion and the kindness of a pussycat—unless someone winds you up.

life path ★ You are a motivator and love to rally the troops at work. You despise laziness and have a habit of telling people exactly what you think of them. Try to be a little more careful in how you express yourself; constructive criticism is fine but character assassination is not good for you or your targets.

love ★ You are drawn to committed, long-term relationships after the age of 30, but you have a roving eye and need to look at what it is that your heart really wants. Why not focus on a Capricorn, whose ruling planet, Saturn, is also your birth date ruler?

best present ★ Spy novel, watercolors.

birthday share ★ 1770 Ludwig van Beethoven, composer; 1778 Sir Humphry Davy, chemist and inventor; 1807 John Greenleaf Whittier, poet; 1975 Milla Jovovich, model and actress.

on this day ★ In 1903, Wilbur and Orville Wright made the first successful controlled flight in a powered aircraft, the *Wright Flyer*, on the beach at Kitty Hawk, North Carolina.

color red ★ number 9, 36, 90 ★ stone ruby—increases your passion for life ★ flora radish ★ animal bull ★ occupation basketball player, filmmaker, pilot ★ key features assertive, dedicated, commanding ★ naturally good at turning fantasy into reality

december 18

character ★ You have a gift for turning your ideas into practical reality. Once you feel passionately about a scheme or task you give it 100 percent dedication. You should have a clear idea about where you want to get in life but you also appreciate that the journey is the destination. You are an inventive genius and will succeed at most things.

life path ★ Your personality is sturdy and you are unwavering in your enthusiasm for life. You can be serious and pensive if you have a problem to resolve, but basically you're an optimist and believe that life will lead you in the right direction. You have more energy than most people and are great at sports and outdoor pursuits.

love ★ Naturally demonstrative, you find loving as natural as eating or breathing. You have an earthy approach and need daily affection to be truly happy. Some of your partners may struggle to keep up with you.

Whether you are male or female you like to take the lead in a relationship but always strive to please your lover before yourself. Go catch an Aries, whose ruling planet, Mars, is your birth date ruler.

best present ★ Pair of boxing gloves, surfboard.

birthday share ★ 1946 Steven Spielberg, director; 1955 Ray Liotta, actor; 1963 Brad Pitt, actor; 1980 Christina Aguilera, singer.

on this day ★ In 1865, slavery was abolished in the United States by the 13th Amendment.

color orange ★ **number** 1, 10, 11 ★ **stone** red jasper—helps you make decisions ★ **flora** cornflower ★ **animal** horse ★ **occupation** singer, performer, airline steward/ stewardess ★ **key features** spontaneous, impulsive, freedom loving ★ **naturally good at** drawing attention to yourself

december 19

character ★ Your foxy nature does not go unnoticed. You have a dazzling smile and a glint in your eyes. Your compelling and captivating manner makes you the focus of interest in a crowd. You love to have a good time and hate early mornings because you're more of a night owl. You have strong female friendships and see your friends as family.

life path ★ Your optimistic and sunny personality tends to encourage good things to come your way, and you are usually a lucky person. You love to be in the moment and don't plan ahead enough. You have confidence and an assured nature, but you can be affected by other people's reactions to you and take it very personally if someone does not like you.

love ★ You love to be in love, and you attract lovers easily. You need someone who enjoys your larger-than-life personality but is strong enough to deal with you, or you can

prove a bit of a loose cannon and a big flirt. Why not look out for a Leo, whose ruling planet is the Sun, your birth date ruler?

best present ★ Expensive scent, silk underwear.

birthday share ★ 1820 Mary Ashton Rice Livermore, women's rights activist, suffragist, author; 1906 Leonid Brezhnev, former Soviet leader; 1915 Edith Piaf, singer; 1972 Alyssa Milano, actress.

on this day ★ In 1941, Adolf Hitler took over as commander-in-chief of the German Army after sacking Field Marshal von Brauchitsch.

december 20

character ★ Perceptive and responsive, you have the ability to heal others in crisis. You're a natural shoulder for troubled souls to cry on. You may have found having such insight hard in your childhood; no one, including your parents, could pull the wool over your eyes. You are honest to a fault and have a genuine love of humanity.

life path ★ You can get caught up in other people's lives and need to be a little more selfish sometimes. You have a mystical, indefinable quality that can make some lesser mortals uncomfortable. You are able to make people think on a deeper level and stir up their unconscious. You have vivid dreams and should keep a dream journal to record them in because they can be prophetic.

love ★ This is the one area in which you can be insecure or even give your power away. You need to work on this and then you will be fulfilled beyond your expectations. You have so much to offer a partner that they will be overwhelmed by your generous heart. A Cancer, whose ruling planet, the Moon, is your birth date ruler would be a perfect match.

best present ★ Candlestick holder, Buddha figurine.

birthday share ★ 1868 Harvey Firestone, founder, Firestone Tire and Rubber Company; 1911 Hortense Calisher, author; 1946 Uri Geller, psychic and illusionist; 1956 Blanche Baker, actress.

on this day ★ In 1860, South Carolina became the first state to secede from the American Union. It was not re-admitted until 1868.

color purple ★ **number** 3, 12, 30 ★ **stone** amethyst—sometimes known as the sobriety stone, this gem will heighten your intuition ★ **flora** cherry blossom ★ **animal** tiger ★ **occupation** drummer, astronaut, politician ★ **key features** wild, fun, full of life ★ **naturally good at** doing things your way

character ★ You're a nonconformist who seeks to sculpt a unique life. You can be hedonistic and overindulgent but you are also not one to shy away from work. You might have a passion for politics or music but, whatever area your unconquerable spirit is drawn to, you go for it. Public recognition may come your way.

life path ★ You may be thirsty for recognition, but not at any cost. You would never sell yourself out, and consequently it may take you longer to succeed than you would like, but you will find lasting success in the end. As you have Jupiter, planet of good fortune, as your ruling planet and also your birth date ruler, you will have unexpected windfalls just when you need them.

love ★ You're attractive, if a little unsettling as a lover. You whiz around and like to do your own thing. You won't allow others to dictate the rules of engagement in your relationships, and if they don't like what you have to offer, you move on. Compromise is essential in all relationships, so work on it! You may like to try another Sagittarius, who is also ruled by Jupiter.

best present ★ Horseback-riding lessons, tickets to a rock concert.

birthday share ★ 1879 Joseph Stalin, Soviet dictator; 1937 Jane Fonda, actress; 1940 Frank Zappa, musician and singer; 1966 Kiefer Sutherland, actor.

on this day ★ In 1913, the first crossword puzzle, compiled by Liverpool-born Arthur Wynne, was published in the weekend edition of the *New York World*.

sagittarius

your ruling planet Your ruler is the wonderfully optimistic and stunningly lucky **jupiter**, planet of expansion and good fortune. This benevolent ruler is protective of you and allows you to be impulsive and spontaneous. Should you have the misfortune to lose out from your rash actions, lovely Jupiter will shove some other good fortune your way, as if to compensate for your bravery of spirit. Jupiter is a huge planet (nearly twice the size of all the other planets combined and 318 times bigger than Earth), which is one of the reasons why it is seen as the planet of expansion, and your character has this quality. Jupiter is 90 percent hydrogen, which no doubt gives you your volatility. In many ways it is the best planet to have as a ruler because it makes you so lucky and gives you the ability always to push yourself beyond your boundaries. Your personality and strength can eclipse those of other people, but usually in a beneficial manner. You are never limited or repressed and this makes you the wondrous and unusual creature that you are.

your natural habitat

Your idea of a dream home is somewhere with exotic, vibrant colors, filled with treasures and paintings brought back from your travels. If you haven't yet traveled much you will still have representations of other cultures in your home. You like it to be painted in rich, deep colors and need it to feel alive. You may have lots of plants or natural ornaments like driftwood, shells, or crystals. You have a deep respect for and love of the natural world. You are probably slightly unconventional and your home is unique. Your bedroom is romantic but you probably leave your bed unmade when you get up. You are a little untidy but your home pulsates with energy. Smell is very important to you, so you like to have essential oils or incense burning or spray your favorite fragrance about to give your rooms an uplifting ambience. You may take a long time to buy a property because you love traveling so much and don't like to be too tied down. You are the most likely sign to live abroad and ultimately to settle in a country other than the one in which you were born.

are you a typical sagittarius?

Wild and loving freedom, you are the more intellectual of the fire signs. You like to study philosophy and are fascinated by life and different cultures. You want to explore the world and everything in it. You are extremely broad-minded and believe we are all equal and have the right to express ourselves whatever our origins or status. You are unusually fit and love to work out or do physical things.

Why you're wonderful! You allow others to be themselves and encourage people to express their true essence. You are generally nonjudgmental and fun to be with. Expansive, affectionate, and a fine lover, you have more staying power and energy for relationships than people of most other signs. You are also adventurous and generous and will not give up until you satisfy your partner. You like the finer things in life but are not materialistic.

Why you're impossible! You can be changeable and irrational, leaping from mood to mood. You might go to bed happy and fulfilled but then wake up like a bear with a sore head. You are liable to take quite innocent comments or gestures personally, which leaves your partner or loved ones scratching their heads trying to figure you out. When you lose your cool you are like an erupting volcano, very fierce and loud.

Your secret side You're so much more vulnerable than you appear to be. You feel things deeply and can often jump to the wrong conclusions or become a little paranoid. If in doubt, *ask*, don't assume! You have a spiritual edge, and it would benefit you to discover more about this side of yourself. You are very good at writing and pondering and may have amassed pages of poetry or philosophical observations that you have never had the courage to share.

sagittarius love compatibility chart

	aries	taurus	gemini	cancer	leo	virgo	
	fun	fun	fun	fun	fun	fun	
	romance		romance		romance	romance	
						loyalty	
	adventure	adventure	adventure	adventure	adventure	adventure	
	kiss		kiss		kiss	kiss	
	relax	relax	relax		relax	relax	
	idea		idea	idea	idea	idea	
					dinner	dinner	

love compatibility chart **sagittarius**

	libra	scorpio	sagittarius	capricorn	aquarius	pisces
passion	✓	✓	✓	✓	✓	
chilling out	✓		✓		✓	✓
spontaneity	✓		✓		✓	✓

 passion chilling out spontaneity attentiveness

capricorn

december 22–january 20

color silver ★ number 4, 13, 22 ★ stone malachite—helps you deal with your fears ★ flora hellebore ★ animal goat ★ occupation astronaut, scientist, architect ★ key features cautious, ingenious, secure ★ naturally good at inventing new gadgets

december 22

character ★ Settled, secure, but a little zany, you have a brilliant and unusual mind. You like to think of new ways to resolve old problems and have a lateral way of thinking. You give your career and family total commitment, but you find it difficult to get in touch with your emotions and tend to intellectualize your feelings.

life path ★ You have an active mind and rarely stop thinking, which can make you appear serious and sometimes grumpy. Lighten up, learn to play, and take some time out to focus on your feelings rather than your thoughts. Balance the two sides of your personality and you will find the inner peace you sometimes lack.

love ★ You are a traditionalist when it comes to love and require commitment and security from your partner. You also tend to be the boss. Sometimes you withdraw and stop sharing, but when you go into this hermit mode it is essential that you tell your partner not to take it personally, as they can find it torture and wonder what is in your head. Why not try an Aquarius, whose ruling planet is also your birth date ruler, Uranus?

best present ★ Body paint, jewelry.

birthday share ★ 1858 Giacomo Puccini, composer; 1949 Robin and Morris Gibb, musicians; 1962 Ralph Fiennes, actor; 1974 Heather Donahue, actress.

on this day ★ In 1990, Lech Walesa was sworn in as Poland's first democratically elected president.

color green ★ **number** 5, 14, 50 ★ **stone** marcasite—helps you evolve as a person ★ **flora** fern ★ **animal** adder ★ **occupation** researcher, journalist, banker ★ **key features** hardworking, academic, serious ★ **naturally good at** writing business proposals

december 23

character ★ Studious and conscientious, you tend to put a lot of your time and effort into your career as well as personal interests that involve some element of reading or writing. You are skillful in all things literary and value the mind above everything. You would benefit from a bit of exercise and focusing on your body a little more.

life path ★ You can get caught in a routine that makes you feel comfortable but is ultimately limiting. You do not like change unless it is a step up the ladder that you had planned and worked for. You love to get away from it all, but you rarely have time for the more whimsical side of your personality.

love ★ You tend to be very serious and quite shy at the start of relationships, but once you know where you stand you find it easy to talk and flirt. However, taking things a step further can create deep anxiety. When you do find the right partner you are stable and devoted. Try a Gemini, whose ruling planet, Mercury, is also your birth date ruler.

best present ★ Tape recorder, sketch pad.

birthday share ★ 1870 John Marin, artist; 1933 Akihito, emperor of Japan; 1964 Eddie Vedder, musician; 1971 Corey Haim, actor.

on this day ★ In 1986, the experimental *Voyager* airplane completed the first nonstop flight around the world without refueling.

december 24

character ★ Self-protective and proud, you find that a lot of your life revolves around your personal relationships. However, you don't demonstrate any preoccupation with your love life, hiding behind a façade of control so that only those who have known you for many years are privileged enough to catch glimpses of your vulnerability.

life path ★ Your karma and life path are connected to your love relationships with family as well as lovers. It is seemingly impossible for you to have a lighthearted romance. This is because you have shared other "past lives" with many of the people you meet; these were often tempestuous and there is some deep healing to be done. The plus side is your feeling that you have known them always.

love ★ For you love is a battleground that you don't quite understand. You have a huge capacity to give love but you are blocked on some level. Do not give in—keep going. Love is your destiny. Look for a Libra, whose ruling planet, Venus, is also your birth date ruler.

best present ★ Day at a carnival, candy.

birthday share ★ 1809 Kit Carson, frontiersman; 1905 Howard Hughes, tycoon and producer; 1922 Ava Gardner, actress; 1971 Ricky Martin, singer.

on this day ★ In 1871, Giuseppe Verdi's opera *Aida* premiered in Egypt at the opening of the Suez Canal.

color indigo ★ **number** 7, 34, 70 ★ **stone** sodalite—grounds you and gives you a sense of security ★ **flora** poinsettia ★ **animal** donkey ★ **occupation** healer, church minister, philosopher ★ **key features** otherworldly, mysterious, intense ★ **naturally good at** entering into secrets

december 25

character ★ You're rather a mysterious creature. You seem very down to earth and practical in some ways yet beneath that sensible exterior lies the heart of a spiritual warrior. You're deep, dreamy, and intense. Your mind travels to unknown depths and you tend to live in a fantasy world, but don't worry—no one else would ever guess.

life path ★ You need to balance the practical with the magical, the serious with the sensuous, and the deep with the light and fluffy. These are hard tasks, particularly as you do not like to reveal your true nature. Open up, free yourself, and life should be much more real and fun. Find a balance between all your conflicting elements rather than expressing different aspects to different people or you will start to fear that you don't know your true identity.

love ★ You have strong fantasies and longings but can see this as a weakness. Indulge a little in your desires and explore your physicality with an open heart. Plan romantic nights in with scented candles, mood music, and a meal for two. Why not try a Pisces lover, whose ruling planet, Neptune, is also your birth date ruler?

best present ★ Shower gel, bed linen.

birthday share ★ 1642 Sir Isaac Newton, scientist; 1887 Conrad Hilton, hotelier; 1899 Humphrey Bogart, actor; 1954 Annie Lennox, singer.

on this day ★ In 1926, Hirohito became the emperor of Japan after the death of his father Emperor Yoshihito.

color burgundy ★ **number** 8, 35, 44 ★ **stone** tiger's eye—for psychic protection and mental stimulation ★ **flora** holly ★ **animal** tarantula ★ **occupation** spy, cabdriver, charity worker ★ **key features** powerful, dogmatic, hard-headed ★ **naturally good at** laying down the law

december 26

character ★ You spend a lot of time feeling stressed out and uptight because you take on too many obligations and spend far too much time under pressure. Take some time out—yes, you can! You need to realize that you are not the only person who can do a job and that you can have the down time you so desperately need.

life path ★ Let's be blunt—you can be a bit of a control freak. You like everything done your way and you can be very judgmental. This is bad news for loved ones because they genuinely care for you but you can make their lives impossible with your demands. Chill out and learn that we all have the right to personal freedom and that all our choices are valid.

love ★ Allow your partner off the leash more and you will be pleasantly surprised. Loved ones are not your property. The more freedom you give your partner, the more true love will be returned. You are strong and loving and you should allow yourself to receive love as well. You would suit another Capricorn, as your birth date ruler is the same as your ruling planet, Saturn.

best present ★ Binoculars, romantic meal.

birthday share ★ 1791 Charles Babbage, inventor; 1891 Henry Miller, author; 1893 Mao Tse-tung, Chinese leader; 1940 Phil Spector, songwriter and record producer.

on this day ★ In 1620, the Pilgrim Fathers, passengers on the *Mayflower*, landed at New Plymouth, Massachusetts, to found the Plymouth Colony.

color red ★ number 9, 45, 90 ★ stone fire opal—brings passion into your life ★ flora african daisy ★ animal boxer dog ★ occupation athlete, entrepreneur, paramedic ★ key features vigorous, faithful, dogmatic ★ naturally good at never giving in until you succeed

character ★ You are sturdy and powerful and have a rather rugged persona, but you have a heart of gold, and although you can be stubborn and pig-headed you are a giver, not a taker. You are also quite a hero and are always going to someone's aid.

life path ★ You need to make sure that you move around enough because your birthday ruler is vigorous Mars. This makes you crave action and excitement, but your ruling planet, Saturn, is much more conservative so you feel pulled in two directions. Why not just leap in and go with the flow? Caution doesn't suit you.

love ★ You are an extremely passionate person, but you can sometimes be a bit lazy. You need to learn the tender art of love. It's important to take your time and enjoy the moment. Search for an Aries who also likes to get physical, as they, too, are ruled by energetic Mars.

best present ★ Boots, cowboy hat.

birthday share ★ 1571 Johannes Kepler, astronomer; 1822 Louis Pasteur, scientist; 1901 Marlene Dietrich, singer and actress; 1948 Gerard Depardieu, actor.

on this day ★ In 1945, the World Bank was created with the signing of an agreement by 28 nations.

december 28

character ★ Glamorous and well dressed, you like the finer things in life. Your classical style suits you and is admired by all your friends. You love to make your home look wonderful and are good at doing it yourself. You have a talent for throwing a meal together and are quite a homemaker, but you also long to be in the limelight.

life path ★ You can push yourself too hard to succeed. You take life very seriously, and if you think you aren't succeeding you can get depressed and reclusive. This strong desire to make it to the big time is almost childlike. You were born to be admired and are heading in the right direction.

love ★ Lovers often try to control you or pin you down, but your stubborn streak prevents this. Your relationships can be marred by conflict and power struggles. When you are ready for love or want to leave a relationship new lovers pop up at just the right time. A Leo lover, whose ruling planet, the Sun, is your birth date ruler, would make a good match.

best present ★ Video camera, favorite fragrance.

birthday share ★ 1856 Woodrow Wilson, 28th U.S. president; 1921 Johnny Otis, musician; 1922 Stan Lee, creator of comic book superheroes; 1954 Denzel Washington, actor.

on this day ★ In 1993, after 2,000 years of often hostile Christian-Jewish relations, the Vatican and Israel approved a document in which the Holy See and the Jewish state recognized each other.

color silvery white ★ **number** 2, 11, 20 ★ **stone** moonstone—connects you with the cycles of the moon, your birth date ruler ★ **flora** snowdrop ★ **animal** dolphin ★ **occupation** singer, violinist, astrologer ★ **key features** sensitive, self-indulgent, intuitive ★ **naturally good at** recognizing the patterns in others' lives

december 29

character ★ You are sensitive to criticism but are actually a powerful, perceptive, and strong person. You can get caught up in your emotions and swept away by a sense of sadness whose source baffles you. This angst can be cured if you build up your relationship with yourself.

life path ★ Wake up, wake up from that lovely dream! You are here in the present not elsewhere in the past or the future! You tend to hold yourself back with things that are history, but move on and you can be anything you want to be. You are great at helping and supporting other people, and it's time to apply all that wisdom to yourself.

love ★ You feel love deeply and have a romantic nature, but you may try to hide this or become cynical about love. That would be a shame, as you have such a lot of affection to give. You need someone who can see all sides of you and not expect you to be the strong one in the relationship. Why not try a Cancer, whose ruling planet, the Moon, is your birth date ruler?

best present ★ Set of runes, white church candle.

birthday share ★ 1808 Andrew Johnson, 17th U.S. president; 1936 Mary Tyler Moore, actress; 1938 Jon Voight, actor; 1972 Jude Law, actor.

on this day ★ In 1890, the last major battle between Native Americans and U.S. troops took place at Wounded Knee Creek in South Dakota.

color purple ★ **number** 3, 12, 30 ★ **stone** turquoise—a stone sacred to native americans that will lead you to your right path ★ **flora** buttercup ★ **animal** panther ★ **occupation** pilot, engineer, boss of your own company ★ **key features** adventurous, well traveled, bold ★ **naturally good at** working abroad

december 30

character ★ Expansive and well rounded, you have managed to balance your outgoing nature with responsibility. You have the ability to work for long hours yet still take time out to have adventures or to cut yourself off from the rat race in a log cabin in the woods. You are luckier than most Capricorns and do well in the stock market or with your own business.

life path ★ You are frustrated by those you assume to be less intelligent than you, but this is usually more a case of a lack of practical application. You have a quick and logical mind but you shouldn't dismiss people who may lack this skill—they often have a different sort of genius. This tendency to throw the baby out with the bathwater can result in your being surrounded by friends who are too similar to you.

love ★ You are a good teacher and nurturer and tend to attract younger lovers.

You particularly enjoy intimate moments in foreign or unusual places or in the open air. Look out for a Sagittarius partner, whose ruling planet, Jupiter, is also your birth date ruler.

best present ★ Cruise, pajamas.

birthday share ★ 1865 Rudyard Kipling, author; 1928 Bo Diddley, singer; 1959 Tracey Ullman, comedienne; 1975 Tiger Woods, golfer.

on this day ★ In 1853, the United States bought 30,000 square miles of land from Mexico for $10 million. The area is now Southern New Mexico and Arizona.

color silver ★ **number** 4, 22, 40 ★ **stone** topaz—lightens you up and teaches you to play ★ **flora** pansy ★ **animal** elephant ★ **occupation** astronomer, attorney, scientist ★ **key features** pragmatic, insightful, judgmental ★ **naturally good at** defending your opinions

december 31

character ★ You have an active and inventive mind that zooms from subject to subject, which means you can take on several tasks at once without making any errors. You like to be in charge and need to be in a prominent position. Your ideas may be a little unusual but you always know how to implement them.

life path ★ You are fascinated by space travel and may yearn to go in a rocket, but you're far too serious to share this dream with people, tending to keep your eccentricity to yourself. On the whole you are very conservative, yet you can go the opposite way and be an over-the-top individualist. Either way, you will always stick to your position and refuse to budge.

love ★ You find it hard to bond with people emotionally and can be celibate for long periods of time. You love almost from a distance and need gentle coaxing to be demonstrative. Why not try an Aquarius, whose ruling planet, Uranus, is also your birth date ruler?

best present ★ Telescope, globe.

birthday share ★ 1869 Henri Matisse, artist; 1937 Sir Anthony Hopkins, actor; 1943 John Denver, singer; 1959 Val Kilmer, actor.

on this day ★ In 1938, Dr. R. N. Harger's "drunkometer," the forerunner of the modern Breathalyzer for car drivers, was officially introduced in Indianapolis.

color orange ★ **number** 1, 10, 100 ★ **stone** clear quartz—the magic wand of crystals, so that what you wish for will be drawn to you ★ **flora** red-hot poker ★ **animal** lion ★ **occupation** magician, model, actor ★ **key features** tenacious, stubborn, strong-willed ★ **naturally good at** going after your dreams

january 1

character ★ You are a shining light in the dim, dark crowd of humanity—you give off that extra charge and sparkle. However, you can get so caught up in other people's needs that you neglect your own. You were born to excel and rise above your beginnings. Sometimes you think it is foolish to want more, but you were born an achiever.

life path ★ It may often feel as if you are stumbling toward a certain goal but don't have full control of your destiny. You may have been burdened with family or other responsibilities, but whatever is holding you back, don't let it! You have a magnetic charm and hidden abilities—explore them, and success is sure to appear.

love ★ You are drawn to the security of a relationship from a very young age, and once you get involved with someone you tend to stay involved. You usually make sensible choices, but a part of you would love to meet a crazy creative person, who will free you and release all your potential. Try a lively and adventurous Leo, whose ruling planet is the same as your birth date ruler, the Sun.

best present ★ Funky jeans, motorbike.

birthday share ★ 1879 E. M. Forster, author; 1895 J. Edgar Hoover, former head of the FBI; 1919 J. D. Salinger, author, and Rocky Graziano, boxer and actor.

on this day ★ In 1962, the Beatles auditioned for Decca records, only to be rejected because the company felt "groups of guitars are on the way out."

color silver ★ **number** 2, 11, 20 ★ **stone** opal—exaggerates your emotions and makes you aware of the truth ★ **flora** jasmine ★ **animal** polar bear ★ **occupation** store owner, fashion designer, bookmaker ★ **key features** fair, kind, responsible ★ **naturally good at** expressing your emotional needs

january 2

character ★ *Balance* is the key word for you; you are often torn between two different paths. You may find yourself in love with two people or be unsure about what sort of relationship you want. You need to make sure that you focus on what your instincts and inner voice are saying rather than relying on your voice of reason.

life path ★ Decisions, decisions! You are always in a dilemma about where you want your life to go. You need security and structure, but you also desire freedom and spontaneity. You have many close friends who rely on you and you're particularly drawn to emotional connections with women. Your mother may feature strongly in your life and hold you back a little.

love ★ You know that love holds mystery and magic. You want to live love to its limits and be carried away on an ocean of desire, but it also scares you. You are vulnerable

and sensitive so may stay in relationships long after they should have finished. Try a Cancer, whose ruling planet, the Moon, is also your birth date ruler.

best present ★ Crystals, diary.

birthday share ★ 1920 Isaac Asimov, science fiction author; 1951 Bill Madlock, baseball player; 1968 Cuba Gooding Jr., actor; 1969 Christy Turlington, model.

on this day ★ In 1900, the first electric omnibus began to run in New York City.

color purple ★ **number** 3, 12, 21 ★ **stone** citrine—boosts your self-esteem ★ **flora** lavender ★ **animal** tortoise ★ **occupation** football star, jockey, full-time parent ★ **key features** committed, loyal, independent ★ **naturally good at** remaining on your path

january 3

character ★ Failure is not an option and you always go the whole way with a project or relationship. You are not a quitter and can overcome any odds with your persistent nature. Sometimes you need to temper this and admit defeat, but your gut instincts are generally right and you have an unlimited capacity to make money.

life path ★ If you keep your eye on the goal you will get there. You always have the support of the people you care about because they marvel at your resolve. You are generally loved and respected and will not let anyone down if you can help it. As you like to be surrounded by people you know well, you would be happiest in a small community. You're an open book: good, honest, and wholesome.

love ★ You love family life and are drawn to having loads of children. You like the whole routine of a family and cherish it as the treasure it is. You will not let anyone threaten your security and need to watch out that you don't overprotect your loved ones. Try a Sagittarius, whose ruling planet, Jupiter, is also your birth date ruler.

best present ★ Badminton set, picnic on a prairie.

birthday share ★ 1892 J. R. R. Tolkien, author; 1909 Victor Borge, pianist and comedian; 1956 Mel Gibson, actor; 1969 Michael Schumacher, race-car driver.

on this day ★ In 1924, British egyptologist Howard Carter found the sarcophagus of Tutankhamen in the Valley of the Kings near Luxor.

color silver ★ **number** 4, 13, 22 ★ **stone** silver—although not strictly a stone, it will inspire and protect you ★ **flora** primrose ★ **animal** jaguar ★ **occupation** choreographer, medium, mathematician ★ **key features** determined, foolhardy, exceptional ★ **naturally good at** using your imagination

character ★ You have a far-out attitude toward life. On the one hand you are quite sensible, but given the right mood you can go off on a wacky tangent. You need inspiration and constant stimulation. You are quite hard on yourself and push yourself to discover life's mysteries, but you are also practical and realistic—which is a challenge in itself.

life path ★ You are no stranger to confrontation and will stick to your guns if you believe you are right. Ironically, you can change your mind at the drop of a hat, which can confuse those around you. You have vision and insight, but other people find it hard to follow your thinking. However, at the end of the day your ideas usually prove to be correct, much to the surprise of colleagues.

love ★ You may have been a bit hit and miss in the love stakes, but you will end up with a lover who adores you. Not everyone can follow where you are coming from because you are so changeable. Why not look for an Aquarius, whose ruling planet, Uranus, is your birth date ruler?

best present ★ Remote-control boat, turquoise bangle.

birthday share ★ 1935 Floyd Patterson, boxer and heavyweight champion; 1937 Dyan Cannon, actress; 1960 Michael Stipe, singer; 1965 Julia Ormond, actress.

on this day ★ In 1863, the four-wheeled roller skate was patented by James Plimpton of New York.

january 5

character ★ You have lofty ideals and you approach life with a certain amount of rigidity. You feel that discipline is the key to growth, although in reality this is not always true for you. There are many ways for you to succeed, and opening up to other opinions and experiences will transform your life more quickly. You're a fussy eater and probably have an interest in nutrition.

life path ★ You are trustworthy and generally honest. You have a way of talking to other people that makes them feel connected with you. Although wise beyond your years, you need to remain flexible and nonjudgmental. You are an enlightened being who has the capacity to attain much knowledge.

love ★ You form good relationships and take great pains to understand your partner. Communication is the key to happy relationships for you, and if you feel you can't be open or talkative, you are liable to leave. Why not try a relationship with a Gemini, whose ruling planet, Mercury, planet of communication, is also your birth date ruler?

best present ★ Ankh pendant, book on growing organic vegetables.

birthday share ★ 1931 Robert Duvall, actor; 1932 Umberto Eco, author; 1946 Diane Keaton, actress; 1969 Marilyn Manson, singer.

on this day ★ In 1925, Nellie Taylor Ross became the first female governor in the United States, serving the people of Wyoming.

color pink ★ **number** 24, 33, 60 ★ **stone** rose-quartz—the universal love stone that draws love to you ★ **flora** petunia ★ **animal** pony ★ **occupation** philosopher, poet, marriage guidance counselor ★ **key features** romantic, strong, susceptible ★ **naturally good at** seeing the bigger picture

character ★ You are a deep-feeling individual who may have had challenges in the area of love, with both family and personal relationships in which you felt love was conditional on being good or working hard. You have had to be more responsible than others and may not have felt free. You are very giving and instinctively care for others.

life path ★ Your life lessons are all focused on love and on understanding exactly what unconditional love is. It is important for you to love yourself unconditionally as well as others. Finding time for yourself and space in which to be playful and excited about life is vital. You will be rewarded in the long run for all you have put in.

love ★ Venus is your birth date ruler, so love is a loaded area for you. Relationships seem to have a powerful effect on you and you can get lost in them. You often become the giver and need to learn how to receive as well. Why not seek out a Libra or a Taurus, whose ruling planet is also Venus, planet of love?

best present ★ Heart-shaped cushion, box of chocolates.

birthday share ★ 1412 Joan of Arc, saint and martyr; 1878 Carl Sandburg, poet; 1913 Loretta Young, actress; 1944 Bonnie Franklin, actress.

on this day ★ In 1941, President Franklin D. Roosevelt addressed Congress, offering support for all who strove for four essential freedoms—freedom of speech and religion, and freedom from want and fear.

january 7

character ★ On first impressions you can appear to be terribly serious and official. Underneath that composed exterior lies a sensitive, creative, and somewhat vulnerable creature. You tend to live up to your responsibilities but may secretly desire a more unconventional existence in which you have more time to sit and daydream. You use your armor to cover up your natural shyness.

life path ★ You're a dreamer, but don't let yourself get carried away. You feel you have a duty to be rational and dependable, but just below the surface a little voice is calling you to explore your vivid and abundant imagination. A part of you would like to discover your spirituality, as you have the mind of a philosopher. Let yourself go a little and release some of the inner you.

love ★ You have intense relationships with unusual or inventive partners, but you are not very good at asking for what you want physically and emotionally. You need to be gently assertive and show some of that vulnerability. When you are secure in a relationship it acts as an anchor and you are much happier in the world. Try to find a Pisces whose ruling planet, Neptune, is also your birth date ruler.

best present ★ Engraved silver pen, leather notebook.

birthday share ★ 1844 Bernadette of Lourdes, saint; 1891 Zora Neale Hurston, author; 1938 Lou Graham, golfer; 1964 Nicolas Cage, actor.

on this day ★ In 1610, the astronomer Galileo Galilei discovered four of Jupiter's moons with his newly invented telescope.

color burgundy ★ **number** 17, 35, 44 ★ **stone** diamond—gives you courage and strength ★ **flora** orchid ★ **animal** crocodile ★ **occupation** rock star, drawing instructor, teacher ★ **key features** determined, relentless, charismatic ★ **naturally good at** achieving the seemingly impossible

january 8

character ★ You were born on a day of stunning potential, so you have the ability to achieve all of your desires even against the odds. If there is genius in you it will come out. You have a gift for teaching others through your example. You are meant to shine and to rise above all obstacles.

life path ★ You probably had a rough start and have had to become tough to get where you are now. You must remember that your possibilities are endless and that if you keep positive you will be triumphant. You do have a tendency to slip into dark moods and become despondent and demanding. Don't give in to this—glimmer like the star that you are.

love ★ You are a little controlling and needy and can get very possessive and jealous in relationships. You need to watch this tendency, as it can push lovers away. However, you are also truly gorgeous and

giving, with the ability to transform others. Try another Capricorn, as both your birth date ruler and your ruling planet is Saturn.

best present ★ Karaoke machine, black shirt.

birthday share ★ 1935 Elvis Presley, singer; 1937 Shirley Bassey, singer; 1942 Stephen Hawking, physicist; 1947 David Bowie, singer and actor.

on this day ★ In 1918, President Woodrow Wilson presented to Congress his "14 Points," a peace plan aimed at a new world order after World War I.

january 9

character ★ You are a force to be reckoned with. You storm through life like a tornado and take no prisoners. You are quick to anger and it seems to be your first response. Chill out and learn some objectivity. Life is not a battle unless you choose to see it that way. You have admirable qualities such as a strong heroic streak, and you are totally fearless.

life path ★ You may enjoy dangerous sports or taking risks because you thrive on adrenaline. Slowing down a little will help you see things differently. You're such a primal being that you very rarely examine your motives. Allow some of that compassion buried deep within to guide you. It is not good for you to spend too much time alone, and women have a soothing effect on you, whether you are male or female.

love ★ Forceful and hot, you are a great and ardent lover. You're like a hungry, insatiable wolf and need a partner who can understand that energy. You love getting physical but need to balance it with spiritual love. Aim for an Aries whose ruling planet, Mars, is also your birth date ruler.

best present ★ Paintball game, pinball machine.

birthday share ★ 1898 Gracie Fields, singer; 1908 Simone de Beauvoir, author and feminist; 1913 Richard Nixon, 37th U.S. president; 1935 Bob Denver, actor.

on this day ★ In 1788, Connecticut ratified the U.S. Constitution and became the fifth member of the United States.

january 10

character ★ Alluring and powerful, you have an air of sophistication and glamour and love material things, even if you are a bit rough and ready. You are extremely determined, have an amazing physical prowess, and vibrate with a strong physical aura. You won't stand for any nonsense and always speak your mind.

life path ★ You are meant to achieve success on your chosen path but will be sent obstacles early on. You have been set a challenging task because your expectations are so high. When you do make it, try not to become too materialistic or take it all for granted. You adore fine jewelry and clothes and can be a bit of a peacock.

love ★ You may imagine it would be exciting to have more than one lover at a time—perhaps one for security and several others for pleasure. Don't go there—it would all become a tangled mess with dramatic scenes and tears. Instead, hunt out a Leo, whose ruling planet, the Sun, is also your birth date ruler.

best present ★ Karate lessons, mirror.

birthday share ★ 1843 Frank James, outlaw; 1927 Johnnie Ray, singer; 1945 Rod Stewart, singer; 1949 George Foreman, boxer.

on this day ★ In 1920, the League of Nations was formally established when the Treaty of Versailles officially came into effect, ending World War I.

january 11

character ★ You have a caring and compassionate nature and a nurturing personality, so you may find yourself drawn to working with children. You have a strong sense of justice and strive always to be fair. You are the host with the most; cooking is your forte and you have the best dinner parties for your many close friends.

life path ★ You feel compelled to do the right thing in life but are uncertain as to what the right thing is. The right thing for you or for other people? You are easily manipulated into thinking you have to take responsibility for everyone in your life. When you learn to free yourself from the bonds of this self-sacrifice your life will take off. You are intuitive—let this guide you.

love ★ You pour love into your family and partner and try to make everything perfect for them. You delight in looking after your partner and are always thinking of little things to make them happy. Stand back and let them have the pleasure of pleasing you sometimes. Why not try a Cancer, whose ruling planet, the Moon, is also your birth date ruler?

best present ★ Tickets for a sentimental movie, swimming with dolphins.

birthday share ★ 1757 Alexander Hamilton, U.S. founding father; 1930, Rod Taylor, actor; 1956 Robert Earl Keen, singer; 1971 Mary J. Blige, singer.

on this day ★ In 1963, the first U.S. discotheque, the Whiskey-A-Go-Go, opened in Los Angeles.

color purple ★ **number** 3, 21, 30 ★ **stone** celestite—this angelic stone brings you confidence and purity ★ **flora** delphinium ★ **animal** sheep ★ **occupation** manager, radio dj, forestry worker ★ **key features** lively, determined, patient ★ **naturally good at** persistence—you head for your goal and never give in

january 12

character ★ You are exuberant and upbeat, although you may have the tendency to bulldoze your way ahead. You know what you want and need to go for it. You may find that catastrophe and good fortune go hand in hand, so that when you lose something, life presents you with something better.

life path ★ As Jupiter is your birth date ruler, you will be bestowed with the odd supreme good fortune. Out of the blue, and no doubt when you are least expecting it, life will give you a whopping great gift. This may be a promotion, a sudden windfall, or a dramatic love affair. You can swing between wild optimism and dark pessimism, and should try to find your balance.

love ★ Love will come to you and it will be beyond what you thought possible. You are destined for a fantastic lover, but this may come only after a run of disappointments.

Hang in there—it will be worth the wait. Try a Sagittarius, whose ruling planet is the same as your birth date ruler, Jupiter.

best present ★ Pair of Rollerblades, vintage jeans.

birthday share ★ 1856 John Singer Sargent, painter; 1876 Jack London, author; 1954 Howard Stern, radio personality; 1955 Kirstie Alley, actress.

on this day ★ In 1932, after winning a special election to fill the remaining months of her late husband's term, Hattie Caraway, a Democrat from Arkansas, became the first woman to be elected to the U.S. Senate.

january 13

character ★ You can be extremely unpredictable for a Capricorn; you don't ever know what you are going to do next. You see yourself as stable but can blow up or change direction completely out of the blue. Use this forceful energy to make positive changes and you could find yourself achieving whatever you desire.

life path ★ You have an inventive and agile mind; you tend to flit from idea to idea and need to work on your focus. You make friends easily but can also cut them off if they don't live up to your expectations. With such an unusual mind you could make your fortune if you train it to work for you rather than against you.

love ★ You may have had an erratic love life full of ups and downs. You like to be in charge in relationships and don't let your guard down easily. There may be times when you have many flirtations going at the same time but you would never two-time a partner. Why not go for an Aquarius, whose ruling planet, Uranus, is also your birth date ruler?

best present ★ Model airplane kit, chocolate body paint.

birthday share ★ 1919 Robert Stack, actor; 1961 Julia Louis-Dreyfus, actress; 1966 Patrick Dempsey, actor; 1977 Orlando Bloom, actor.

on this day ★ In 1910, New York's Metropolitan Opera took part in the first live radio broadcast of opera, presenting "Pagliacci" and "Cavalleria Rusticana."

color green ★ number 5, 23, 50 ★ stone euchroite—fills you with a sense of enthusiasm and joy ★ flora fern ★ animal bulldog ★ occupation war reporter, archaeologist, pr executive ★ key features powerful, fearless, articulate ★ naturally good at dodging life's bullets

character ★ Handsome or beautiful, you have a solid and strong image. You love danger and rarely avoid a challenge. You are rather maverick and some people misunderstand you, seeing you as hard or cruel. Yes, you are self-protective and independent, but you love the company of people of like mind. You would risk life and limb to help someone in trouble.

life path ★ You tend to push yourself and can get tired and withdrawn as a result. You want to be fit and toned, and your body image is important to you. You believe the body should be like a well-oiled machine, and even if you are unfit or overweight you sense that your body could be transformed simply by applying the power of your mind.

love ★ You like to be demonstrative but can be clumsy or overpowering because you don't know your own strength. It would be better if you refined your technique and became more tenderly affectionate. You are very careful about who you let in, but when you give your heart you are solid as a rock. Seek out a Gemini, whose ruling planet is Mercury, your birth date ruler.

best present ★ Astrological chart, skateboard.

birthday share ★ 1941 Faye Dunaway, actress; 1963 Steven Soderbergh, film director; 1968 LL Cool J, rap artist; 1969 Dave Grohl, musician.

on this day ★ In 1954, actress Marilyn Monroe married baseball star Joe DiMaggio.

january 15

character ★ When you love something—be it an idea, philosophy, or person—you do it to the max. There are very few topics on which you have a neutral view. You live your life to the fullest and follow your convictions to the bitter end. Others may find your uncompromising attitude challenging, but they will admire your power.

life path ★ You have a huge heart and are full of love, but you can have trouble showing it in a conventional fashion. You tend to keep your softness hidden from view. Only those close to you get to see your playful side and know that you're a real softie. You feel that the rest of the world has to see you as invincible, but projecting this image creates problems because people will then treat you as if you are.

love ★ You give your loved one all of your body and soul. You may have messed around a lot between relationships, but you are faithful and adoring when you commit yourself. You are a masterful lover and need lots of attention in return. You would do well with a Libra or Taurus, whose ruling planet is Venus, your birth date ruler.

best present ★ Locket, silver photo frame.

birthday share ★ 1906 Aristotle Onassis, shipping magnate; 1913 Lloyd Bridges, actor; 1929 Martin Luther King Jr., civil rights campaigner; 1937 Margaret O'Brien, actress.

on this day ★ In 1870, a donkey first appeared in a cartoon to symbolize the U.S. Democratic Party. Published in *Harper's Weekly*, it criticized ex-secretary of war Edwin Stanton and was captioned "A Live Jackass Kicking a Dead Lion."

color blue ★ number 7, 34, 70 ★ stone lazulite—this gorgeous stone will uplift your spirits ★ flora forget-me-not ★ animal badger ★ occupation fortune-teller, psychologist, playwright ★ key features unfathomable, secretive, sensitive ★ naturally good at understanding other people's vision

character ★ You are seeking the meaning of life and like to dig deeper than most people. You ponder why you are here and get flashes of revelation about what your life is about but can never quite pin them down. Perceptive and creative, you want to build something important with your life. You can get lost in your imagination but do strive to be practical.

life path ★ You have a remarkable capacity to understand other people and are very helpful in encouraging them to follow their dreams. You love to talk about other people's pasts with them but never reveal much about your own. You would make a good psychologist because you tend to know what hidden motivations people have.

love ★ You're very loving but often have trouble admitting to or exposing your feelings, preferring to show your love in useful ways with small acts intended to please. You do caring things for your beloved and try always to be there when they need you. However, you can be led off on a tangent sometimes and appear rather irresponsible. Fish for a Pisces, whose ruling planet, Neptune, is also your birth date ruler.

best present ★ Barbecue set, computer game.

birthday share ★ 1948 John Carpenter, director; 1959 Sade, singer; 1974 Kate Moss, model; 1979 Aaliyah, singer and actress.

on this day ★ In 1920, Prohibition took effect in the United States, forbidding the sale and manufacture of alcohol.

color dark green ★ **number** 8, 44, 80 ★ **stone** malachite—helps you confront your fears ★ **flora** pine tree ★ **animal** rabbit ★ **occupation** builder, church minister, teacher ★ **key features** serious, reflective, determined ★ **naturally good at** battling against the odds

january 17

character ★ Stern but fair would be a good way of describing you. Solid as a rock, you are probably built like one as well. You will face challenges and may have suffered some kind of loss or disaster that has made you stronger but also makes you hide some of those raw emotions. You have the potential to be very wealthy but may have seen money or success drain away in the past.

life path ★ You tend not to show fear in any circumstances. You face life's battles head on and know the meaning of the word *struggle*. Eventually you will reach a point where you have attained great wisdom and can learn to step out of the way of an oncoming crisis; life will then flow easily and you will be able to relax and become healed and optimistic.

love ★ You are loyal and loving to your partner but can inadvertently keep them from doing their own thing. You are so protective that you worry when they are out of your sight, but instead of explaining this, you will argue about your lover's personal freedom, which can be very annoying for them. Why not try another Capricorn, as your birth date ruler is the same as your ruling planet, Saturn?

best present ★ CD player, digital watch.

birthday share ★ 1706 Benjamin Franklin, statesman, author, and inventor; 1899 Al Capone, gangster; 1942 Muhammad Ali, boxer; 1962 Jim Carrey, comedian and actor.

on this day ★ In 1912, the explorer Robert F. Scott reached the South Pole.

january 18

character ★ You are far less serious than most Capricorns and love nothing better than having a good laugh and a joke. Your practical jokes are notorious, but if you suppress this playful side you could end up expressing an angry and irritable persona instead, so keep laughing. You have a strong aura of friendliness, but this conceals quite a few secrets and you never reveal all of who you are.

life path ★ You have boundless energy and drive and go for it in life. You usually have a cheery front and rarely show sadness when you feel it. Determined and conscientious, you want to follow your own path and should be your own boss. You can get into conflicts with rivals in love or career but this only serves to spur you on.

love ★ You're passionate and love deeply. You love to spend hours on end in the company of your loved one, but some partners can find you too demanding of their attention. This may have made you hold back later in life or feel frustrated that you would not find a lover to suit you. You will, so relax. Why not choose an Aries, whose ruling planet, Mars, is also your birth date ruler?

best present ★ Stereo system, football.

birthday share ★ 1882 A. A. Milne, poet and humorist; 1892 Oliver Hardy, comedian and actor; 1904 Cary Grant, actor; 1955 Kevin Costner, actor.

on this day ★ In 1993, the holiday honoring Martin Luther King Jr. was officially observed in all 50 U.S. states for the first time.

color orange ★ **number** 1, 11, 100 ★ **stone** cherry opal—balances your physical and mental energy ★ **flora** sunflower ★ **animal** goose ★ **occupation** rock star, model, entrepreneur ★ **key features** flamboyant, free-spirited, strong ★ **naturally good at** causing a stir

january 19

character ★ You have an independent nature and don't give a fig what other people think of you. You have more front than a department store and display your outrageous nature whenever possible. Even if you look respectable on the surface, anyone who has known you a short while will soon be treated to your party-animal routine. You can be hedonistic and a little self-destructive because you want to experience all of life now.

life path ★ You may fight against your wild side but it is instinctive, so why not just balance and incorporate it? You can find other outlets for your fiercely passionate personality—why not take up some kind of creative pursuit that allows you to express your need for attention, such as acting classes or singing lessons?

love ★ You love attention and the finer things in life and get frustrated if you are not treated like a king or queen. You have so many aspects to your character that you need a grounded and loyal partner to keep you on the straight and narrow. Look for a Leo, whose ruling planet, the Sun, is also your birth date ruler.

best present ★ Acting lessons, karaoke machine.

birthday share ★ 1809 Edgar Allan Poe, author and poet; 1943 Janis Joplin, singer; 1946 Dolly Parton, country singer; 1949 Robert Palmer, singer.

on this day ★ In 1966, Indira Gandhi was sworn in as India's first female prime minister.

color silvery white ★ **number** 2, 11, 20 ★ **stone** white coral—connects you to your spirituality ★ **flora** jasmine ★ **animal** meerkat ★ **occupation** hairdresser, midwife, doctor ★ **key features** focused, caring, understanding ★ **naturally good at** listening to people's problems

january 20

character ★ You're a real softie and have genuine compassion and love for other people, spending time supporting those close to you. You are sensitive to others' opinions but show a strong face. You have a deep need to be secure with those you love and don't function as well when you feel alone. Building up a strong sense of self is essential for your growth.

life path ★ Getting in touch with your spirituality will be a great help. You are naturally interested in mystical things and should trust your gut feelings. You have a karmic connection to women and will find that it is women who have the most to teach you. Some of these lessons will be painful, others liberating. Your relationship with your mother was also intense, for good or bad.

love ★ You tend to get deeply involved in relationships but also can become insecure for no reason. You can overanalyze each word your partner says, or think too much about where the relationship is heading rather than just going with the flow. Why not try a Cancer, whose ruling planet, the Moon, is also your birth date ruler?

best present ★ Charm bracelet, deck of tarot cards.

birthday share ★ 1896 George Burns, comedian; 1926 Patricia Neal, actress; 1930 Edwin "Buzz" Aldrin, astronaut; 1946 David Lynch, director.

on this day ★ In 1981, former actor Ronald Reagan was inaugurated as president of the United States. At age 69, he was the oldest candidate ever to take office.

capricorn

your ruling planet Saturn is a grumpy old taskmaster or stern father. Having such a stern planet governing you may sound scary but actually Saturn has its plus points. It teaches you about limitation and about laying foundations. It fills you with a sense of duty and responsibility and makes you aware of the consequences of your actions. Saturn gives you the stamina and power to compete and to complete. You have self-discipline, thanks to Saturn, and it does bestow upon you a certain charisma. More good news is that Saturn, like the best fathers, is supportive and provides a sense of surety that shores you up. You know you can do it even if it is a bit tough now, and this inner confidence keeps you going against all the odds. With Saturn at your feet you can achieve beyond even your own wildest expectations.

your natural habitat You have very traditional tastes in your home environment. You like quality not quantity and prefer to drink from the finest cut glass and bone china. Even if you are broke you will keep nice things around you and would rather have nothing than cheap imitations. You like the finer things in life but usually avoid paying by credit card because you like to know purchases are truly yours. You may have a city apartment, a country cottage, or a suburban box but whatever shape your home takes it will be exquisite and perfect in its own right. You always remember details like nice towels and good soap. You are proud of your home and will no doubt keep moving up the ladder to bigger and better. You can be trendy and happening, but again it has to be done properly or not at all. You are fond of real art and love to surround yourself with beautiful original oil paintings or sketches. You love your garden, if you have one, but with so many other responsibilities you rarely get the time to do as much gardening as you would like.

are you a typical capricorn?

If you are **practical, hardworking**, and **earthy** you fit the stereotype of your sign. You are the **salt of the earth** and as **honest** as the day is long. You don't like arty types or people with pretensions. You are very **blunt** when you speak and think that emotional analysis is for wimps. If you are an evolved Capricorn you can discuss emotions when it is important to do so, but generally you prefer simply to get on with life. You have no time to contemplate your navel.

Why you're wonderful! Loyal and a workhorse, you will complete a job or honor a commitment even if you have to use your last breath. You don't give up and you don't give in; like the packhorse that you are, you will patiently and diligently walk up that mountain until you get to the top. You are family oriented and take promises and responsibilities seriously. Your word is your bond.

Why you're impossible! Stubborn and belligerent, you rarely admit defeat or admit that you are in the wrong. You find it hard to apologize and can give your partners and family a headache with your refusal to budge on issues you feel even remotely strongly about. You will bury your head in the sand and stick to a fixed routine rather than be flexible. You don't like change and can be a workaholic.

Your secret side You can suddenly be turned on by the idea of a gamble and fantasize about get-rich-quick schemes, but these rarely—if ever—work out for you so are best avoided. You are tenacious but would love to be lazy and cruise the world living in the lap of luxury. If things come too easily, you tend to take them for granted. You love grandeur and wealth and can find yourself indulging in overspending just to show off, but at other times you can be considered quite mean, so you need to find a balance here.

	aries	taurus	gemini	cancer	leo	virgo
fun		🍾		🍾	🍾	🍾
romance	❤	❤		❤	❤	❤
loyalty		🔗		🔗	🔗	🔗
adventure		🎈		🎈	🎈	🎈
	💋	💋		💋	💋	💋
		🪑		🪑		🪑
				💡		
		👥		👥		👥

KEY ▷ fun romance loyalty adventure

libra	scorpio	sagittarius	capricorn	aquarius	pisces
🍾	🍾		🍾		🍾
💘	💘	💘	💘		💘
⭕	⭕		⭕		⭕
🎈	🎈	🎈	🎈		🎈
	👄	👄	👄		👄
🪑	🪑		🪑		🪑
👥	👥		👥		👥

 passion  **chilling out** **spontaneity** **attentiveness**

aquarius

january 21–february 19

january 21

character ★ You can be a little hard to handle if people aren't used to you, as you have a very vibrant and speedy nature. You speak quickly, spilling out all your ideas in a jumble, and sometimes people can make the mistake of underestimating you. Actually, you are something of a genius and always manage to pull your ideas together to succeed.

life path ★ You are probably not only gorgeous but also incredibly lucky—life may have thrown you a few curve balls but you always land on your feet and keep going. Your unusual personality and electric charm has enabled you to fast-forward in your life. Even if you are weighed down with responsibilities now, you are just waiting for the right moment to launch yourself … and believe me, you will.

love ★ You don't like to be tied down and want to be a free spirit who explores all that life has to offer. You want to see the world and make your mark. If you do settle down early you will still venture forth when you're older, because nothing will quell that sense of adventure. Why not try a Sagittarius, whose ruling planet, Jupiter, is your birth date ruler?

best present ★ Ticket to any foreign destination, globe.

birthday share ★ 1905 Christian Dior, fashion designer; 1940 Jack Nicklaus, golfer; 1941 Placido Domingo, opera singer; 1956 Geena Davis, actress.

on this day ★ In 1954, USS *Nautilus*, the first nuclear-powered submarine, was launched in Groton, Connecticut.

color silver ★ **number** 4, 22, 40 ★ **stone** hematite—gives you the confidence to follow your dreams ★ **flora** orchid ★ **animal** whippet ★ **occupation** Inventor, writer, adventurer ★ **key features** unusual, awesome, groundbreaking ★ **naturally good at** making your mark

january 22

character ★ Wow! You're a special character. Not only are you ruled by Uranus twice, but you were born on the 22nd, which is a master number. What all this means is that you are either a visionary, quite crazy, or both! You were born ahead of your time and have ideas and thoughts that most of the world is not ready for. However, believe in yourself, write them down, follow your dreams, and go for it; eventually the world will catch up.

life path ★ Rasputin was born on this day and so was the Romantic poet Byron. Rasputin, for all his faults, did have the ability to predict the future, and Byron was able to capture the intense feelings of all-consuming love in immortal poetry. Like these two you can reach out to explain, experience, or present something unique, deep, and most of all original. Don't be scared to be yourself—others will love you for it.

love ★ You find long-term relationships challenging, as your head goes off in so many directions. You zoom around, flitting from emotion to emotion, and your lovers feel on the outside of it all. Look out for another Aquarius, who may be able to cope.

best present ★ Amethyst crystal ball, astrological chart.

birthday share ★ 1788 Lord Byron, poet; 1935 Sam Cooke, singer; 1965 Jazzy Jeff, singer and rap artist, and Diane Lane, actress.

on this day ★ In 1907, the first senator of American Indian ancestry, Charles Curtis of Kansas, began his term in office.

january 23

character ★ You can be a little insecure about yourself, but once you are brave and follow through on some of your bright ideas, you will soon realize you are destined to achieve beyond your dreams. You are not motivated by money but by inspired ideals. You want more than wealth—you want to live a life full of intellectual adventures in which you are on a voyage of discovery of the mind.

life path ★ You are different from the majority, but that is a good thing. You like meeting people who come from all walks of life and can get along with just about anyone. However, you find selfish or materialistic people a challenge and big spenders a turn-off, unless they have made their money in some unusual fashion. You are a bit of a rebel.

love ★ You need someone who challenges your mind and makes you think. You love to sit up late into the night, perhaps with a bottle of wine, chatting and delving into all sorts of diverse topics. Perhaps you should find a Gemini, whose ruling planet is your birth date ruler, Mercury.

best present ★ Bottle of tequila, lava lamp.

birthday share ★ 1832 Edouard Manet, impressionist painter; 1928 Jeanne Moreau, actress; 1944 Rutger Hauer, actor; 1957 Princess Caroline of Monaco.

on this day ★ In 1973, President Richard Nixon announced the end of U.S. involvement in Vietnam.

color cerise ★ **number** 6, 33, 60 ★ **stone** rose-quartz—the unconditional love stone that attracts love to you ★ **flora** pink rose ★ **animal** koala bear ★ **occupation** poet, dancer, performance artist ★ **key features** inspirational, stunning, distant ★ **naturally good at** capturing the hearts of strangers

january 24

character ★ You have a free and artistic spirit and admire people in history who have been rebellious or creative geniuses. You flirt with people but with an odd detachment. You are drawn to romance but usually daydream about it more than live it, even though you have no shortage of offers and people often become infatuated with you.

life path ★ You're a bit of a muse, so others are inspired just by being around you. You excite and enthrall all those you meet. You can suffer from nervous energy or get the odd panic attack. You need to ground yourself and get back to nature if you feel out of sorts. You are a genuine delight to have around and rarely allow yourself to lose control.

love ★ You were born to be loved, but although your birth date ruler is Venus, planet of love, you rarely engage in all-out passion. Why is this? Well, you have a loving spirit and heart and a very charitable nature but are fearful of the intensity of your own emotions. Find a Taurus or Libra, whose ruling planet is also Venus and who will help you give yourself fully.

best present ★ Book by Virginia Woolf, tickets to the ballet.

birthday share ★ 1892 Edith Wharton, author; 1941 Neil Diamond, singer; 1949 John Belushi, comedian and actor; 1959 Nastassja Kinski, actress.

on this day ★ In 1989, serial killer Ted Bundy was executed in Florida's electric chair.

january 25

character ★ You become completely immersed in whatever you are interested in and lose yourself in grand plans and wild imaginings. You refuse to conform and must have your personal freedom. You have a brilliant mind and a sweet manner. You like to talk about life's mysteries and tend to have a gang of special friends who are all rather hip or extraordinary.

life path ★ You are always moving on toward the next trend and are one step ahead of the game, sensing where the cutting edge is. You push yourself to your limits, testing out what you feel, and will probably experiment with your appearance as well as your ideas. You have a bohemian aura about you and hate to be judged, as you see yourself as many different things that cannot be put into a box.

love ★ You succumb to many different types of love. You can be wild and free and have brief flings; you can have platonic and intense friendships as well as obsessions and infatuations. Wherever the mood takes you, you will go. Why not try a Pisces, whose ruling planet, Neptune, is your birth date ruler?

best present ★ Tickets to a poetry reading, rare plant.

birthday share ★ 1759 Robert Burns, poet; 1874 W. Somerset Maugham, author; 1882 Virginia Woolf, author; 1981 Alicia Keys, singer.

on this day ★ In 1924, the first Winter Olympic Games opened at Chamonix, France.

color dark green ★ **number** 8, 44, 62 ★ **stone** chrysocolla—brings emotional calm and frees you of guilt ★ **flora** wild garlic ★ **animal** anteater ★ **occupation** navy SEAL, musician, administrator ★ **key features** tenacious, uncompromising, determined ★ **naturally good at** triumphing over disaster

january 26

character ★ You have had your share of trials and tribulations. At various points in your life you will feel that every time you get up, you will be knocked back down. But this roller coaster existence is fortunately temporary and seems only to make you more determined than ever to push through and make it.

life path ★ At certain times you may feel you bit off more than you could chew in the University of Life but hey, you have made it so far and the best is yet to come. You have the ability to surprise all your doubters and suddenly leap forward with renewed vigor. You are talented and easily stimulated, you come up with the goods when attacking any task, and if you are sure you want something, nothing can get in your way.

love ★ You may end up with a partner for the wrong reason. Perhaps you have been hurt in the past so are going for a safe bet or someone who can help you in some way. You trust friendship more than romance, but also have it in you to be very flirtatious indeed. Why not go for a Capricorn, whose ruling planet, Saturn, is your birth date ruler?

best present ★ Signet ring, silk sheets.

birthday share ★ 1925 Paul Newman, actor; 1955 Eddie Van Halen, rock guitarist; 1958 Ellen DeGeneres, actress and comedienne; 1961 Wayne Gretzky, hockey player.

on this day ★ In 1788, the first European settlers arrived in Australia.

color scarlet ★ number 9, 45, 90 ★ stone red jasper—grounds you and gives you a sense of security ★ flora red tulip ★ animal wildebeest ★ occupation composer, race-car driver, musician ★ key features impetuous, reckless, inspired ★ naturally good at being stunning at at least one thing

january 27

character ★ Unusually bright and precocious, you pick things up very easily and when shown a new task are able to master it within minutes. You have dynamic flair and verve and love the thrill of the chase, either for a career highlight or to capture a love interest. You are extremely flirtatious and funny but somewhat aloof.

life path ★ Your energetic and enthusiastic approach to life is great, but you can also have an erratic temper that seems to pop up out of nowhere like a rampaging Tasmanian devil. You can be calm and cheerful one minute and then—boom! You're off. Astonished onlookers can only take a step back until you have calmed down.

love ★ You can be excited by the hint of a flirtation. You are very tactile and physical and like a partner who can respond with equal ardor and abandon. Sometimes you can be a little too boisterous and would both benefit from taking things softly and slowly for a change. Hunt for an Aries, whose ruling planet, Mars, is your birth date ruler.

best present ★ MP3 player, pool table.

birthday share ★ 1756 Wolfgang Amadeus Mozart, composer; 1832 Lewis Carroll, author; 1885 Jerome Kern, composer; 1964 Bridget Fonda, actress.

on this day ★ In 1888, the National Geographic Society was founded in Washington, D.C.

color orange ★ **number** 1, 10, 55 ★ **stone** carnelian—the romans favored this as an amulet and lucky charm ★ **flora** geranium ★ **animal** lion ★ **occupation** magician, performer, athlete ★ **key features** eccentric, funny, stellar ★ **naturally good at** following your passion

character ★ You have such conviction that you don't care what other people say. You will be you, and nothing and no one will deter you. You tend to hover on the fringes of society, or if you don't you probably have a secret habit or foible that is slightly outrageous.

life path ★ You love exhibitionists and have been known to be one yourself. You are attracted to arty types and hang out in the trendiest places. However, you are deeper than this implies, and although you do like to be talked about and admired, you have genuine depth. You may become famous or infamous and you will never be ignored.

love ★ You can be a little too free with your love and may acquire a reputation for being anyone's for the taking. In fact, it is simply that you don't like to hurt people's feelings by saying no. You don't like to be bound by society's ideas of what love should be and refuse to be labeled or controlled. You might like to try a Leo, whose ruling planet, the Sun, is also your birth date ruler.

best present ★ Top hat, unicycle.

birthday share ★ 1912 Jackson Pollock, artist; 1936 Alan Alda, actor; 1980 Nick Carter, singer; 1981 Elijah Wood, actor.

on this day ★ In 1986, seven astronauts died after the *Challenger* space shuttle exploded 72 seconds after lift-off.

january 29

character ★ You are intuitive, compassionate, creative, and a little wacky. You say what you think and defend everyone's right to be an individual. You have a soft heart and can be overgenerous, but that is why you're so loved. Life will become easier for you after the age of 25, when you start to be aware that anything is possible.

life path ★ You should always trust your gut instincts, as you have a well-developed sixth sense that will have saved your skin on a number of occasions. Listening to that inner voice will guide you to your destiny. You may feel that you have something important to do with your life and you could be right.

love ★ You are quite cautious about who you let into your heart but are very good at giving love to others, particularly friends whom you can consider family. It is likely you will find enduring love later on in life. This will shore you up and enhance your inner strength. Why not try a Cancer, whose ruling planet, the Moon, is your birth date ruler?

best present ★ Night out at a soul music concert, radio.

birthday share ★ 1916 Victor Mature, actor; 1939 Germaine Greer, author and feminist; 1945 Tom Selleck, actor; 1954 Oprah Winfrey, television host.

on this day ★ In 1900, the American Baseball League, composed of eight teams, was organized in Philadelphia.

color purple ★ **number** 3, 12, 21 ★ **stone** fluorite—opens you up to your inner guide ★ **flora** daisy ★ **animal** pot-bellied pig ★ **occupation** social activist, governor, rebel ★ **key features** rebellious, troublemaker, big-hearted ★ **naturally good at** leading an uprising

january 30

character ★ You're swift to defend the underdog and you live your life according to your own moral code. You have a talent for bringing groups together for good or bad and may fancy living in a commune. You would like to have been a 1960s rebel but will settle for turning the world of the new millennium inside out.

life path ★ You have the potential to be wealthy and a person with a strong social conscience, so if you do have money, you will probably give some of it away to good causes, because no matter how hard you try to wreck your own life or be self-destructive, you're incredibly lucky and attract rewards for very little output.

love ★ Male or female, you are seeking a comrade in arms. When you find this twin soul you will remain loyal and loving. You will need to have many joint plans for it to work, though, because you love to get up to mischief, and what better fun could there be than to have another mischief-maker to share life with? Search for a Sagittarius, whose ruling planet, Jupiter, is your birth date ruler.

best present ★ Oil paints, biker jacket.

birthday share ★ 1882 Franklin Delano Roosevelt, 32nd U.S. president; 1930 Gene Hackman, actor; 1937 Vanessa Redgrave, actress; 1941 Dick Cheney, U.S. vice president and former secretary of defense.

on this day ★ In 1948, Mahatma Gandhi, Indian political and spiritual leader, was assassinated by a Hindu extremist.

january 31

character ★ You are strong and quite grounded for someone with so much Uranus energy. You reign supreme in your tendency to daydream and manage to be original and ingenious. You may discover a new way for cars to run without gasoline or a lipstick that truly doesn't come off when you kiss. You can be messy and always late, but you have much to offer.

life path ★ A lot of the time you rush around in fast-forward mode and can make mistakes in your sheer eagerness to get along. You may be neglectful of your home, which can put lovers off if they are coming for a romantic liaison.

love ★ You can get overexcited if you like someone, but this can be endearing. You can make a rocket out of champagne wire and are very entertaining. Calm down a bit and let your partner get a word in edgewise; you will find that if they stay after a month it could be for life. Why not try another Aquarius, as Uranus is both your birth date ruler and your ruling planet?

best present ★ Train set, board game.

birthday share ★ 1921 Carol Channing, singer; 1923 Norman Mailer, author; 1970 Minnie Driver, actress; 1981 Justin Timberlake, singer and dancer.

on this day ★ In 1950, President Harry S. Truman announced he had ordered the development of the hydrogen bomb.

color orange ★ **number** 1, 10, 100 ★ **stone** chalcedony—sacred to the native americans, this gives you balance and grounds your grand plans ★ **flora** hydrangea ★ **animal** eagle ★ **occupation** director, producer, aerobics instructor ★ **key features** original, buzzing, hot ★ **naturally good at** strutting your stuff

february 1

character ★ You're one-of-a-kind, and they sure broke the mold when they made you. You are humble and charismatic and have amazing electricity all around you giving off sparks to the unsuspecting public. If what you have could be put in a bottle and sold, you would be staggeringly rich. Funnily enough, you don't believe you are gorgeous. Come on, wake up! You're delicious!

life path ★ It would be fitting for you to have a job in the public eye. You are kind and will talk to anyone; you open doors for whoever is following behind and are exceptionally polite and courteous. So what are your bad points? You need to get more in touch with who you are and what you want and be aware that you have a strong effect on others.

love ★ You will be adored and you need a partner you can look up to and respect as well as one who is always honest with you.

You cannot bear secrets and like everything to be out in the open in your relationships. Why not lasso a Leo, whose ruling planet, the Sun, is your birth date ruler?

best present ★ Pewter goblet, meditation CD.

birthday share ★ 1901 Clark Gable, actor; 1931 Boris Yeltsin, Russian president; 1965 Brandon Lee, actor; 1968 Lisa Marie Presley, actress and heiress.

on this day ★ In 1893, Thomas Edison opened the first movie studio, in New Jersey.

february 2

character ★ You are drawn to the mysterious and have a very perceptive personality. You should explore your spirituality; if you already have, you will be pretty enlightened. You have the ability to soothe people when they are in pain or trouble. You believe in a higher power and fate, and what you believe in you will, to a certain extent, ordain, so keep positive and serene.

life path ★ Even if you downplay your spiritual side you use your intuition to make decisions more than you use your rational mind. You are drawn to the sea but also like to be in the countryside, especially under the stars on a summer's evening. You have your finger on the beat and rhythm of nature and should be good with animals.

love ★ You want a transcendent love that whisks you off to the heavens where you travel to other realms locked in each other's eyes. You see the soul and spirit of your lover. A celestial match would be a Cancer, whose ruling planet, the Moon, is also your birth date ruler.

best present ★ Set of runes, scented candle.

birthday share ★ 1882 James Joyce, author; 1927 Stan Getz, jazz saxophonist; 1947 Farah Fawcett, actress; 1954 Christie Brinkley, supermodel.

on this day ★ In 1950, U.S. Senator Joseph McCarthy announced he had evidence there were individuals in the State Department who were card-carrying members of the Communist Party.

color purple ★ number 12, 21, 30 ★ stone amazonite—gives you courage ★ flora cactus ★ animal chameleon ★ occupation zoologist, explorer, composer ★ key features inventive, dynamic, magnanimous ★ naturally good at breaking down boundaries

february 3

character ★ You love to feast on life and like nothing more than a new experience. You can smash through frontiers and develop new techniques in whichever career path you choose. You are intellectual and have a probing mind. Financially lucky, you do love to spend.

life path ★ Easily bored, you sometimes make life more difficult for yourself just for the heck of it. You make friends easily and have a good laugh when you're in form. You can also squirrel yourself away to read or indulge in some obscure hobby or interest. You are exceptionally good at all forms of research.

love ★ You like relationships but tend not to be consumed by them. You have so much to do that you need a lot of personal freedom in romantic encounters. Fortunately you tend to meet people who give you what

you need. Why not try a Sagittarius, whose ruling planet is Jupiter, your birth date ruler?

best present ★ Encyclopedia, pastels.

birthday share ★ 1809 Felix Mendelssohn, composer; 1894 Norman Rockwell, artist; 1943 Blythe Danner, actress; 1950 Morgan Fairchild, actress.

on this day ★ In 1969, Yasser Arafat became leader of the Palestine Liberation Organization (PLO).

color silver ★ **number** 4, 13, 22 ★ **stone** labradorite—pushes you to be more than you think you are ★ **flora** fig tree ★ **animal** collie dog ★ **occupation** scientist, neurologist, researcher ★ **key features** dazzling, unconventional, enigmatic ★ **naturally good at** having flashes of brilliance

february 4

character ★ You have an off-the-wall, unusual mind. You spend hours thinking strange and magnificent thoughts and are something of a genius. Because you have your head in the clouds so much, you can pay little attention to your eating habits, but you still manage to have endless energy and are very fit from dashing about.

life path ★ It is difficult for you to get in touch with your emotions because you live in your head and analyze your feelings. You can be too hard on and controlling of yourself but still respect other people's freedom. You believe all people are special, unique, and gifted, and you have an optimistic outlook.

love ★ You are quite difficult to understand yet inspiring and exciting. You love to explore romance and intimacy to the limit and break through taboos and boundaries, as you do in all things in life. A tame partner is not for you. Look out for another Aquarius, as your ruling planet and your birth date ruler are both Uranus.

best present ★ Telescope, trip to NASA.

birthday share ★ 1902 Charles Lindbergh, aviator; 1948 Alice Cooper, singer; 1962 Clint Black, country singer; 1975 Natalie Imbruglia, singer.

on this day ★ In 1927, a new land-speed record was set in Wales, when Malcolm Campbell reached 174 mph in his car *Bluebird*.

color green ★ **number** 14, 23, 50 ★ **stone** lapis lazuli—this sacred stone helps you speak your higher truth ★ **flora** rhubarb ★ **animal** parrot ★ **occupation** writer, journalist, singer ★ **key features** expressive, articulate, thinking ★ **naturally good at** writing short stories

february 5

character ★ You are incredibly bright and have a razor-sharp wit. You express yourself with ease and are drawn to academics and those with any kind of brilliance. You are rarely jealous and approach your own emotions like a psychologist, but you would benefit from feeling more and thinking less. You would be wise to take a writing course because you have a gift for writing.

life path ★ Follow your mind and you shall have the answer. You are a thinker and were born to use that head of yours to capture life's mysteries, intrigues, and pleasures. You may occasionally feel as if you are going around the bend with all those ideas, in which case take time out, go to the beach, and chill out.

love ★ You are a real lover of people and are not at all superficial in your choice of partner. You are searching for a lover with a dazzling wit and an equal mind. Why not try a Gemini, whose ruling planet is also your birth date ruler, Mercury?

best present ★ Silver fountain pen, trip to Hawaii.

birthday share ★ 1914 William Burroughs, author; 1948 Barbara Hershey, actress; 1962 Jennifer Jason Leigh, actress; 1969 Bobby Brown, singer.

on this day ★ In 1922, the first *Reader's Digest* magazine hit the shelves.

color pink ★ **number** 6, 24, 33 ★ **stone** rhodochrosite—the healing stone that calms you and invites love ★ **flora** carnation ★ **animal** penguin ★ **occupation** entertainer, drummer, personal coach ★ **key features** loving, philosophical, perky ★ **naturally good at** communicating your desire

february 6

character ★ Life for you is one long love affair; for good or bad you treat your day-to-day experience as if it were your lover. Because of this you may appear a little dramatic or overemotional, which is very rare for an Aquarius. You want life to be good to you, and even though you have sometimes been disillusioned like the rest of us, life tends to love you back.

life path ★ When you are attracted to someone, you woo with your mind, charming and cajoling your unsuspecting prey with your honey words and endless allure. You probably have a mesmerizing speaking voice that hypnotizes your quarry. You can be fickle and adore the chase but you are not unkind.

love ★ You flit from lover to lover, getting dizzy in the spin cycle of your rather frenzied love life. Love is your oxygen and you keep seeking that elusive high. You may well find it with a Taurus or Libra, whose ruling planet, Venus, is your birth date ruler.

best present ★ Book of Shakespeare sonnets, riding boots.

birthday share ★ 1895 Babe Ruth, baseball player; 1911 Ronald Reagan, 40th U.S. president; 1917 Zsa Zsa Gabor, actress; 1945 Bob Marley, singer.

on this day ★ In 1788, Massachusetts became the sixth member of the United States.

february 7

character ★ You have a fanciful nature and walk around delighting in observing life's little details. You're a prophet and a dreamer and have every intention of sharing your high ideals with others. The difference between you and other dreamers is that you may actually achieve something quite profound with your life if you fully commit to it.

life path ★ You can be quite elfish and fantastic and need to guard against embellishing stories until they bear little relation to the reality. Your imagination is a gift from the universe and ought to be used wisely. You have a strong connection to spirituality and to your higher self. You like quirky, offbeat spiritual paths.

love ★ As long as you are clear about what is fantasy and what is reality, all is well. You can paint a marvelous mask on the face of mere mortal love interests and turn them into gods or goddesses, but you get very annoyed when the mask slips, even though it was you who placed it there in the first place! Why not try a Pisces, whose ruling planet, Neptune, is also your birth date ruler?

best present ★ Scuba-diving lessons, an original poem written for you.

birthday share ★ 1812 Charles Dickens, author; 1945 Pete Postlethwaite, actor; 1962 Garth Brooks, country singer; 1966 Chris Rock, comedian.

on this day ★ In 1964, the Beatles arrived in the United States for the first time.

february 8

character ★ You are driven and determined and have a very serious persona. You may be a creative soul but you always take life gravely; you are not one for idle chitchat or superficial nonsense. You have a plan and a goal, and you want to get your teeth into life's problems to solve them quickly. You are very hard on yourself and need to be kinder and more compassionate to yourself.

life path ★ You are drawn to the seedier aspects of life—you like to take a peek at the underbelly of humanity, perhaps because you have not yet come to terms with or integrated your "shadow side." We are all very complex and have the good, the bad, and the ugly in us, so accept all aspects of yourself and avoid being self-destructive.

love ★ You seem unable to give your all to a partner and are often wrapped up in your own thoughts to the exclusion of other people. Your loved ones can get frustrated with you but are often doting. A good choice would be a Capricorn, whose ruling planet, Saturn, is also your birth date ruler.

best present ★ Trip to a comedy club, toy sports car.

birthday share ★ 1921 Lana Turner, actress; 1925 Jack Lemmon, actor; 1931 James Dean, actor; 1941 Nick Nolte, actor.

on this day ★ In 1910, the Boy Scouts of America organization was founded in the District of Colombia.

color red ★ **number** 18, 45, 90 ★ **stone** carnelian—a roman amulet for protection and good fortune ★ **flora** delphinium ★ **animal** badger ★ **occupation** artist, lifeguard, pilot ★ **key features** driven, powerful, kind ★ **naturally good at** risking your security for advancement in work

february 9

character ★ You're a lethal combination of striking good looks and irresistible charisma. Your strong aura can make people think you are aggressive or too forceful, but you are soft inside and take criticism personally. You are brave enough to go for what you want in life eventually, but may not feel you have achieved what you desire until after you are 30.

life path ★ You can be hot-headed and impulsive and may inadvertently hurt someone close to you with your rash decisions. You tend to chastise yourself for this because you can empathize with others. You like the great outdoors and are more into achievement than money. Success for you is about doing something you love, not how much you have in the bank.

love ★ You are very focused on where you want to be in life but passion can and does knock you off course. You have such a craving for romance that it can override everything else. Why not try a fiery Aries, whose ruling planet, Mars, is also your birth date ruler and who shares your intensity?

best present ★ Weekend in the mountains, denim jacket.

birthday share ★ 1942 Carole King, singer; 1943 Joe Pesci, actor; 1944 Alice Walker, author; 1945 Mia Farrow, actress.

on this day ★ In 1964, the Beatles made their U.S. TV debut on *The Ed Sullivan Show*.

color orange ★ **number** 1, 10, 100 ★ **stone** fire opal—sparks you into action ★ **flora** orange blossom ★ **animal** jaguar ★ **occupation** model, designer, artist ★ **key features** creative, admired, bold ★ **naturally good at** standing out in a crowd

february 10

character ★ You have flair and vision and an original outlook. You have an eclectic mix of friends who are also eccentric and slightly strange, but you wouldn't have them any other way. Although you love attention you don't seek it in an obvious manner, simply using your style to capture interest.

life path ★ You love diversity. Walking in the park in the city and going to see an art-house movie are favorite pastimes. You enjoy the simple pleasures in life like coffee in the morning, and your unconventional style means you look glamorous even in thrift store clothes. This refreshing individuality is delightful to others.

love ★ You have a feline magnetism that draws many admirers to you. At some point in your life you may be torn between two lovers who have very different attractions. You like to experience the extraordinary in love and are very broad-minded. A Leo, whose ruling planet, the Sun, is also your birth date ruler would most fulfill you.

best present ★ Leather boots, retro clothes.

birthday share ★ 1898 Bertolt Brecht, dramatist; 1930 Robert Wagner, actor; 1950 Mark Spitz, swimmer and Olympic Games gold medalist; 1967 Laura Dern, actress.

on this day ★ In 1942, Glenn Miller received the first gold record for selling a million copies of "Chattanooga Choo Choo."

color silvery white ★ **number** 2, 11, 20 ★ **stone** opal—accentuates your feelings, so handle it with care ★ **flora** orchid ★ **animal** owl ★ **occupation** lawyer, astrologer, fortune-teller ★ **key features** magical, mysterious, knowing ★ **naturally good at** falling in love at first sight

february 11

character ★ You have a spooky way of assessing people on first meeting and are rarely wrong. You are mystifying and elusive and like to spend time exploring your intuition. Your home is your temple and you probably have candles and oils burning while a wind chime softly tinkles a tune. You are delicate yet powerful and can be trusted.

life path ★ You have a strong sense of justice and will always speak your mind, although gently and persuasively. You cannot abide conflict and are quite sensitive. You appreciate beauty, and as your birth date number is a master number, you are here on Earth to find a higher purpose.

love ★ You love tenderly and evenly and will always treat your loved ones with care and consideration. You need space to breathe but are a firm believer in monogamy. Easygoing, enlightening relationships that take in lots of entertaining and culture are your ideal. Why not try a Cancer, whose ruling planet, the Moon, is also your birth date ruler?

best present ★ Incense holder, book about India.

birthday share ★ 1847 Thomas Edison, inventor; 1934 Mary Quant, fashion designer; 1936 Burt Reynolds, actor; 1969 Jennifer Aniston, actress.

on this day ★ In 1812, Massachusetts governor Elbridge Gerry signed a law changing the state's electoral boundaries to ensure a Republican majority. The move gave rise to the term *gerrymandering*.

color purple ★ **number** 3, 12, 21 ★ **stone** citrine—gives you a stronger sense of self
★ **flora** iris ★ **animal** goldfish ★ **occupation** builder, stockbroker, social worker ★
key features lucky, purposeful, ingenious ★ **naturally good at** biding your time

february 12

character ★ You're focused on your career, not for the salary but because it interests you and you genuinely enjoy working and problem solving. You have good self-esteem and tend to plow into life with enthusiasm. You exude passion and gusto but are sometimes not in touch with your body or your true energy levels.

life path ★ You make a good adjudicator and are trusted by your compatriots to make fair decisions, but this can frustrate you sometimes because you carry too many responsibilities. Everyone wants your advice or counsel because you are a fabulous listener. Take heart; you will no doubt be rewarded for all your fine deeds one day.

love ★ You don't get too wrapped up in love and take it a little for granted. Is this perhaps because love comes easily to you?

If you are single maybe you are spending too much time on your work. Make time to find a Sagittarius, whose ruling planet is also your birth date ruler, Jupiter.

best present ★ Trumpet, tickets to a basketball game.

birthday share ★ 1809 Charles Darwin, scientist, and Abraham Lincoln, 16th U.S. president; 1938 Judy Blume, author; 1980 Christina Ricci, actress.

on this day ★ In 1924, George Gershwin's "Rhapsody in Blue" premiered in New York.

february 13

character ★ You live in a self-constructed world and get so overtaken by your unique view of things that you may even mutter to yourself as you wander around preoccupied with plans and ideas. This special talent for seeing things differently may end up making you your fortune, so don't let others put you down.

life path ★ Never mind born to be wild—you were born to be diverse. You're a special and rare creature because you really don't conform, not out of rebelliousness but out of originality. However, it's difficult for you to maintain lasting friendships because you are so unpredictable and inconsistent.

love ★ You find it hard to stick to relationships, as you like your freedom too much. You can fall in and out of love quickly and prefer other elusive creatures like yourself. It might be good to try another Aquarius, as both your birth date ruler and your ruling planet are Uranus.

best present ★ Go-kart, punching bag.

birthday share ★ 1934 George Segal, actor; 1944 Jerry Springer, television host; 1950 Peter Gabriel, singer; 1974 Robbie Williams, singer.

on this day ★ In 1990, roaring crowds gave Nelson Mandela a hero's welcome when he returned to the black township of Soweto with a pledge to end "the dark hell of apartheid."

color green ★ **number** 5, 23, 50 ★ **stone** amber—soaks up negativity ★ **flora** gardenia ★ **animal** hyena ★ **occupation** bookstore owner, electrician, talk show host ★ **key features** witty, engaging, piercing ★ **naturally good at** telling people how it is

february 14

character ★ You are great company and spend most of your time having a good old banter. You can be blunt to the point of being rude, but as you have such a cute smile you get away with it. Being so entertaining and jovial, you make an excellent dinner-party guest.

life path ★ You have the ability to get information out of people and must be careful not to be a gossip. Everyone wants to tell you their business because you appear to be open. Your dream job would be a radio show host, and you certainly have the talent for it. You suffered from shyness when you were young but overcame it by the time you were 20, and now have innate confidence.

love ★ You like balance in relationships and are after commitment eventually, but you are also a mischievous flirt! You are faithful and true when you finally fall in love, but you may be tempted to have several flings when you are single, thinking, what the heck, life is for living! Just be honest with everyone concerned because dishonesty is never a good policy. Try to find love with a Gemini, whose ruling planet, Mercury, is also your birth date ruler.

best present ★ Digital radio, theater tickets.

birthday share ★ 1859 George Ferris, inventor of the Ferris wheel; 1894 Jack Benny, comedian; 1944 Alan Parker, director; 1946 Gregory Hines, dancer and actor.

on this day ★ In 1929, the St. Valentine's Day Massacre took place in Chicago.

color pink ★ **number** 6, 33, 60 ★ **stone** amethyst—to balance your energy ★ **flora** amaryllis ★ **animal** bloodhound ★ **occupation** actor, skier, dancer ★ **key features** wild, fun loving, physical ★ **naturally good at** getting yourself into trouble

february 15

character ★ You're a dazzling creature full of vitality and fizz. You love overindulgence and being very naughty. But although you live for the pleasures of the flesh, you do have a deeper side that perhaps needs some more attention. You don't know when to stop or how far you should go, so perhaps try to establish some boundaries for yourself.

life path ★ You streak along in life—talk about va-va-voom! You want to feast on life and don't intend to slow down or monitor yourself. At some point you may take the opposite stance and become totally clean living and self-disciplined, but this is unlikely until you are much older.

love ★ You love to get yourself into all sorts of sticky situations and dilemmas. Nothing is straightforward in your love life but you don't seem to mind too much.

A Libra or Taurus, whose ruling planet, Venus, is also your birth date ruler, may one day ensnare you for good.

best present ★ Coffee grinding machine, eye mask.

birthday share ★ 1564 Galileo Galilei, astronomer; 1927 Harvey Korman, actor and comedian; 1951 Jane Seymour, actress; 1954 Matt Groening, cartoonist.

on this day ★ In 1898, the Spanish-American War began after the battleship USS *Maine* blew up in Havana harbor. The cause of the explosion still remains a mystery.

february 16

character ★ If people don't know you they may think you're not very bright because you don't speak unless you are sure about something. However, all your brightness lies under the surface. You are a philosopher and a scholar and like to get a good grasp of things, not just on an intellectual but also on a practical level.

life path ★ You are something of an alchemist; you turn dubious situations into positive experiences through this ability to sense the ultimate truth of circumstances. You have experienced many upheavals and traumas but took them in your stride and have used them as fertilizer to grow. You need a lot of good loving but find it hard to receive.

love ★ You're a wounded soldier and have found that love was not returned when you gave it. Earlier disappointments have turned you off to the reality of love but not the fantasy. Let the past go—you deserve all the love the world can give you. Why not try a Pisces, whose ruling planet, Neptune, is also your birth date ruler?

best present ★ Amber necklace, dream catcher.

birthday share ★ 1935 Sonny Bono, singer, television host and U.S. congressman; 1957 LeVar Burton, actor; 1958 Lisa Loring, actress; 1959 John McEnroe, tennis player, journalist, and commentator.

on this day ★ In 1959, Fidel Castro became leader of Cuba after having ousted the right-wing dictator Fulgencio Batista.

color maroon ★ **number** 8, 44, 80 ★ **stone** diamond—as tough, rare, and valuable as you ★ **flora** mistletoe ★ **animal** doberman dog ★ **occupation** lecturer, football player, journalist ★ **key features** hard-hitting, sturdy, insightful ★ **naturally good at** finding out the truth

february 17

character ★ You are true to yourself and have strict guidelines about how you should behave and be in the world. You are determined and ambitious and ultimately seeking answers. Writing is one of your talents and you may be called upon to write about social injustice. You sometimes come across as a tough cookie and can seem suspicious, but you're really just curious.

life path ★ Your life has taken some dramatic twists and turns but you have always advanced like a Trojan warrior. Your appearance of invulnerability is deceptive, though. You are stunning to look at, if a little quirky, and exhibit great stamina and nerve.

love ★ You can be stern and unbending in relationships and distance yourself, especially if there are problems. Loosen up and open up, and you will get much more from them. You value long-term commitment but can fall into bad patterns. Find a Capricorn, whose ruling planet, Saturn is also your birth date ruler.

best present ★ Sheepskin rug, massage oil.

birthday share ★ 1934 Barry Humphries, entertainer and creator of Dame Edna Everage; 1941 Gene Pitney, singer; 1954 Rene Russo, actress; 1963 Michael Jordan, basketball player.

on this day ★ In 1904, Puccini's opera *Madame Butterfly* premiered in Milan.

color red ★ **number** 9, 54, 90 ★ **stone** ruby—represents loyalty and passion ★ **flora** stargazer lily ★ **animal** hippopotamus ★ **occupation** circus performer, stuntperson, limbo dancer ★ **key features** impulsive, reckless, dynamic ★ **naturally good at** being fired out of a cannon, metaphorically and literally

february 18

character ★ You're one crazy dude! You will try anything for the sheer thrill of it. You like to live by the seat of your pants and have unlimited potential. You're not focused enough to have a standard job and your life fizzes with adventure. You see a risky situation and you go for it. Try to avoid gambling, as you would not know when to stop.

life path ★ You will always go one step further in a dare and need to watch this tendency to feel indestructible. Why do you need this high-octane life? Your dramatic and dynamic personality craves love, but you look in the wrong direction and the friends around you encourage you to misbehave.

love ★ You tend to show off when you first meet someone, and your adolescent jokes and party tricks often don't hit the right note. Try being a bit quieter and talk more about the inner you. Why not go for an Aries, whose ruling planet, Mars, is also your birth date ruler?

best present ★ Trampoline, scooter.

birthday share ★ 1932 Milos Forman, director; 1933 Yoko Ono, singer and artist; 1954 John Travolta, actor; 1964 Matt Dillon, actor.

on this day ★ In 1930, Clyde William Tombaugh, working with photographic plates at the Lowell Observatory in Flagstaff, Arizona, discovered the planet Pluto.

color orange ★ **number** 1, 10, 100 ★ **stone** blue lace agate—helps you express your emotions ★ **flora** yucca plant ★ **animal** cocker spaniel ★ **occupation** jockey, interior designer, performer ★ **key features** glowing, radiant, inspiring ★ **naturally good at** entering into the spirit of things

february 19

character ★ You're an individual who adores your independence. You like to do things your way and won't let anyone order you around. You have a strong need to prove yourself and generally do. You should be successful in whichever field you choose, but if you're in a dead end job it will wear you down.

life path ★ Your path is to dance to your own tune and find your voice. You might have been disciplined when you were younger or rejected for your willful and forceful nature, but you never let it get you down or stop you. You are on your way up and this should continue. You hate being in a rut but, luckily, your ruts are not as deep as everyone else's, so count your blessings.

love ★ People tend to fall in love with you easily and you were born to be worshiped and loved. You like the attention as long as it isn't suffocating and will be very protective of your partner. Look out for a Leo, whose ruling planet, the Sun, is also your birth date ruler.

best present ★ Body lotion, trip to Arizona.

birthday share ★ 1473 Nicolas Copernicus, astronomer; 1924 Lee Marvin, actor; 1960 Holly Johnson, singer; 1967 Benicio Del Toro, actor.

on this day ★ In 1918, in Russia, a decree abolishing all private ownership of land, water, and natural resources was issued by the Soviet Central Executive Committee.

aquarius

your ruling planet Kooky **uranus** is a wild and unpredictable planet—
it can shake up the world and suddenly change all the rules, just like you. Erratic, some say
a little crazy, Uranus holds the key to change through unconventional action. Discovered in
1781, it was first thought to be a comet. The atmosphere on Uranus is bleak, with winds
gusting at more than 600 miles per hour. This fast-moving but cool atmosphere is often seen
in those ruled by this planet. It also has 20 moons that are named after Shakespearean
characters, and you may well have been accused of being a drama queen! To have 20 moons
would certainly make you prone to sudden mood changes. Fundamentally, it is the planet of
rebellion, and this energy will not be controlled by anyone, nor can its actions be foreseen.
Uranus is so extraordinary that a typical Uranus day and night can last 42 years. It is unique,
different, and unstoppable.

your natural habitat You are perfectly happy in a teepee or a cave with a bunch of hippies and a root beer, and you're also so flexible that you can travel with just a rucksack on your back and see the whole universe as your natural habitat. You hate to be penned in, and your idea of a nightmare would be a house in the suburbs with matching curtains and carpets. Ideally your home would have an inventive and unusual decor and each room would be different. You are likely to be untidy and have books, magazines, and sketches strewn around the place. However, your bedroom is usually quite bare, possibly minimalist and painted white. You like this space to be free and uncluttered so that you can lie down calmly and think. You probably have a music system in more than one room, with an eclectic music collection. You are drawn to computers, and especially the Internet, which you explore with fascination, downloading vast quantities of information.

are you a typical aquarius?

So are you an archetypal water-bearer? Do you like to be surrounded by diverse friends? Aquarians are liberal minded and very forward thinking. Your friends will be from all cultures and backgrounds. They may wear suits or have body piercings and tattoos. You're not bothered about what is on the outside as long as your buddies are real underneath. You are exciting and different.

Why you're wonderful! You have an innate sense of freedom and an unconventional approach to life. You mix well with both sexes. You admire others who have the courage to be unique and individual and you, too, strive to express your original thoughts. You have the potential to be a genius and may experience eureka moments when everything in the universe makes sense for a split second. You're a great and possibly unusual dancer and love all forms of creativity—the weirder the better. You make an excellent but unthreatening rebel and are ahead of your time.

Why you're impossible! You're such a free spirit that you find it impossible to make firm commitments. You know what you think from one moment to the next but may find it hard to pin down emotions. Freedom is everything to you and friends may feel you are there mentally but don't understand extreme emotions. You can be strangely detached at the most crucial times. You tend to put your foot in it by speaking your mind in a cool fashion, unaware that you may be treading on people's toes.

Your secret side You are fascinated by the phenomemon of love and romantically adventurous; you would happily date people with intriguingly different lifestyles, exotic looks, or mysterious backgrounds. You think about other people's motivation and weigh what you feel about them by careful observation. You have a need to be different and so may do things purely because others won't.

aquarius love compatibility chart

	aries	taurus	gemini	cancer	leo	virgo
	🍾		🍾		🍾	🍾
			❤		❤	
			🔗		🔗	
	🎈		🎈	🎈	🎈	🎈
			💋		💋	
			🪑	🪑	🪑	
	💡		💡	💡	💡	💡
			👥		👥	

KEY ▷ fun   romance   loyalty   adventure

	libra	scorpio	sagittarius	capricorn	aquarius	pisces
	🍾		🍾		🍾	
	💘		💘		💘	💘
	💍				💍	
	🎈		🎈		🎈	🎈
	👄				👄	👄
	🪑		🪑		🪑	
	💡		💡		💡	💡
					👥	

👄 passion   🪑 chilling out   💡 spontaneity   👥 attentiveness

pisces

february 20–march 20

color silver ★ number 2, 11, 20 ★ stone rose-quartz—a heart-healing stone that brings unconditional love ★ flora gladioli ★ animal labrador retriever ★ occupation healer, psychic, nurse ★ key features intuitive, caring, sensitive ★ naturally good at dreaming of the future

february 20

character ★ You have a compassionate nature and deal with people with empathy and warmth. You can suffer from being a little paranoid and self-conscious as you get confused between your own emotions and the emotions of other people; this is because you merge so completely with people.

life path ★ Your healing ability always comes out somehow, even if you don't explore it in a traditional way. You make a difference and those around you feel better just by being in your presence. On the down side you can become drained because you don't know when to stop giving. Try to build up some boundaries and devote at least one day a week to treating yourself.

love ★ You're a sensitive little flower in love and get swept away in the fantasy of it all. You initially create a gorgeous dream of what your partner is like, but to guard against becoming disillusioned later on you need to be aware that we all have our faults. Why not try a Cancer, whose ruling planet, the Moon, is your birth date ruler?

best present ★ Crystal ball, aquarium.

birthday share ★ 1927 Sidney Poitier, actor; 1954 Patty Hearst, kidnapped heiress; 1966 Cindy Crawford, model; 1967 Kurt Cobain, singer.

on this day ★ In 1962, John Glenn became the first U.S. astronaut in the Earth's orbit when the Mercury capsule *Friendship VII* carried him into space for a five-hour voyage.

color purple ★ **number** 3, 12, 33 ★ **stone** amber—soaks up negativity and heals the past ★ **flora** geranium ★ **animal** cockatiel ★ **occupation** singer, speech writer, drama student ★ **key features** wild, overemotional, freedom loving ★ **naturally good at** making money through creative pursuits

february 21

character ★ You tend to keep pushing yourself forward even when you feel it is hopeless. You have a creative and original mind and are destined to be a real individual. You cannot dance to another's tune but many have tried to control you. You seem gentle and laid-back but are actually quite tough.

life path ★ You have flashes of inspiration that are essential for you to develop. You are not one to stand still and daydream, despite being a Pisces, but perhaps you need to take the time to observe your fantasies to increase your chances of conjuring them into reality. Money is attracted to you, but you like to squander it.

love ★ You need freedom and commitment. You are a natural lover and have probably had quite a few romantic adventures. Even when you settle down, you can have a wandering eye. A Sagittarius, whose ruling planet, Jupiter, is also your birth date ruler, would suit you well.

best present ★ Incense burner, relaxation CD.

birthday share ★ 1933 Nina Simone, singer; 1955 Kelsey Grammer, actor; 1958 Alan Trammell, baseball player; 1979 Jennifer Love Hewitt, actress and singer.

on this day ★ In 1885, the Washington Monument was dedicated, one of the world's tallest masonry structures at 555 feet (169.29 meters).

color chrome ★ **number** 4, 13, 22 ★ **stone** hematite—gives you self-confidence ★ **flora** daisy ★ **animal** mongoose ★ **occupation** inventor, playwright, circus performer ★ **key features** dynamic, unconventional, generous ★ **naturally good at** discovering and unearthing mysteries

february 22

character ★ Strong-willed and individual, you can be argumentative and challenging. You have many different ideas about what you want to do with your life and can travel in many different directions all at the same time, making others feel that you are chasing your tail. You will never have a conventional life and may have two seemingly opposing interests or jobs.

life path ★ Allow yourself to flow and know that diversity is your gift. You have the capacity to understand complex emotions and situations. You may find that once you accept yourself as you are you will go on to heal others who have suffered in life. You have a big heart and the ability to love unconditionally.

love ★ You like to be free and may be quite changeable in the area of love. You can fall in love at the drop of a hat but really need a grounded lover who can accept your odd take on life. Try an Aquarius, whose ruling planet, Uranus, is your birth date ruler.

best present ★ Day at the races, Scrabble board game.

birthday share ★ 1732 George Washington, 1st U.S. president; 1908 John Mills, actor; 1932 Edward Kennedy, U.S. politician; 1975 Drew Barrymore, actress.

on this day ★ In 1879, Frank Winfield Woolworth opened his first Five Cent Store in Utica, New York.

color green ★ **number** 5, 14, 50 ★ **stone** green aventurine—for protection during travel ★ **flora** stargazer lily ★ **animal** black cat ★ **occupation** journalist, psychiatrist, nurse ★ **key features** articulate, empathetic, forthcoming ★ **naturally good at** talking about emotions

february 23

character ★ You have a lot to say but are also a good listener, a rather unusual combination. A love of literature is matched by a good grasp of foreign languages. You find it strange that some people can't communicate and get frustrated if others hold back from you emotionally. You are open and caring.

life path ★ Your strength is how you express yourself. You are a channel for spiritual wisdom, and if you are ever in trouble or have a problem you simply ask for an answer and it always comes to you. You can feel reserved and shy and need to overcome this to truly be the vibrant person you are.

love ★ You are looking for a lover to merge with, someone who will understand you and walk side by side with you through stormy weather. Try ducking into a cellar occasionally rather than ambling straight into the storm and you may find a partner who's prepared to take the journey! Why not try a Gemini, whose ruling planet, Mercury, is your birth date ruler?

best present ★ Walkie-talkie, canoe.

birthday share ★ 1633 Samuel Pepys, diarist; 1685 George Frederic Handel, composer; 1939 Peter Fonda, actor; 1955 Howard Jones, singer.

on this day ★ In 1874, Walter Winfield patented a game called Sphairistike, more widely known as lawn tennis.

february 24

character ★ Romantic and obsessed with relationships, you have unrealistic expectations that can cause a constant craving for intimacy. You long to meet your twin soul, but because you were crushed emotionally at an early age, you may have suppressed this extreme desire. Either way, your life is ruled by fighting or yearning for love.

life path ★ You're very sensitive to your environment and the emotional moods of others. This sensitivity can make you a little unstable as you lurch from mood to mood. You need to find a way to be grounded and open. You hate confrontation and may be tempted to lie rather than get into an argument.

love ★ Loving yourself is fundamental to your survival in the poker game of love. For you, love is a high-stakes affair, with your soul bet on the last card. If you build up your relationship with yourself you will find you glide through to win a prize that fulfills you. Why not try a Libra, whose ruling planet is Venus, your birth date ruler?

best present ★ Print of a Pre-Raphaelite painting, book of love poetry.

birthday share ★ 1938 James Farentino, actor; 1955 Alain Prost, racing driver; 1965 Kristin Davis, actress; 1966 Billy Zane, actor.

on this day ★ In 1981, Buckingham Palace announced the engagement of Prince Charles and Lady Diana Spencer.

color indigo ★ **number** 7, 16, 70 ★ **stone** red jasper—to help ground you ★ **flora** seaweed ★ **animal** owl ★ **occupation** mystic, personal coach, healer ★ **key features** spiritual, imaginative, intense ★ **naturally good at** transcendental meditation

february 25

character ★ Your life is mysterious and unusual. It's as if you are being led, and all sorts of bizarre adventures and meetings map out the direction you feel you should take. You are a strong believer in fate but strive to be a sorcerer. You want to master this life and inspire others to transform their own circumstances.

life path ★ You're destined to be a bit of a guru: you are self-absorbed but can suddenly utter the most profound thoughts and observations. Although you come across as quiet and unobtrusive, there is more to you than meets the eye. Be careful not to get lost in your mind or become too consumed by your spiritual side, or you could lose touch with reality.

love ★ Love for you is a minefield. On the one hand you want to play it safe, staying shy and reserved, but on the other hand you long to take a risk with a mysterious stranger. Passion will do you good, so seek lots of it. Why not try another Pisces, as both your Sun sign and your birth date are ruled by Neptune?

best present ★ Book on astrology, massage roller.

birthday share ★ 1841 Pierre-Auguste Renoir, Impressionist painter; 1935 Sally Jessy Raphael, talk show host; 1943 George Harrison, musician; 1966 Tea Leoni, actress.

on this day ★ In 1964, Cassius Clay, (Muhammad Ali) became world heavyweight boxing champion for the first time.

color brown ★ number 8, 17, 80 ★ stone ruby—to give you strength and passion ★ flora hemp ★ animal scottish terrier ★ occupation property developer, fashion designer, security guard ★ key features confused, powerful, hypnotic ★ naturally good at running your own business

february 26

character ★ You can swing from sweet and kind to domineering and cut off. You are often unaware of showing your harsh side and believe you have reason to be cold or aloof. In fact you are oversensitive and tend to judge a situation without seeing your part in it. However, you are generous and kind and will give your last dollar to a beggar.

life path ★ It is as if you have been here and done this before. You have insight and empathy, but you tend to preach or be rigid in your views. The beauty of you is that you can change. If someone special touches you emotionally, you will prove able to transform into a truly enlightened and accepting human being.

love ★ You hate to lose control of your emotions so can keep partners on a string, not allowing them too close. Your love is enormous but you see it as a weakness and keep it bottled up in your heart, allowing out only a measured amount. Throw caution to the wind and let it gush free! Choose a Capricorn, whose ruling planet, Saturn, is your birth date ruler.

best present ★ Trip to a botanical garden, yoga mat.

birthday share ★ 1802 Victor Hugo, author and poet; 1829 Levi Strauss, founder of the Levi Strauss clothing company; 1928 Fats Domino, singer and pianist; 1932 Johnny Cash, singer.

on this day ★ In 1936, Adolf Hitler opened the first factory for the production of the "People's Car," the Volkswagen Beetle, in Saxony, Germany.

color red ★ **number** 9, 45, 90 ★ **stone** garnet—fires you up and gets you going ★ **flora** tulip ★ **animal** racehorse ★ **occupation** rock singer, model, athlete ★ **key features** vibrant, flirtatious, extreme ★ **naturally good at** losing your cool

character ★ Emotional and slightly highly strung, you are a hopeless romantic but can be high maintenance as a friend because you are so intense. You need a lot of attention and tend to take things personally. Lovable and spontaneous, you are ruled by your feelings and find it hard to be objective.

life path ★ You are striking, with a magnetic allure. You can get confused about whom you fancy and relish a romantic challenge. Once you are loved you are never forgotten, but former lovers say you are a little crazy. Invest that enchanting energy in your work and you will really go places.

love ★ You are intoxicated by infatuations and can be quite a handful! You are not one to avoid temptation, and can be far more impulsive than you intend to be. Why not try an Aries, who will give you a run for your money, as their ruling planet, Mars, is also your birth date ruler?

best present ★ CD of love songs, candles.

birthday share ★ 1807 Henry Longfellow, poet; 1902 John Steinbeck, author; 1932 Elizabeth Taylor, actress; 1980 Chelsea Clinton, daughter of former President Bill Clinton and senator Hillary Rodham Clinton.

on this day ★ In 1991, the Persian Gulf war ended as Kuwait was liberated.

color orange ★ **number** 1, 10, 100 ★ **stone** carnelian—a roman good luck talisman ★ **flora** orchid ★ **animal** jaguar ★ **occupation** scientist, painter, performer ★ **key features** unique, charming, glowing ★ **naturally good at** charming the birds out of the trees

february 28

character ★ Cute and appealing, you have no shortage of admirers. You can be somewhat over the top, but you tend to get away with it. You have a glint in your eye and the polish of a 1950s movie star. You like lots of notoriety and can have a reputation as a heartbreaker. You were shy when you were young but should come into yourself after the age of 23.

life path ★ You are a natural actor or performer and would shine on the stage. You are articulate and funny, to the point of exaggerating to get a laugh. You hate to make mistakes and always feel you have to achieve more and more to give you confidence. Self-esteem is not created by success but by who you are as a person.

love ★ You will stick with a lover who is loyal and glamorous. You are quite fussy about who you choose and have high expectations. You tend to be a bit of a flirt, which can irritate your partners. Search for a Leo, whose ruling planet, the Sun, is your birth date ruler.

best present ★ Gold mirror, photograph album.

birthday share ★ 1824 Charles Blondin, high-wire acrobat; 1939 Tommy Tune, dancer and actor; 1940 Mario Andretti, race-car driver; 1957 John Turturro, actor.

on this day ★ In 1912, the first parachute jump from an aircraft was made in Missouri by Albert Berry.

color silver ★ number 2, 11, 20 ★ stone moonstone—connects you to your natural rhythm ★ flora lotus ★ animal lamb ★ occupation author, opera singer, midwife ★ key features authentic, kind, delicate ★ naturally good at drawing cartoons

february 29

character ★ Wistful and dreamy, you waft through life in a bubble of positive feelings, but unfortunately when your bubble is pricked by some cynical fool you can be very disheartened. You see the best in people and talk directly to their soul, looking them firmly in the eye. As a result, your love gets through.

life path ★ You're marvelous with young children and are maternal and caring. Family is important to you but you can feel neglected; perhaps you put too much emphasis on this and need more independence? You are a real softie when it comes to helping others out in times of crisis and often have friends around to take comfort from your care and nurturing.

love ★ When you commit you want it to be for life. You can get too clingy and insecure in a relationship, which can jeopardize the very security you are so desperate to keep. Try to

keep some of your life separate or you may become a slave to the home. Your perfect partner would be a Cancer, whose ruling planet, the Moon, is your birth date ruler.

best present ★ Recipe book, CD of classical music.

birthday share ★ 1736 Anne Lee, founder of the society of Shakers; 1792 Gioacchino Rossini, operatic composer; 1904 Jimmy Dorsey, bandleader; 1916 Dinah Shore, singer.

on this day ★ In 1940, Hattie McDaniel became the first black woman to win an Oscar, for her role as Mammy in *Gone With the Wind*.

color orange ★ **number** 1, 10, 100 ★ **stone** fire opal—gets you going and stirs up your passion ★ **flora** gerbera ★ **animal** tiger ★ **occupation** talk show host, bar manager, magician ★ **key features** sweet, loving, magnetic ★ **naturally good at** making others feel good

march 1

character ★ You have a creative nature and like to be around sensitive individuals who follow their dreams. You are easily influenced and may in the past have drawn people to you who have wanted to take control of your very being and talents. Try not to give your power away but build up your own influence so as to be able to steer your own ship in life.

life path ★ You slip and slide your way toward your artistic goal. You don't want a normal job but one that can make your soul sing. You sometimes hide these high ideals from others but spend hours fantasizing about your future global success. Inject some practicality into those plans and get on with them.

love ★ You have always been loved or adored by your friends but your love life has been more haphazard. You are secretly a bit of a loner and are stronger than you think in

relationships. You like things your way and can get insular if a lover goes against your wishes. Why not try a Leo, whose ruling planet is the Sun, your birth date ruler?

best present ★ Cocktail recipe book, firework display.

birthday share ★ 1904 Glenn Miller, musician; 1910 David Niven, actor; 1927 Harry Belafonte, singer; 1954 Ron Howard, actor and director.

on this day ★ In 1961, the Peace Corps was established by President John F. Kennedy.

color silver ★ number 11, 20, 200 ★ stone clear quartz—the magic wand of crystals, will magnify your desires ★ flora lavender ★ animal tropical fish ★ occupation rebel, jewelry maker, artist ★ key features outgoing, feeling, strange ★ naturally good at expressing your emotions

march 2

character ★ You like to say what you think and you like to shock. You have a slightly eccentric feel about you that is charming, as you have the attractiveness to carry it off. You may want to get involved with a charity because you have a yearning to change and save the world. You are a bit of an extremist and either party like mad or stay at home reading and writing poetry.

life path ★ You are seeking a special someone who is like a twin soul; this may be a friend or a lover, but you have a feeling that you are just half a person with something missing until you find this mysterious person to dock with you and make you whole. In fact, the wholeness is inside you all along; the other person just wakes you up and brings you some sort of confirmation.

love ★ You flourish in the right relationship and reveal the softer side of yourself when you truly love. Partnerships are important to you, and you will give and take 50/50. Communication is essential and you can chitchat for hours with your loved one. Narrow your search to a Cancer, whose ruling planet, the Moon, is also your birth date ruler.

best present ★ Shaker wooden box, fountain pen.

birthday share ★ 1931 Tom Wolfe, author, and Mikhail Gorbachev, former Soviet leader; 1942 Lou Reed, singer; 1962 Jon Bon Jovi, singer.

on this day ★ In 1949, Captain James Gallagher completed the first nonstop around-the-world flight in 94 hours, one minute.

march 3

character ★ Quick witted and expansive, you capture the attention of strangers quite easily. You often chat to people you don't know and your open manner is appealing. You can be seen as a bit of a klutz because you are not very practical—you live in your mind and heart and forget to focus on what your hands are doing. You have a sense of style but your clothes are always in disarray as you rush from meeting to meeting.

life path ★ You have so much potential to develop that the question is where to begin. You may fancy becoming a scriptwriter, as you have a great sense of humor and acute observational skills. You like to earn your money through a job with an important message to spread, and you want to make others' lives easier.

love ★ You are always stunned when any potential partner expresses interest in you. Your natural friendliness and generosity may attract partners who later take advantage of you, so you need to be alert to warning signs. A Sagittarius, whose ruling planet is also your birth date ruler, Jupiter, would be a wise choice.

best present ★ Kaleidoscope, crystal wand.

birthday share ★ 1831 George Pullman, designer of luxury railway cars; 1847 Alexander Graham Bell, inventor of the telephone; 1911 Jean Harlow, actress; 1958 Miranda Richardson, actress.

on this day ★ In 1931, the "Star-Spangled Banner," originally the "Defense of Fort McHenry," was adopted as the national anthem of the United States.

color gray ★ **number** 4, 13, 22 ★ **stone** hematite—increases your self-esteem ★ **flora** sunflower ★ **animal** sea lion ★ **occupation** scientist, astronomer, fortune-teller ★ **key features** distracted, erratic, virtuoso ★ **naturally good at** conducting music in front of an orchestra or alone in your living room

character ★ You are quite difficult to understand, as your mind is far ahead of the rest of us mere mortals. You have the hint of a mad professor about you. You are fascinated by time travel or science fiction and would love to tour space in a rocket. If you're female this may be less pronounced and you will turn your attention to astrology or spirituality.

life path ★ You're completely crazy but harmless and great fun. You love way-out music and would make a brilliant DJ because you have a good ear for music. You act in an unpredictable way and need a lot of space. You hate to be confined or closed in and feel trapped if you are made to obey any one ruler. Your free spirit cannot be contained, nor should it be.

love ★ You may have gaps between long-term relationships and need a lover who will give you space and not expect a traditional relationship. You admire people who are free-spirited like you and are not attracted to suburbanites. Why not try an Aquarius, whose ruling planet, Uranus, is also your birth date ruler?

best present ★ Trip to NASA, telescope.

birthday share ★ 1678 Antonio Vivaldi, composer; 1944 Bobby Womack, musician and singer; 1967 Evan Dando, singer; 1969 Chastity Bono, daughter of Sonny and Cher.

on this day ★ In 1933, Franklin D. Roosevelt was sworn in as the 32nd President and the first to be elected for a third and fourth term.

color green ★ number 7, 14, 50 ★ stone turquoise—this sacred native american stone brings protection ★ flora wild orchid ★ animal shark ★ occupation radio dj, director, advertising creative ★ key features chatty, funny, neurotic ★ naturally good at painting the town red

march 5

character ★ You love to have a good time and don't know when to stop. You can drink and cavort until the early hours and may find this has a negative effect on your work. You just about keep things together but you cannot resist excitement. You need to watch your health if you surrender to this lifestyle for any length of time.

life path ★ You find it difficult to sleep, and wake up with a hundred ideas rampaging through your head. Your mind is fast and furious and needs an outlet. You can be sloppy around the house and are hopeless at doing your washing—you often rush around crumpled in last night's clothes. You will attract partners who want to mother you, which helps, but it is up to you to grow up.

love ★ You are very impulsive and can love one person one day, only to change your mind a few days later. You need someone who is quite firm with you and doesn't let you get away with too much, but who also respects your individual style. Why not try a Gemini, whose ruling planet, Mercury, is also your birth date ruler?

best present ★ Clothes press, video camera.

birthday share ★ 1908 Rex Harrison, actor; 1936 Dean Stockwell, actor; 1948 Eddy Grant, singer; 1958 Andy Gibb, singer.

on this day ★ In 1918, Moscow became the new capital city of Russia.

color pink ★ **number** 6, 15, 33 ★ **stone** tiger's eye—gives you protection ★ **flora** tulip ★ **animal** dolphin ★ **occupation** waiter/waitress, model, zookeeper ★ **key features** sensual, childlike, delicate ★ **naturally good at** encouraging others to flirt with you

character ★ You can play the part of the airhead, whether male or female. You like others to appreciate your beauty and are quick to turn on the magic. You perhaps need to take more responsibility for your life and practice standing on your own two feet. In the past you may have been supported by your parents, or a benefactor, so you now find responsibility tough.

life path ★ You have a vivid imagination that could be used in your career. You have real depth underneath that frivolous exterior and want to be loved and to love (perhaps a little too freely!) If you have evolved, you may become a spiritual leader or workshop leader and be able to transform others with your unconditional love.

love ★ You are perpetually in love and have a strong romantic streak. You can associate sex with love and vice versa, which can be confusing. In rarer instances you may suppress your sexuality because you fear its power. Look for a Libra, whose ruling planet, Venus, is also your birth date ruler.

best present ★ Diamond ring, bottle of champagne.

birthday share ★ 1475 Michelangelo, Renaissance artist; 1806 Elizabeth Barrett Browning, poet; 1944 Dame Kiri Te Kanawa, opera singer; 1959 Tom Arnold, actor.

on this day ★ In 1836, frontiersman Davy Crockett died as the Alamo fell to Mexican troops, ending a 13-day siege in San Antonio, Texas.

color blue ★ number 16, 25, 70 ★ stone blue lace agate—helps you communicate clearly ★ flora strawberry blossom ★ animal black cat ★ occupation film editor, casting agent, marine biologist ★ key features flirty, intangible, absentminded ★ naturally good at diving and swimming

march 7

character ★ You can often feel like the proverbial fish out of water, particularly if you live in the city. You need water around you, or at least the countryside, as you are so sensitive to your environment. Ironically a lot of you March 7th people choose to live in big cities like New York or London, as though you feel a need to push or test yourself in the big bad world. Make time to retreat to the country whenever you can.

life path ★ You are clever and inventive but sometimes lack the confidence to follow your ideas through. You can get a job in the media or filmmaking but then rarely receive the acclaim you deserve for your talents; you need to find someone who will recognize your skills and promote you. You have an understanding of life's mysteries.

love ★ Your lovers often appear out of nowhere or you find them through a peculiar chain of coincidences. Fate plays a large part in your love life in particular. You learn loads by falling in love and are never single for long. Why not try another Pisces, as Neptune is both your ruling planet and your birth date ruler?

best present ★ Computer, cruise.

birthday share ★ 1849 Luther Burbank, naturalist; 1942 Tammy Faye Bakker, talk show host; 1960 Ivan Lendl, tennis player; 1964 Bret Easton Ellis, author.

on this day ★ In 1917, the world's first jazz record, "The Dixie Jazz Band One Step," recorded by Nick LaRocca's Original Dixieland Jazz Band, was released by RCA Victor in Camden, New Jersey.

color racing green ★ number 26, 35, 44 ★ stone diamond—represents loyalty and power ★ flora african daisy ★ animal alsatian ★ occupation printer, gardener, race-car driver ★ key features uncompromising, charismatic, hypnotic ★ naturally good at being in tune with nature

march 8

character ★ You can be controlling and rigid and have a tendency to be judgmental. You don't like this side to your personality but find it impossible to give in or admit when you are wrong. You have a kind heart for strangers yet are very self-possessed and rarely, if ever, share your inner world with others, no matter how seemingly close.

life path ★ You are a loner and may be afraid of intimacy even though you crave it. You are passionate but even in this you fear losing that precious control. If you took more risks with your heart and trusted more, you would find that life is quite a delightful place full of joyful surprises and a lot of love. You inspire adoration.

love ★ You may choose a safe bet because you have problems surrendering to others and see this as some sort of weakness. You have impossible expectations and tend to try to contain your partner. You have the potential to experience profound and enlightening romantic experiences if you remain open and don't slam the door in true love's face. Why not surrender to an Aries, who will shake you up and love you eternally?

best present ★ Magnificent flowers, rose-gold ring.

birthday share ★ 1921 Cyd Charisse, actress and dancer; 1943 Lynn Redgrave, actress; 1959 Aidan Quinn, actor; 1963 Kathy Ireland, actress.

on this day ★ In 1948, the Supreme Court ruled that religious instruction in public schools violated the Constitution.

march 9

character ★ Scorching and fiery, you really rock. You have loads of energy and masses of enthusiasm; in fact you never know when to stop and can get totally worn out every month or so without realizing why. Calm down and plot your rise to stardom so that success will come more easily.

life path ★ You could be described as over the top but you are quiet sometimes, so that would not be fair. You are sensitive to others' opinions and can get a little paranoid if you are not greeted with open arms. You have an argumentative streak but feel wounded if you are criticized, so give up quarreling, as it is counter-productive. We all have our own truth, and life is not black and white.

love ★ You are a great lover and you put your heart and soul into a relationship. You can be somewhat demanding and want romance and fireworks every time. Why not try an Aries, whose ruling planet is Mars, your birth date ruler?

best present ★ silk bed linens, tape of positive affirmations.

birthday share ★ 1918 Mickey Spillane, author; 1934 Yuri Gagarin, astronaut; 1940 Raul Julia, actor; 1943 Bobby Fischer, chess player.

on this day ★ In 1796, Napoleon Bonaparte married Josephine de Beauharnais, widow of a former officer executed during the French Revolution.

march 10

character ★ Cheerful and joyous, you are likable and funny. You love to entertain people and have a childlike goofiness, yet you manage to be ultracool at the same time. You belong to the "in crowd" but also like to spend quiet times gazing at the Moon and coming up with elaborate plans to sail around the world painting butterflies or some such gentle pursuit.

life path ★ You have such a great way with people that you really should do something with it if you aren't already. People like you and believe in you. Combine this with your creative bent and you're onto a winner. You are naturally psychic and could perhaps become well known in this field.

love ★ You find it easy to have relationships but can get too drawn into your dreams or spirituality and then have no time for such basic human needs. This could be a mistake, because a lover makes a good sounding board for you to work on those grand plans. Find a Leo, whose ruling planet, the Sun, is your birth date ruler.

best present ★ Camera, trip to a Caribbean island.

birthday share ★ 1940 Chuck Norris, actor and kickboxer; 1958 Sharon Stone, actress; 1966 Edie Brickell, singer; 1977 Shannon Miller, gymnast.

on this day ★ In 1990, American Jennifer Capriati, at 13 years and 11 months, became the youngest player ever to reach the final of a professional tennis tournament in an event held in Florida.

march 11

character ★ You have always felt you have a higher purpose, and you have a stronger connection than most with your higher power/God/the universe—whatever you call it. You are on a path that was always going to lead somewhere, and you have probably already achieved more than you thought you would. If you haven't, you will!

life path ★ The universe has something special in store for you. You were born on a master number, 11, which means you are a bit of a magician; this, combined with your ruling planet, Neptune, a magical planet, and your birth date ruler, the Moon, means you can work miracles if only you believe it. Remember to be careful what you ask for, though, because you might just get it.

love ★ You become a little insecure in relationships so it is important not to feel submissive or that your partner is better than you. You're a fine catch once you feel stronger emotionally. Why not go for a Cancer, whose ruler, the Moon, is also your birth date ruler?

best present ★ Writing set, trip to Hawaii.

birthday share ★ 1931 Rupert Murdoch, media mogul, 1950 Bobby McFerrin, singer; 1952 Susan Richardson, actress; 1982 Thora Birch, actress.

on this day ★ In 1888, a torrential rainstorm hit the East Coast of the United States—then the rain turned to snow and became a blizzard, the most famous snowstorm in U.S. history.

color purple ★ number 3, 21, 30 ★ stone amazonite—gives you courage ★ flora gladioli ★ animal giraffe ★ occupation publisher, comedian, ballet dancer ★ key features eccentric, spontaneous, wild ★ naturally good at breaking free of convention

march 12

character ★ You're an untamed sprite who likes to cause mischief, and you often get yourself into trouble. You have tremendous spirit and may have had hardships when growing up that made you strong but still intensely vulnerable and needy. You fight those you love because you fear your own fragility, but you encourage commitment.

life path ★ You have to be allowed to follow your own wacky path but you avoid being self-destructive. You tend to feel misunderstood and crave adulation and attention. You are special and do not need to have a hissy fit or be outlandish to prove it. You tend to land on your feet and get noticed eventually, but you may give up success for love.

love ★ You're difficult but gorgeous. You like to set traps and tests for those you love but still seem to attract saints and genuinely loving individuals who adore your kookiness. Why not try an equally crazy Sagittarius, whose ruling planet is Jupiter, your birth date ruler?

best present ★ Retro sunglasses, yo-yo.

birthday share ★ 1922 Jack Kerouac, author; 1946 Liza Minnelli, singer and actress; 1948 James Taylor, musician; 1957 Marlon Jackson, singer.

on this day ★ In 1945, Anne Frank, the Dutch Jewish teenager who kept a diary of her wartime experiences, died in the Bergen-Belsen concentration camp in Germany. She was 15.

color silver ★ **number** 4, 13, 22 ★ **stone** lapis lazuli—to enlighten you; this magical stone was worn by egyptian high priests ★ **flora** primrose ★ **animal** cocker spaniel ★ **occupation** guru, salesperson, astrologer ★ **key features** unconventional, visionary, puzzling ★ **naturally good at** making drastic changes

march 13

character ★ You can be outlandish and far out. Your views border on the extreme and sometimes tip right over. You have unshakable belief in your eccentric views, and although sometimes this can be dangerous, you are capable of truly unique thought that could be groundbreaking. If you do conform too much or appear normal, you are probably unhappy because you are suppressing your true exotic nature.

life path ★ It's hard to tell what your life path is as you veer from one direction to another. Perhaps you need to sit still for a minute and decide where it is you want to go. Life is a magical mystery tour for you but it could be more productive.

love ★ You inspire followers, but can also draw people to you who are cynical about your nature, which is not helpful. Stick with those who accept and admire you, because cynics make bad partners. Why not acquire an Aquarius, whose ruling planet, Uranus, is also your birth date ruler?

best present ★ Cell phone, computer game.

birthday share ★ 1733 Joseph Priestley, scientist; 1911 L. Ron Hubbard, author; 1939 Neil Sedaka, singer; 1960 Adam Clayton, bassist.

on this day ★ In 1781, the planet Uranus was discovered by the German astronomer Herschel.

color green ★ **number** 14, 23, 50 ★ **stone** emerald—keeps you true to yourself ★ **flora** fern ★ **animal** bear ★ **occupation** mathematician, inventor, researcher ★ **key features** brilliant, original, fast ★ **naturally good at** coming up with unique theories

march 14

character ★ Albert Einstein was born on this day, and you too have a dash of the genius about you. You are a little self-effacing, though, and don't believe in yourself enough. You may turn your talent to comedy or a similarly surprising career—nothing can disguise the spark within you.

life path ★ Be bold, be confident, and go for it! Trust what you feel and allow your mind to take you to places where others could never follow. You're excellent with words and can explain clearly and precisely what you think and feel. Do not underestimate this gift, as it is probably the skill that will fulfill you and draw wealth and prosperity to you.

love ★ You need someone strong and loyal who can be your anchor. You do go off on romantic tangents but will find a lover who can sit through the night talking and laughing with you. What you need is a Gemini, whose ruling planet, Mercury, is also your birth date ruler.

best present ★ Thesaurus, trip to a science museum.

birthday share ★ 1879 Albert Einstein, scientist; 1933 Quincy Jones, composer, and Michael Caine, actor; 1958 Prince Albert of Monaco.

on this day ★ In 1883, political philosopher and social theorist Karl Marx died in London.

color pink ★ number 6, 33, 42 ★ stone polka-dot agate—cheers you up and makes you giggle ★ flora buttercup ★ animal afghan hound ★ occupation astronaut, dating agency consultant, songwriter ★ key features captivating, addictive, hectic ★ naturally good at drawing people to you like a flame draws moths

march 15

character ★ You're intriguing, beguiling, and very, very tempting. You could arouse a hermit with your puppy-dog eyes and husky voice. You have an excessive streak, though, which makes you slightly dangerous. Work on tempering this and you will evolve into a kind and spiritually leveled lover.

life path ★ Try to avoid overindulgence, at least some of the time, as you have genuine ability and the power of personality to achieve your goals. You need to focus and force yourself to channel some of your energy into your innovative pursuits to succeed in life.

love ★ You have a problem remaining faithful unless you're obsessed, in which case you can pursue the object of your affection to the top of Everest if need be and still refuse to see a chill wind if there is one. Try a Libra for balance, as their ruling planet, Venus, is also your birth date ruler.

best present ★ Sheepskin rug, Pisces pendant.

birthday share ★ 1932 Alan Bean, astronaut; 1933 Roy Clark, musician, country singer, and comedian; 1941 Mike Love, singer; 1947 Ry Cooder, guitarist and producer.

on this day ★ In 1964, actress Elizabeth Taylor married Richard Burton in Montreal.

color blue ★ number 7, 34, 70 ★ stone aquamarine—allows you to speak your inner truth ★ flora lavender ★ animal piranha ★ occupation diver, pianist, bomb-disposal expert ★ key features fearless, foolish, dreamy ★ naturally good at tackling danger unawares

march 16

character ★ You can be very subjective, and as you are so in tune with other people's emotions and thoughts, you must avoid jumping to conclusions. We all think random and fleeting thoughts that change, and to latch onto some unsuspecting person's momentary lapse will leave you with a distorted perception of the truth.

life path ★ Yours is likely to be a productive but painful existence; if you could learn not to take life so personally it would be an easier ride. You have an incredible imagination and a good way of interacting with others as long as you don't get caught up in a sea of feelings. You can leap into the future, dazzling others with your ideas, if you let go of the past.

love ★ You are rather extreme in love and can be consumed by it to the detriment of everything else. You have felt devastated when things don't work out, but you need to

see the bigger picture. The next love could be fuller, so celebrate and trust. Try another Pisces, as both your ruling planet and birth date ruler are Neptune.

best present ★ Parachute jump, fish tank with exotic fish.

birthday share ★ 1926 Jerry Lewis, comedian and actor; 1932 R. Walter Cunningham, astronaut; 1940 Bernardo Bertolucci, director; 1949 Erik Estrada, actor.

on this day ★ In 1802, the U.S. Military Academy was founded at West Point, New York.

color maroon ★ number 8, 35, 44 ★ stone red jasper—grounds you ★ flora ivy ★ animal llama ★ occupation banker, pr executive, agent ★ key features expressive, hardworking, complex ★ naturally good at putting your nose to the grindstone

march 17

character ★ You have a loving and gentle nature but you try to be tougher than you are, tougher on yourself and tougher on others. People do not necessarily see this side of you unless they get really close. You treat lovers as an extension of yourself and want them to be perfect.

life path ★ You are inspired and talented, and whatever path you choose, you will be relentless until you get success. You may have felt unloved as a child and now feel you have to overcompensate. You are fantastic as you are and truly lovable, so let in the love that surrounds you and don't give in to cynicism or paranoia.

love ★ You can resist love because you find it quite challenging. You want a good, honest partner and may be a little puritanical (that or the other extreme but rarely in the middle). When love does eventually grip you, it will be like the inescapable coils of an anaconda. It could well be with a Capricorn, whose ruling planet, Saturn, is also your birth date ruler.

best present ★ Jasper ring, silver letter-opener.

birthday share ★ 1919 Nat King Cole, singer; 1938 Rudolf Nureyev, ballet dancer; 1951 Kurt Russell, actor; 1964 Rob Lowe, actor.

on this day ★ In 1969, Golda Meir, a 70-year-old grandmother, took office as Israel's first woman prime minister.

color scarlet ★ **number** 9, 72, 90 ★ **stone** garnet—brings you passion ★ **flora** bird of paradise ★ **animal** german shepherd ★ **occupation** director, painter, athlete ★ **key features** passionate, extrovert, excitable ★ **naturally good at** doing your own thing

character ★ You are like molten lava and rarely cool down. You live life to the max and want to jam it full of delicious and delightful experiences. You are not afraid to live life for today, so go, cat, go! Perhaps that is the only way for you to be fully in the present. Be aware of how this affects your acquaintances and loved ones, though.

life path ★ How can anyone keep up with you? You could set a record for stamina and enthusiasm. You are usually surrounded by hangers-on and people you have taken under your extensive wing. Take time out occasionally to reflect and be alone.

love ★ You're a big romantic—a person who's in love with love. You are drawn to mysterious affairs and like to dabble with dangerous partners who test you to the limit. This is your choice. If you don't like it, change it. Why not hunt out an Aries, whose ruling planet, Mars, is your birth date ruler?

best present ★ Disco ball, whiskey.

birthday share ★ 1932 John Updike, author; 1936 F. W. de Klerk, South African president; 1952 Will Durst, comedian; 1970 Queen Latifah, rap artist and talk show host.

on this day ★ In 1965, Soviet cosmonaut Alexei Leonov made the first spacewalk.

march 19

character ★ You may be rather a drama queen and have a tendency to be extravagant with your money, time, and words. You captivate people and have no problem getting what you want. You may come across as a little aloof or austere, but this couldn't be further from the truth— you're a pussycat, really.

life path ★ You will want to be in the public eye in some way and were born for it. If you have repressed your outgoing personality maybe it is time to shock the world with your glamorous side. No one does glamour quite like you do, sweetie! Fly free and explore yourself—all the answers are inside you.

love ★ You command love even if you are insecure. You enjoy relationships and are fairly easygoing and generous with your partners. Romance and intimacy are as essential to you as the air you breathe. Search for a Leo, whose ruling planet is the Sun, your birth date ruler.

best present ★ Original painting, trip to a museum of modern art.

birthday share ★ 1933 Philip Roth, author; 1936 Ursula Andress, actress; 1947 Glenn Close, actress; 1955 Bruce Willis, actor.

on this day ★ In 1920, the United States refused to sign the Versailles Treaty and join the League of Nations, for fear of being drawn into a war if another member country was invaded.

color silver ★ **number** 2, 11, 20 ★ **stone** moonstone—connects you with your natural rhythm ★ **flora** foxglove ★ **animal** white tiger ★ **occupation** astronomer, producer, nursery school teacher ★ **key features** kind, unusual, liberated ★ **naturally good at** changing your life

march 20

character ★ You are caring and compassionate, open and pleasing. You treat other people as you want to be treated yourself, but find it hard to say exactly what it is you need or desire. You grow more confident as you get older and will make a very wise sage in your latter years.

life path ★ You were born on the last day of the zodiac wheel and as a result have tremendous potential for an all-or-nothing existence. It is not an easy ride, in many ways, as you will be forced to confront who you really are and what you really want. There will come a time in your life when you will be called upon to make a drastic change, and at this point it is essential that you follow your heart.

love ★ Loyalty and love become very confused in your mind and you can stay in a relationship for the wrong reasons—or perhaps for you they are the right reasons? You will not let someone down if you can help it, but remember that it is your life and that your first responsibility should be to yourself. If you are single, why not try a Cancer, whose ruling planet, the Moon, is your birth date ruler?

best present ★ Digital camera, trip to Arizona.

birthday share ★ 1828 Henrik Ibsen, playwright; 1950 William Hurt, actor; 1957 Spike Lee, director; 1958 Holly Hunter, actress.

on this day ★ In 1997, Liggett Group, the maker of Chesterfield cigarettes, settled 22 state lawsuits by agreeing to warn on every pack that smoking is addictive and admitting the industry markets cigarettes to teenagers.

pisces

your ruling planet **Neptune** is the planet of illusion and dreams. It is the blue planet and in mythology Neptune was the Roman equivalent of Poseidon, Greek god of the sea. Neptune has the fastest wind speeds in the solar system, and these, coupled with a changeable atmosphere, symbolize your ability to change within the blink of an eye. Neptune is shrouded in mystery; it has a big dark spot that comes and goes for no apparent reason and baffles astronomers. You are also prone to enter into dark moments when you are overwhelmed by your emotions and feel powerless. Fortunately this is balanced by other periods in your life of childlike joy and optimism. Carl Jung said that Neptune rules the subconscious mind and inspires creativity. Neptune also provides you with an idealistic streak and can throw you the odd curveball of belief in a fantasy rather than reality. It is a planet of divine perception, but you have to be grounded enough to be able to deal with all the profound truth Neptune offers or you will lose yourself in an airy, delusional dream world.

your natural habitat

Ideally you would like to live in a perfect country cottage or castle, somewhere steeped in history and surrounded by beauty. Your cottage would be on a clifftop overlooking the sea or on a private beach. Water soothes you, and you are drawn to settle near it or overlooking it. You like to have peace and tranquility and lots of animals. A farm would do, as long as you did not have to do the practical work of running it. You would much rather sit around gazing at the countryside and writing romantic novels. Your home will have gorgeous pictures on the walls, soft lighting, scented candles, and open fires. You pay special attention to your bedroom, favoring pink or a similar soft color to nurture your emotions. Your attraction to water means you like to have a big bathroom and bath. You appreciate antique furniture that is classic but individual, and your prized possessions have been passed down through generations. Framed photographs of your family and friends are everywhere. You love history and enjoy hearing tales of your ancestors. You are affected by the energy in your home and would benefit from smudging, the Native American practice of space clearing with a stick of sage, to clear your space of any feelings you need to shift. Do this once a week and your home will feel much calmer.

are you a typical pisces?

Soft, kind-hearted, and deliciously romantic, you are caught in a nebulous state where you need everything to be like a fairy tale. You have high expectations about love and crave a partner who will be your knight in shining armor or your maiden fair who you can dote on and read Shakespeare to. You have a vivid imagination and are very sensitive to your environment and other people's moods. You appear to be very gentle and ethereal and like to be surrounded by animals.

Why you're wonderful! You are sweet and gentle and have a huge amount of empathy for your friends and fellow man. You listen to people's problems and are always on the telephone. You have a highly developed creative bent and the ability to write or perform, although you are naturally quite shy. You are also intuitive and psychic and may have prophetic dreams. You would give your last five dollars to a beggar and probably your coat as well.

Why you're impossible! Because you live in a hazy universe of soft-focus lighting and the odd illusion, you can be changeable and untrustworthy. This is not intentional but you can in the heat of the moment be unfaithful, tell a lie, or betray a confidence. You don't ever see it like that, though, as it is not in your nature to be duplicitous. You are so affected by your surroundings and present circumstances that you can lose touch with what you truly hold dear.

Your secret side You long to find someone strong enough to hold and contain you. Like the two Pisces fish swimming in different directions, you rarely ever make up your mind about anything and are frequently led by your emotions. You might make a decision, but then something happens, and with a swish of your tail you've changed direction. You need a partner who can be an anchor yet not restrict this natural twisting and turning completely or make you feel bad about your imagination and sensitivity.

pisces love compatibility chart

	aries	taurus	gemini	cancer	leo	virgo
fun	🍾	🍾	🍾	🍾	🍾	🍾
romance		❤️	❤️	❤️	❤️	❤️
loyalty		🔗		🔗	🔗	🔗
adventure		🎈	🎈	🎈	🎈	🎈
		💋	💋	💋	💋	💋
		🪑	🪑	🪑		🪑
	💡		💡	💡	💡	💡
		👥		👥		👥

	libra	scorpio	sagittarius	capricorn	aquarius	pisces
	🍾	🍾	🍾	🍾		🍾
	💘	💘	💘	💘	💘	💘
		💍		💍		
	🎈	🎈	🎈	🎈	🎈	🎈
	💋	💋	💋	💋	💋	💋
	🪑	🪑		🪑		🪑
	💡	💡	💡		💡	💡
		👥		👥		👥

 passion chilling out spontaneity  attentiveness

dedication

In memory of my beloved mother, Bruna Ida Saunders, born May 9, 1928 died December 11, 2002. Your indomitable spirit lives on in our hearts.

Huge blessings to Kalina and Dot, guardian angels.

With thanks to: Tara, a star and a Goddess; Minty, for the gift; Julie P, for her unerring friendship; Cazza and Matty, for their research skills; and Sarah D, for being my guru.

And finally, as always, to that unpredictable but alluring Pisces, Marie. What dreams may come…

about the author

Michele Knight (www.micheleknight.com) is a wild
Aries woman who has been a psychic since birth.
Her mother was a well-known Italian psychic and
medium. Michele has been a media psychic for
many years, regularly appears on television, and is
astrologer for a magazine. She has been practicing
intuitive astrology since the age of thirteen
and lives in a country cottage nestled in
the English hills.

An Hachette Livre UK Company
First published in Great Britain in 2004 by Spruce
a division of Octopus Publishing Group Ltd
2–4 Heron Quays, London E14 4JP
www.octopusbooks.co.uk

Distributed in the United States and Canada by
Hachette Book Group USA
237 Park Avenue
New York
NY 10017

ISBN 13 978-1-84601-294-5
ISBN 10 1-84601-294-5

Printed and bound in China
10 9 8 7 6 5 4 3 2

This book contains the opinions and ideas of the author. It is intended to provide helpful and informative material
on the subjects addressed in this book and is sold with the understanding that the author and publisher
are not engaged in rendering any kind of personal professional services in this book. The author and publisher
disclaim all responsibility for any liability, loss or risk, personal or otherwise, which is incurred as a consequence,
directly or indirectly, of the use and application of any of the contents of this book.